The Shadow of the Galilean

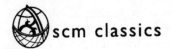
scm classics

The Shadow of the Galilean

*The quest of the historical Jesus
in narrative form*

Gerd Theissen

scm press

Translated by John Bowden from the German
Der Schatten des Galiläers.
Historische Jesusforschung in erzählender Form
Published by Christian Kaiser Verlag, Munich 1986

A catalogue record for this book is available
from the British Library

0 334 02852 3

First published in English by SCM Press in 1987
This edition first published in 2001 by SCM Press
9–17 St Albans Place London N1 0NX

Second impression 2004

SCM Press is a division of
SCM-Canterbury Press Ltd

Typeset in Ehrhardt by MATS, Southend-on-Sea, Essex
and printed in Great Britain by
Bookmarque Ltd, Croydon, Surrey

For Oliver and Gunnar

Contents

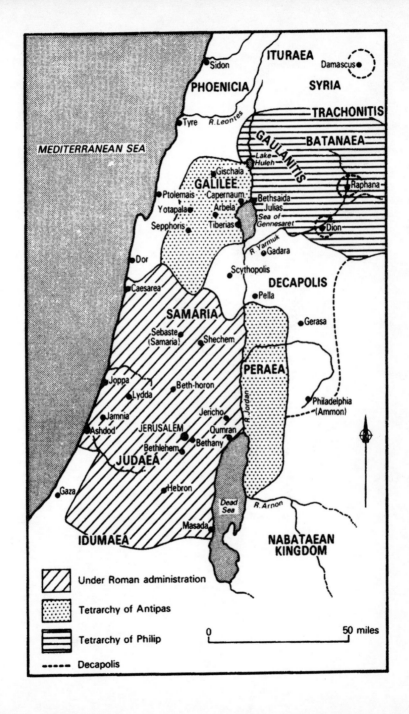

ITURAEA

Damascus

SYRIA

Sidon

PHOENICIA

TRACHONITIS

Tyre   R. Leontes

GAULANITIS   BATANAEA

MEDITERRANEAN SEA

Lake
Huleh

Gischala

GALILEE

Raphana

Ptolemais   Capernaum

Bethsaida-
Julias

Yotapala   Arbela

Sea of
Gennesaret

Sepphoris   Tiberias

Dion

R. Yarmuk

Dor

Gadara

Caesarea

Scythopolis

DECAPOLIS

Pella

SAMARIA

Gerasa

Sebaste
(Samaria)

Shechem

PERAEA

Joppa

Beth-horon

Lydda

R. Jordan

Jericho

Jamnia

Philadelphia
(Ammon)

Ashdod

JERUSALEM   Qumran

Bethlehem   Bethany

JUDAEA

Gaza   Hebron

Dead
Sea   R. Arnon

Masada

IDUMAEA

NABATAEAN
KINGDOM

Under Roman administration

Tetrarchy of Antipas

Tetrarchy of Philip

----- Decapolis

0   50 miles

Preface

There are not many books on the New Testament in general, or the historical Jesus in particular, to which one could give the accolade: 'I found it difficult to put down'. But that was just my experience when I first read Gerd Theissen's *The Shadow of the Galilean* some fourteen years ago. For sheer readability Theissen's *Shadow* can easily stand alongside the massive Jesus books of Dominic Crossan in the US and Tom Wright in the UK. But for inventiveness in presentation he pulls ahead of both. And for compactness and the compelling power of the narrative he weaves, Theissen stands alone.

The Shadow of the Galilean has the two great strengths of a good historical novel. By that I mean, first, that Theissen has created a credibly historical character – Andreas – who as autobiographical storyteller maintains the narrative flow. Andreas is a fruit and grain merchant from Sepphoris, the administrative capital of Galilee, who is blackmailed by Pilate, Roman governor (prefect) of Judea, to gather information on the Jesus movement. It is through the information and rumours that come to Andreas that the reader is enabled to trace out 'the shadow' of the Galilean. The element of intrigue and hint of danger is just the spice that the narrative needs.

Second, good historical novelists should be master of their sources: the invented characters and episodes should fit seamlessly into the historical facts known to us, integrated into the historical data as though wholly of a piece with it. Theissen passes this test with flying colours as well. No question, Theissen knows his sources – not just the Gospels, but the Jewish historian Josephus, and the complementary information which enables historians to reconstruct a reliable picture of what happened in the past. The reader can be confident of historical authenticity, for example, that references to

Qumran draw on the best information available, and that the social and political contexts are credible. There is a historical 'concreteness' in 'the shadow' which most studies of the historical Jesus fail to achieve. Through the character of Andreas the reader can begin to experience something of the reality of Second-Temple Judaism as a living religion, including its diversity, something of the real politics of first-century Israel, and something of the social tensions particularly between city and village.

Part of the genius of *The Shadow* is that it enables the twenty-first-century reader to gain a more realistic sense of how the traditions about Jesus began to take shape. Andreas is not a follower of Jesus, nor does he ever meet him. So there is nothing first hand in his reports back to the Roman authorities. But neither is he merely chasing shadows; he meets, for example, with Chuza and his wife, the latter being a supporter of Jesus. The image is rather of one who is close enough to catch sight of Jesus' shadow, to be overshadowed by Jesus, but never to see him face to face. This also adds to the spice of intrigue.

The point I am making is that Andreas knows about Jesus as the great majority of Jews of the time knew about Jesus. To be sure, Andreas is hunting out the information in order to report on Jesus. But the stories and rumours which he narrates are probably a fair representation of the market-place gossip and campfire tales by which news was popularly disseminated in those days. The picture he builds up is not the same as we would have heard within the groups of Jesus' followers. It is rather lopsided: Andreas' attention is naturally caught by teaching that sounds subversive. But that is part of the point. There would have been no 'right', or no single 'right', picture of Jesus. So much would depend on what the second-hand hearer would hear – and on how he or she heard it. Andreas has to decide how to present Jesus to his spymaster – as a security risk? a philosopher? a poet?

To press the image, the point is that only a shadow is perceptible – not Jesus himself, but only the shadow he cast. And the clarity of the shadow depended on how high the sun was in the sky, whether other items blocked it, and where the viewer stood in relation to it. The weakness of the book is that Theissen filters the information about

Jesus which he records (though in a historically credible way). The strength is that, because Andreas gathers clear reports (drawn in fact directly from the Gospels), he enables the reader both to sympathize with Andreas' dilemma in assessing Jesus and to join with him in the attempt.

Another strength of the book is the very neat way Theissen attempts to bridge the gulf between historical situation and modern scholarship. He uses four techniques. First, the style is often somewhat artificial – probably an inevitable consequence of trying to achieve narrative exegesis. I did not find it a problem. Second, Andreas is himself rather modern (too modern), at times unbelievably sceptical for his age; but if he was successfully to communicate across the centuries that too was probably inevitable. Third, there are some twenty-two pages of notes, plus an eight-page appendix on the most important sources on Jesus and his time. So readers can always follow up details and check them for themselves.

The master stroke, however, is the correspondence with Dr Kratzinger. A letter to this colleague introduces the book, and subsequent letters come after each chapter. In these Theissen explains the perspective he has adopted, answers questions and deals with various points of detail, and thus is able to convey effectively to the reader the scholarly principles and judgments that have informed the writing of each chapter. In this way the reader is made aware that not simply Andreas reacted to the shadow of the Galilean, but Theissen too. In this way, Theissen is able to give voice to the critical questionings which his portrayal was bound to raise. The in-effect dialogue between Andreas and Jesus is thus complemented by the dialogue between Theissen and Kratzinger, and the resulting four-way discussion (however artificial) enables the reader as a twenty-first-century reader to join in. I won't spoil the plot by revealing the identity of Dr Kratzinger. On this too *The Shadow of the Galilean* invites you to read for yourself and to make up your own mind.

James D. G. Dunn
Lightfoot Professor of Divinity
University of Durham

In Place of a Foreword:

Letter to a Colleague

Dear Dr Kratzinger,

Many thanks for your letter. Yes, the rumours that have reached you are true: I'm writing a narrative about Jesus. You beseech me never to publish this book. You're anxious about my scholarly reputation and concerned for the good name of New Testament interpretation. Your worries would be justified if this were the kind of Life of Jesus which imaginatively filled in those areas about which historical sources are silent and sacrificed historical truth to making an effect. Let me reassure you: I am most averse to writing anything about Jesus which is not based on sources. There is nothing about Jesus in my book which I have not also taught at the university.

Of course I have invented the narrative framework. The main figure in the book, Andreas, never lived, but he could have lived in the time of Jesus. I have made use of many historical sources in this story about him, and his experiences are meant to demonstrate the sort of thing that people living in Palestine at that time could expect constantly to happen to them.

You may ask whether the reader will see this web of truth and fiction for what it is, whether he or she will be able to distinguish between what I have made up and what is historical. To make this possible I have added notes to the text in which I cite the sources that I have used. Of course the notes don't have to be read.

You ask what the real purpose of this book is. In essence, I am concerned to do only one thing: to sketch in narrative form a picture of Jesus and his time which both does justice to the present state of scholarly research and is understandable to present-day readers. The narrative has been constructed in such a way as to show not only the results of that research but also how it is carried on. I have chosen the narrative form in order to show readers who have no access to historical studies what scholars think and how they argue.

I hope I may send you the first chapter to see what you think of it. I shall be delighted if after reading it you feel rather more positive about my plans.

All good wishes,
Yours,
Gerd Theissen

I

The Interrogation

The cell was dark. Only a few moments ago people had been thronging round me in a panic. Now I was alone. My head was throbbing. My limbs hurt. The soldiers had looked innocuous; they had joined in the demonstration and the shouting. No one could have guessed that they had been planted there until they took out their concealed clubs and hit us with them. Most of us fled. Some were trampled to death in the rush, others were knocked down by the blows of the soldiers.

There had been no reason for me to run. After all, I was simply there by chance, along with Timon and Malchus. I hadn't been interested in the demonstration. I was interested in Barabbas, whom I had noticed among the demonstrators. I was trying to get to him when panic broke out and everything turned into a confused mixture of cries, blows, whistles and kicks. When I came to, I had been arrested. So had Timon. I wonder whether Malchus escaped?

So now I was squatting in this darkness. I felt the pains in my body. But it was not just the bruises and the fetters which hurt. Something more had made my limbs seize up. It was the humiliation through brute force, and the fear of the further humiliation to which I would be helplessly exposed.

Guards were marching up and down outside. I heard voices. Someone opened the door. I was dragged out in fetters for interrogation, somewhere in the official residence of the Roman prefect in Jerusalem. An officer sat opposite me. A scribe took notes.

'Do you speak Greek?' was the first question.

'All educated people here speak Greek,' I replied.

The man who was interrogating me had clear-cut features. His watchful eyes inspected me in a penetrating way. In other circumstances I might perhaps have liked the look of him.

'What's your name?'

'Andreas, son of John.'

'Where do you come from?'

'Sepphoris in Galilee.'

'Occupation?'

'I deal in fruit and grain.'

The officer paused and waited for the scribe to write all this down with a scratchy pen.

'What are you doing in Jerusalem?', he went on.

'I've come up for Pentecost.'

He raised his head and looked me straight in the eye. 'Why did you demonstrate against Pilate?'

'I wasn't demonstrating. I just happened to get caught up in the demonstration.'

Should I have said that I had recognized an old acquaintance among the crowd of demonstrators? Certainly not! Barabbas was very hostile to Rome. He might well be on the wanted list. I could be associated with him.

'Do you claim that you didn't shout "No money for Pilate!"'

'I've no idea what it's all about,' I lied.

The official laughed derisively. Everyone in Jerusalem at that time knew that the fuss was about money which Pilate wanted to take from the temple treasury for the building of a new aqueduct for Jerusalem.[1]

'You ought to know better than to get mixed up with a crowd of demonstrators.'

'None of them were armed. It was all friendly until the soldiers intervened,' I retorted hastily.

'But the demonstration was against us Romans. That sort of thing is suspicious. Haven't you already been involved in clashes between Jews and non-Jews? Haven't we met before?'

'What kind of clashes?'

'Conflicts in our cities in which hotheads of your age get involved. They begin with stupid tricks and end up with street fights as in Caesarea.'[2]

'My home town, Sepphoris, is quiet. The inhabitants are mostly Jews – but they've had a Greek education.'

'Did you say Sepphoris? Weren't there also disturbances in

Sepphoris? What about the revolt after the death of Herod? Your city was a real nest of terrorists!' he shouted back at me.

'That's not true. Thirty-three years ago there was a rebellion against Romans and Herodians throughout Palestine. The rebels captured our city by a trick and forced the inhabitants to fight against the Romans. The city had to pay the penalty. The Roman general Quintilius Varus sent troops against it, stormed it, burned it and either killed the inhabitants or sold them as slaves. It was a fearful catastrophe for our city.'[3]

How could I get him off this subject? Not everyone had been killed or enslaved at that time. Some had managed to escape, including Barabbas' father. Barabbas had often told me about it. Were they interrogating me because of him? But what could they know of our friendship? At all events, I must distract him from anything connected with Barabbas. Once again I stressed:

'All the inhabitants of Sepphoris had to pay for the rebellion – even Varus soon met his end: not long afterwards he perished in Germany along with three legions!'

'And they liked that in Sepphoris!' The officer's voice still sounded loud and angry.

'There was no one here to like it. They were all dead or in slavery. The city was a pile of ruins. It was rebuilt by Herod's son Herod Antipas. He settled people there who were favourable to the Romans. My father also came to Sepphoris at that time. We are a new city. Ask the Galileans in the neighbourhood. Our city is thought to be friendly to the Romans. That's the Sepphoris I come from.[4]

'We'll look into all that. Another question. What position does your family have in the city?'

'My father is a decurion, a member of the council.'

Our city was organized like a Greek city. There were a civic assembly, a council, elections and city officials. I deliberately referred to this because I knew that the Romans gave support to the republican cities and the well-to-do in them.

'Your father must be rich if he is one of the decurions of Sepphoris. What's his profession?'

'He deals in grain as I do.'

'Who does he deal with?'

'Galilee supplies agricultural produce to the cities on the Mediterranean coast: Caesarea, Dor, Ptolemais, Tyre and Sidon. I've already provided the Roman cohorts in Caesarea with grain.'

'We can check that. Do you have business dealings with Herod Antipas?'

'Of course. He has the biggest estates in Galilee. He used to have his residence in Sepphoris. I often deal with his stewards.'

I noticed how interested the interrogating officer was in Herod Antipas.

'What do they think of Herod Antipas in Sepphoris?'

'He can rely on us in the city, but people in the country still have reservations about the Herodians.'

The officer picked up a piece of paper. He seemed to read it through quickly, gave me a questioning look and went on:

'This is the report on the interrogation of your slave Timon. Some of it reads rather differently. Do you really claim that you are loyal supporters of Herod Antipas?'

I shuddered. They had interrogated Timon! Slaves were interrogated under torture. Timon could have said anything about me and my family. I felt the blood rush to my head and quivered all over in anger.

'Answer me! What do you have against Herod Antipas?'

'We support his rule. All respectable people in Sepphoris and Tiberias support it,' I asserted.

'Then why do people in your house mock him so much?'

'What do you mean?'

'Your slave says that you call him a degenerate king, a reed shaking in the wind, a fox!'

I laughed in relief:

'He was once to have been heir to King Herod. But Herod changed his will regularly. Antipas inherited neither kingly rank nor kingdom, not even the largest and best part, but only a quarter of it: Galilee and Peraea.'

'So now he dreams of possessing all of it one day?' Suddenly there was silence in the room. Even the scribe had stopped writing and looked at me.

'Perhaps. At all events he's dreamed of it,' I replied.

'And what about the reed in the wind?'

I had the comforting feeling that Antipas had become more important than I was. Was the official trying to collect information about him? I continued rather more confidently:

'The "reed in the wind" is a phrase people use of him. There was criticism ten years ago when Antipas moved his capital from our city to Tiberias, a city he had founded in honour of the emperor. Of course we in Sepphoris were unhappy about the transfer. Business is better in a capital than in the provinces. So there was a good deal of criticism of Antipas in Sepphoris.'

'What's that got to do with the "reed in the wind"?'

'That came about like this. Antipas had coins minted in his new capital. Normally coins have portraits of rulers on them, but it is forbidden under Jewish law to depict human beings or animals. So Antipas chose a harmless emblem, one perhaps meant to signify his new capital by the Sea of Galilee: reeds, a reed waving in the wind – and now that is on his first coins, where otherwise his portrait would have been. So he is mocked as being a reed "waving in the wind". That's all.'[5]

'Who is he wavering between?'

'Sepphoris and Tiberias.'

'Only between cities?'

'Also between wives.'

'You mean the affair with Herodias.'

'Yes, his wavering between his first wife, the Nabataean princess, and Herodias.'

'Isn't he also wavering between Nabataeans and Romans? At any rate he was married to a daughter of the king of Nabataea.'

So that was why the Romans were interested in the wavering Antipas! I said quietly – and it was the truth:

'No! Antipas is as pro-Roman through and through as his father Herod.'

'But how does that fit in with the fact that at the same time he's a strict Jew? As you said, he won't have images.'

'Nor will any Jew.'

'Really? Your slave Timon told us that there was a statue in one of the rooms of your house.'

'That's a statue given to us by a Gentile business friend. We didn't want to hurt him by refusing the gift,' I said in confusion.

'That's certainly interesting: you conceal statues of gods in your houses.'

'Antipas himself has statues of animals in his palace![6] And as you know, his brother Philip even has a portrait of the emperor on his coins.'

'Statues of animals? Is that really true?'

'I've seen them myself. They're in his new palace in Tiberias. Well-to-do people are more lax over the Jewish laws in their own houses than in public.'

'So how would it be if we spread rumours among the people that Antipas was practising idolatry in secret, and that some people in Sepphoris are not much better.'

'Statues aren't gods. Statues are made by craftsmen. They're things like anything else. The fact that we have such a "thing" standing around at home doesn't mean that we are practising idolatry.'

'I don't understand. All the world worships the gods by means of statues.'

'We shall never worship what has been made by human hands. God is invisible. It's impossible to make an image of him.'

There was a pause. The officer looked at me thoughtfully. Wasn't it stupid in my situation to stress what distinguishes us Jews from all other peoples – including this Roman official in front of me? Finally he said gently:

'I've heard a story about how this God who has no image came about. It goes like this. A long time ago a plague broke out in Egypt. The Pharaoh turned for advice to the oracle of the god Ammon and was told that he should purge his kingdom of you damnable Jews and then the plague would cease. All the Jews were driven out into the wilderness, where they were left to their fate. Most of them wandered around in the wilderness, demoralized. But then one of you, Moses by name, called on them not to wait for divine intervention or the help of other men. Seeing that in any case they had been forsaken by the gods they were to trust in themselves and rise above the present distress.[7] – When I heard this story I asked myself whether you believe in any god at all.'

What was the purpose of this caricature of the biblical story? Did he want to provoke me? Did he have an interest in our religion? That was hardly likely. What should I say in reply? Something vague and indefinite? Something about the invisible God whom no one, neither he nor I, can understand and comprehend, the one whom no one knows? Something to divert him from the great questions? But then the thought occurred to me that if I could involve him in a debate over basic matters I would finally have distracted him from Barabbas. So I heard myself say stubbornly:

'God is not like the gods of the nations. The invisible God does not deal with the powerful but with the outcast who are driven into the desert.'

I say how the officer winced.

'Do you doubt that the gods are on the side of the Roman empire? How could it have spread so far? How could a small city have become a world empire?'

'All nations think that the gods are on the side of the victors. But we know that the invisible God can be on the side of the losers.'

The officer looked at me in some concern. His voice sounded choked.

'There is something in your faith which rebels against any earthly power. But you too will find your place in the Roman empire like all other peoples. For it is our task to bring some order to the peace of the world, to spare the conquered and to fight against rebels[8] – in this land and all over the world.'

And after a brief pause he added: 'Your case will take some time yet. We shall examine what you've said and then decide whether charges are to be laid against you.'

And with that I was dismissed. I was taken back to my cell. Now I had to wait. How long was it likely to be before they completed their investigations into me? I was basically confident. I came from a well-to-do family which had good relations with the Romans. But there were moments of uncertainty. What else would Timon say? Would he keep his mouth shut about Barabbas? He had never seen him, but he could have heard him mentioned in conversations. If my connections with Barabbas could be kept in the background, not much could really happen – if!

Then I had gloomy forebodings: my fate seemed to me to be the forerunner of a gloomy destiny which would affect all our people. Those tensions between Jews and Romans which had led to the demonstration against Pilate would get greater and greater – to the point of open rebellion against the Romans. Untold misery, war and oppression, would come upon our land.[9] Compared with this misery the misfortune of my arrest was small. But there was not much comfort in that. In Pilate's dark prison the time of waiting seemed to me to be infinitely long. It was a bad time for me.

Dear Dr Kratzinger,

Many thanks for your comments on the first chapter. You say that you can't find anything in it that points to Jesus. Please be patient. By beginning with a picture of the time of Jesus I'm simply doing my duty as a historian, explaining a historical phenomenon in terms of its context. In the case of Jesus this context is the social and religious world of Judaism.

Here the Gospels give us a one-sided picture. They were written at a time (between AD 70 and 100) in which the renewal movement within Judaism centred on Jesus had become a separate religion from Judaism, in competition with its mother religion. Its writings often give us only caricatures of Judaism. It is therefore unclear to the reader of the Bible how deeply Jesus is rooted in Judaism.

The Gospels also suggest that at that time Jesus was the focal point of Palestinian history. From a historical perspective, however, he was a marginal phenomenon. We do not immediately come upon his traces when we look at the Palestine of the first century AD. The historian's experience needs to be communicated to the reader. But I promise you that there will be many pointers to Jesus in my story.

I assume from your letter that you want to read more of my book before finally passing judgment on it. May I take that as an invitation to send you further chapters? I've just finished the second.

All good wishes,
Yours,
Gerd Theissen

2

Blackmail

The worst thing was that there was no one with whom I could discuss my situation. Did anyone even know about it? Did my parents guess where I was? Had Malchus managed to get home? Was Timon lying in another corner of this dark cellar? Gloomy pictures arose in my mind. How many Jews had already been incarcerated here, how many tortured, how many killed? How many had simply disappeared? And what would become of me?

In this hole to which no sun penetrated, and no noise apart from the footsteps of the guards, I lost all sense of time. The cell was like a coffin in which I was buried alive. Fear of death filled the clammy air. In despair I prayed:

Vindicate me, Lord our God,
for I am innocent.
I have trusted in you.
Prove me,
try me.
You know me better than I know myself.
Defend me before their tribunal
against false witnesses and calumniations.
Preserve me from the intrigues of their secret police.
I have no complicity with the powerful.
I despise those who scorn human life,
who treat it as refuse,
who throw us into prison,
who humiliate and ill-treat us.
Let me not perish through their hands.
On those hands there is blood.

They get themselves riches through bribery,
they exercise power through compulsion.
Anyone who criticizes them disappears into their cellars:
anyone who rebels against them is removed.
O God, let me see your house again,
where your glory dwells.
Deliver me from the hands of these bandits.
And I will praise and bless you in the congregation.[1]

I counted the days by the sparse rations which were regularly thrust into the cell. The first week went by. Nothing happened. The second week went by. It seemed like a year. Finally in the third week, I was brought out.

Was I going to be set free? My hopes rose. First of all we went through a labyrinth of corridors. Then I was pushed into a large room. I stood blinded by the light flooding in through the window. Gradually I was able to note details. Before me was a judgment seat on an elevated dais. On it sat a small man. He was wearing an expensive white toga with purple stripes. A golden ring gleamed on his hand – a sign that he was a Roman knight. The soldier who had brought me in whispered to me, 'The prefect.' So this was Pontius Pilate, the prefect of Judaea and Samaria![2]

A hearing at the highest level. My case would certainly be decided here. So long as nothing had come out about Barabbas!

Pilate was reading a scroll as I entered the room. To his right and left stood two soldiers of his bodyguard. A scribe was taking notes. Without raising his eyes Pilate began:

'Andreas, son of John, I have been reading the record of the interrogation. You claim that it was pure chance that you happened to be involved in the demonstration against me. In the meantime we have gained information about you. We have learned a great deal. Why did you conceal important matters from us?'

'I have no idea of anything else that might be particularly important,' I said hesitantly.

'It is important.'

He looked at me unimpressed and continued in a monotone.

'Something has been left out of the account of your career.'

'I don't know anything else in which the Roman authorities might be particularly interested.'

'Where were you after you left the gymnasium?'[3]

So that was it! Someone had told me to tell the truth to the state police, but as little of it as possible. So I said:

'I was in the wilderness for a year with an ascetic, a man called Bannus.'

'Being an ascetic and nothing else?'

'I wanted to find the way to true life. I studied the law of our God.'

'Why did you keep quiet about it?'

'Why should I mention that particular year? It was a purely religious matter.'

'This "purely religious matter" is also open to other interpretations. First, you disappeared to spend a year with the resistance fighters. Secondly, you were arrested at a demonstration against the Roman prefect. Thirdly, this demonstration was directed by some agitators from the underground.'

'And am I supposed to be one of these agitators and string-pullers? That's nonsense!'

'But it's possible.'

'I was in the wilderness to reflect in solitude. Not everyone who puts everyday life behind them for a while is a trouble-maker and a terrorist. I'm for peace.'

'You kept quiet about your time in the desert. That's suspicious.'

I began to sweat. My hair stuck to my brow, my clothes stank. I had not been able to change them for three weeks. I had not been allowed to wash. Outwardly I must have presented a sorry picture. But I was also falling apart inside. Like many other people, I really had gone into the wilderness for religious reasons, to reflect there and seek God's will in the solitude of an oasis.[4] But it was there that I had made the acquaintance of Barabbas. Did Pilate know this? But he simply repeated,

'It's all very suspicious.'

'It's certainly suspicious if you look at it with mistrustful eyes. I only got involved in the demonstration by chance. I've a good conscience. That's why I didn't run away like all the others.'

Pilate still looked utterly unmoved. What did he want of me?

'I could institute proceedings,' he said after a short pause.

'I would be bound to be acquitted!'

'Perhaps. But I could send you to Rome for further investigations.'

'They would acquit me there, too.'

'It takes two years. You would certainly spend two years in prison!'
He looked at me and gave a meaningful laugh.

What was Pilate getting at? He couldn't send every suspect to
Rome. Were he to do so he would be shipping out half Palestine. On
the other hand it was clear that he could damage me, regardless of
whether I was found guilty or not. He continued:

'I'll make you a fair offer. You can go free as soon as you say that
you are ready to provide us with material about certain religious
movements in the country.'

'That's blackmail!'

I was seething with anger and disgust. I would have liked to spit in
Pilate's face. This man was trying shamelessly to blackmail me, and
he spoke of fairness.

'Let's say that it is something which is in both our interests.'

'I will not spy.'

'Don't let's use the word "spy" in this context. Let's call it
"research". You won't be putting a finger on anyone or denouncing
anyone.'

How cynically Pilate spoke! As if he didn't know that to report that
the ideas of a group of people were not in line with those of the Roman
occupying forces was tantamount to denunciation. I pulled myself
together and tried to say as gently as possible,

'None of my fellow countrymen will see the difference between
spying and research.'

'We would regard you as . . .' Pilate thought for a moment; then he
seemed to have found the right word, 'as an adviser in religious
affairs.'

I kept quiet.

'As you like. In that case we will start proceedings against you and
put your time in the desert – or wherever you were – under the
microscope!'

'So it's blackmail!'

Had Pilate discovered something about my connection with

Barabbas? What was he capable of? There were bad rumours about him, rumours of ill-treatment and acts of violence. Couldn't he simply make me disappear? Couldn't he produce false evidence against me at any time? Couldn't he get anything he wanted out of me by torture? And if I gave in? But I continued to fight with all my strength against such an idea.

'Andreas, you're upset. I understand. You're still young. But in a long life I've learnt that it is hard to persuade people to be useful of their own accord. You have to help them along.'

His voice still sounded as detached and matter-of-fact as it had at the beginning of our conversation. I had the impression that my personal fate left him cold. Basically it seemed to him to be a matter of indifference whether or not I accepted his offer. And that worried me.

'Call it blackmail as far as I'm concerned. But try to look at things from my point of view. I'm responsible for law and order in this country. That's a difficult job. Why? Because we Romans constantly hurt your religious sensibilities although we don't want to. Take this aqueduct affair as an example. My idea was to get reasonable water supplies for Jerusalem at last. My best architects and builders were to be employed on the job. But there wasn't enough money to finance it. Experts confirmed that the temple treasury could be used for the supply of water in Jerusalem.[5] There's enough money there. Every Jew pays an annual temple tax. So I approached the temple with the suggestion that they should finance the water supply. Completely in accordance with your laws. And what happened? A few pious fanatics sense disaster. They give the word, "No holy money for unholy Pilate. Not a penny for the Romans from the temple treasure!" As though it were a matter of using the money for ungodly purposes! Ignoring the fact that this is a matter of getting money for an aqueduct from which the temple and all Jerusalem would profit. Now we Romans are again portrayed as tyrannous authorities who do not observe your religious laws – and even want to plunder the temple treasure.'

That's what had happened over his aqueduct. He had wanted to improve his image and the attempt had completely misfired. Was I now to help to make more successful propaganda for him? The excitement which had crept into Pilate's voice for a moment seemed to have been blown away when he continued.

'The whole affair was a setback. But despite such setbacks we must continue to do everything possible to get peace in this land. There's a good chance: my confidence is based on two considerations.

First, on the proven principles of Roman policy towards subject peoples. We see the secret of our success as being our ability to turn enmity into friendship. For what more faithful allies does the Roman people have than those who were its most stubborn enemies? What would the empire be today had not far-sightedness united victors and vanquished?[6] The Jews were not always our enemies. On the contrary, by becoming our allies you freed yourselves from the rule of Syrian kings![7] At that time you succeeded in preserving your own religion and culture with our support. Only later, when your neighbours asked us for protection from your military invasions, did you come under our rule – and at just the right time for us to be able to prevent the threat of a civil war which would have brought deep distress upon your land.[8] But even in this situation we left your religion untouched. So our policy will continue to be respect for your religion, your God, your customs, your sensibilities. We respect even what is alien to us. But we expect you to respect what is holy to us, to note the reverence that our soldiers have for the emperor and allow everyone everywhere to worship his gods. Respect must have a reciprocal basis.

And now my second consideration. I know from conversations with your leading priests that you, too, accept our rule in principle. God has long allowed other peoples to rule over you: you have tolerated Babylonians, Persians and Greeks – why not also the Romans, who are far more obliging towards subject peoples than all previous world empires? You say that everything that happens is controlled by the one and only God who is worshipped in Jerusalem.' He paused, as if he wanted to leave me time to reflect. 'In that case you must also concede that he wanted us Romans to build our world empire. He wanted you to lose through us the independence which you had won from the Syrians with our help.[9] There is no reason why the Jewish people cannot accept us as rulers of the world – especially since we understand that, unlike any other peoples in the East, you cannot worship the emperor as god.

So in principle there should be no problems. But in practice we have great difficulties. Above all we have the problem that what your leading priests say to us is not what moves the people. At the moment much seems to be changing in your religion. There is tumult among the people. New ideas and movements keep arising. Prophets and preachers go through the land. It is difficult for us to get the feel of these new movements. Your leading priests do not do much better. They have lost the spiritual leadership of some groups of the population. Yet on these groups the stability of the land depends. We need information about them. We are ready to respect your religious feelings as far as possible and avoid unnecessary offence. But to do that we need to know what is happening among the people. We have plenty of experts in official Judaism. We need someone whose ear is closer to the ground. Only then can we have further information to damp down conflicts before they get going.'

'But why me? Why do you think that I'm the right man?'

'You are educated. You speak our language and your own. You are well informed on religious matters in Judaism and in our religion. You come from a family which is well disposed towards the Romans. You are not a fanatic. You are for peace. The fact that you have a little idol in a side room gives you added appeal to us. I have long-standing orders that we should look for someone like you. You are the right person.'

'But I don't want to be!'

I really didn't want to be involved. It would be an intolerable double game. How could I combine my friendship for Barabbas with my work for the Romans? How easily I could fall between all the stools! But Pilate said gently,

'Think: there's still something hanging over you, even if you are acquitted. I need only say in Caesarea that you are under suspicion of having dealings with terrorists. That would not do your business much good. It would ruin you – and your father.'

It was blackmail! I felt a deep sense of contempt rising in me. Everything was tactics among these powerful people; they were all-calculating. Their real feelings and attitudes remained hidden. The one certain thing was that they wanted to keep their power. Did Pilate guess my thoughts? He began again:

'Find anyone in this country who will do anything for us without blackmail! You probably think that I'm a quite terrible man, just as others think that I am inhuman. I recently heard what the Jews in Alexandria are saying about my period of office; that it is a chain of acts of bribery, violence, robbery, ill treatment, offence, executions or legal processes, one intolerable cruelty after another.[10] I grant that I am ready to do a good deal in the cause of peace. But I am not as inhuman as that.'

He grinned. He probably noticed that his words were not proving to be particularly convincing. But perhaps that, too, was his tactic. I tried to gain time:

'How am I to get access to all these religious movements?' At all events I did not want to give the impression that I already had contacts with them.

'No problem. You'll stay a little longer in prison. You'll be well treated. All you want. We shall then see that the rumour gets around that the Romans are holding a young man who is outstanding for his steadfastness and faithfulness to the Jewish religion. Things are going badly with him. Nevertheless he makes no secret of his conviction that the Romans are in this land illegitimately and that it belongs only to God. In short, we'll give you a halo. Then we'll let you go. All the pious groups will trust you. All you'll have to do is go round the country and write a report about the religious mood among the people. We're interested in anything that might endanger political stability in the land, anything that puts our rule in question. My official, Metilius, whom you've already met, will explain your task. He will provide you with what information we already have. Do you agree?'

'I'd like to think it over a bit more.'

'All right. Until tomorrow. And remember that despite rumours to the contrary I'm not inhuman.'

Again a grin appeared on his face. Was that the end of the conversation? No. Pilate turned to me again.

'I read in the report something about statues Antipas has in his palace. Have you seen them yourself?'

'Yes, and others could also bear witness to them.'

'The hypocrite! He puts up animal statues at home and protests when I want to hang up shields with the emperor's name on in my Jerusalem residence.[11] He says that that sort of thing is against your laws.

Hypocrisy everywhere! People get excited about my coins with harmless sacrificial symbols on them,[12] but you can only pay the temple tax in coins of Tyre! And what do they have on them? The god Melkart – an idol![13] In the temple forecourt all the money is exchanged for these idolatrous coins. Sometimes when I go through the forecourt I want to overturn the tables of the money-changers! No one gets worked up about them! But there's a great outcry against my harmless copper coins!. But let's leave it at that.'

Pilate had spoken angrily. He seemed almost to have forgotten that I was there. But right at the end he turned to me. Again his voice sounded matter-of-fact, cold and dead. It worried me.

'Ponder your decision well! And do not forget that I am not the inhuman creature others see in me. I am just a Roman prefect who wants to keep his land in order.'

I was led off and again sat in my dark cell. I had been shown a way out. But it was a dead end. I was caught in a trap. I wished I were anywhere else, and in my helplessness I again turned to the God of my fathers.[14]

> Free us, O God, from these scoundrels!
> There are no honest men left,
> and all humanity has disappeared.
> The powerful surround us with propaganda talk,
> they make fun of us.
> Fine words come from their lips,
> but their thoughts are on oppression.
> They talk of peace and threaten with weapons,
> they speak of tolerance and mean their power.
> Let them choke on their speeches,
> on their well-considered words,
> which sound so statesmanlike
> and seek to break our backbones.
> Destroy the arrogance of their power
> and the cynicism of their rule.

Speak, Lord.
'For the sake of the oppressed,
for the sake of the prisoners,
I will arise,
I will save
those who sigh for freedom!'
God, you will preserve and protect us
from criminals and dictators!
You are our support
amongst those to whom nothing is holy.
Vileness spreads among men,
but your word is trustworthy,
a light in the darkness.

Dear Dr Kratzinger,

You are 'amazed' at my boldness in inventing stories about Pilate. It would trouble your conscience as a historian and exegete to do that.

Of course Pilate never had the conversations I attribute to him. But the background to his actions which emerges from this conversation is the one that I analyse in my lectures on the New Testament environment. The subject-matter of history is not only individual events but also typical conflicts and structures. They are the 'rules of the game' which my fictitious narrative follows.

If I may for a moment use our technical academic language, I would say that the presupposition of 'narrative exegesis', which is what narrative like my book is now called – is the step from historical events to structural history. The basic structure of narrative exegesis consists of historical reconstructions of patterns of behaviour, conflicts and tensions, and its superstructure consists of fictitious events in which historical source material is worked over in a poetic way. This definition of narrative exegesis is rather too pretentious for my taste. But you know that things have to be put in a complicated way if they are to be taken seriously in the academic world.

Moreover, in a 'narrative exegesis' one can sometimes neglect chronology in the use of source material. Even events after the death of Jesus can illustrate the structural conditions of events in his time. I have no qualms about, for example, moving back by about twenty-five years the wilderness ascetic 'Bannus', who was active in the wilderness of Jordan in the fifties. You have criticized that as an anachronism. But scholars often act in this anachronistic way. Would we not justifiably criticize an academic dissertation on John the Baptist if it did not indicate that Bannus was the nearest analogy?

I shall be very interested in your views on the next chapter.

All good wishes,
Yours,
Gerd Theissen

3

Andreas' Decision

Andreas – Pilate's spy? Never! My whole being rebelled against it. Though Pilate might imprison me for years in this hole I would never betray anyone to the Romans! All right, the Romans had brought peace and quiet to our country. But what kind of a peace was it that was achieved by oppression and blackmail? What kind of quiet which only existed because people were silenced by force? The thoughts kept whirling around my head.

But what was I do to? What would happen if I said no? Would Pilate have me tortured in order to extract information from me about my friends, my family and possibly also Barabbas? Would he have me secretly executed so that no one learned of his attempts at blackmail? Or would he have me crucified publicly as a deterrent? Would he ruin the family business? What would happen to Timon? His last words rang in my ears: 'I am not the inhuman creature others see in me!' Wasn't that a clear hint? Didn't it mean, 'Watch out, perhaps I am indeed the inhuman creature that I seem to others to be'?

Could I escape this torment? Was there a place where no blackmail could reach me? Where no one commanded and threatened? Where all the tormenting voices in me fell silent and everything was still?

I longed for death. Had I not learned from the philosophers[1] that there is a way out even from the worst situations? One door, death's door, is always open. Through this door one could escape the most cruel tyrannies. But was suicide the right solution? The Romans admired Cato and Brutus, who had killed themselves in a hopeless situation, and this attitude could also be found among Jews. In principle, however, we thought differently. God has given us the task of living and we cannot hand it back to him when we think it too difficult. For who can know what plans God still has for us – God, who gives courage to the lost and outcast? Our ancestors, too, had been abandoned on all sides – abandoned by all men. They had wandered through the wilderness hopelessly and in despair. But they had not given up. They had believed Moses when he told them that they had a task which they could not betray.

If only I had even the freedom to wander in the wilderness! Then a thought went through my mind: why should I not appear to accept Pilate's offer – and then disappear without trace into the wilderness? I had learned how to survive there. Bannus had taught me. I could go to him. Perhaps I was now in a position to understand his teaching. At that time it had been alien to me.

What had driven me out to him? I had been very restless, in a way which I find difficult to explain. I had grown up in a liberal home. We adopted a philosophical approach to Jewish customs and convictions. My father kept saying that the Bible expresses the thought of Greek philosophers. I recall how we once watched the dawn in wonderment. We had climbed a mountain to wait for the sun to rise. Then it broke through the morning mist and transformed the landscape in a marvellous play of colour and light. My father said, 'I can see why pagans worship the sun. It is only a ray of the true God. Through its radiance they detect God. They may indeed confuse the creator with his creatures, but they have a sense of the beauty of this world.'[2]

He loved beautiful things. That's why a guest once gave us a little statue of a god. For my father it was the portrait of a handsome man, nothing more. He put it in a side room. He was convinced that once the idea of the incomparability of God is rooted in all hearts, all things of this world can confidently be depicted in pictures.[3]

That's the kind of atmosphere I had grown up in. But then I had discovered that not everyone thought as my parents did. I got to know the faith of simple people who had no need to demonstrate that their faith was of equal worth to Greek philosophy. They took belief in the uniqueness of God utterly for granted, as something which needed no defence and justification. For them the vital thing was that people should fulfil his will and take his commandments seriously in everyday life. I discovered a new world.

At that time I had a deep longing to get to know my Jewish faith thoroughly. I wanted to go right through it – in utter commitment. I longed for decisiveness and clarity. Then I heard of Bannus. I was attracted by the fact that he taught in the wilderness – away from ordinary life. He, too, thought that we Jews had to begin all over again from the beginning: just as we had come from Egypt through the wilderness to arrive in this land, so we had to go back to the wilderness. In it we had to hear once again the voice of the one who had said in the burning bush, 'I am who I am.'

Bannus' views were radical. Not only the Jews but the whole world had to begin all over again. This existing world had gone wrong. It was a world of injustice and oppression, exploitation and anxiety. It would perish because of its own transgressions in a great divine judgment. But then a new world would begin. I can still hear his voice:

Then God will raise up an eternal kingdom
for all men,
the God who once gave the law.
All men will worship this God and stream to his temple.
And there will be only one temple
and roads everywhere will lead to it.
All the mountains will be easy to climb
and ships will be able to sail over all the seas.
All people will live in peace.
All weapons will disappear.
Riches will be shared justly
and God will be among men.
On the hills, wolves and sheep together
will eat grass.
The panther will graze with the kid,
bears will spend the night with calves.
And the lion will eat straw from the manger
like an ox
and small children will lead him on a rope.
Serpents and asps will sleep with babies
and will do them no harm.
For the hand of God will be upon them.[4]

Those were beautiful dreams! Dreams of escape into a new and better world! Not much better than my dream of a flight into the wilderness! But how unrealistic it was! The Romans knew I had spent time in the desert. They would have search parties out for me everywhere. I would drag down Bannus with me. And they would be all the more likely to come upon the traces of Barabbas.

I had already spent some time with Bannus when Barabbas came upon us. He, too, was from Galilee and came from Sepphoris. As a young couple his parents had just managed to escape the catastrophe which befell our city. They had lost home and possessions. Now they lived in modest circumstances in Gischala in northern Galilee. Their flight from Sepphoris and the barbaric treatment of the city had left its stamp on the life of the family. They rejected the Romans – and the Herodian princes, whom they saw as simply puppets of the Romans. Not that they rejected the foreigners because they were foreigners. They rejected them because they brought slavery and oppression.

What had Barabbas looked for in the wilderness? Did he want to hide from the Romans? Had he committed a crime against them? I didn't know. All that was clear was that while I was on the way towards finding a home in the great world of Judaism he had made his decision. He had found his home. He was intent on affirming it in the face of the seductive world of the Romans and Greeks. He exuded certainty. That attracted me. He knew what would give meaning and content to his life. I was searching.

Our reactions to Bannus' teaching differed. The message of a new world did not attract me to the core. I had learned at home to love this world, whereas Barabbas had learned to despise it. He passionately took up the idea of a new world. He differed from Bannus on only one point. He said that this new world would not come by itself. God wanted us to do something about it. And we might have to bring it in by force.[5] The Jews who escaped from Egypt also travelled into a new world. But it did not come to them as a gift. They had to take hard knocks, had to fight against external enemies and be on guard against traitors in their own camp.

Although Barabbas had my sympathies, I shrank from the idea of bringing in a new world by force. Force degenerates. Force corrupts. Nevertheless I found Barabbas congenial: he wanted to do something.

He didn't want to wait. He was convinced that, evil though the world was, it offered a chance. But I was not convinced that his enterprise could be successful. I thought it unrealistic. The Romans were too powerful.

In my present situation I began to understand my companions in the wilderness better. Bannus wanted to have nothing to do with this world of extortion and oppression. Was it not best to leave it behind, to wash off its dirt and madness in the Jordan? Surely it deserved to perish. Had I had the power, I would have brought down fire from heaven to swallow up Pilate and his soldiers.

And I understood Barabbas. Didn't one have to do something against the Romans? Surely one had to defend oneself? But wasn't open rebellion an act of sheer desperation?

Then I had a new idea. Why not play people like Pilate at their own dirty game? If Pilate worked with blackmail, he deserved to be cheated. Shouldn't I accept his offer but only give him information which we Jews had an interest in the Romans having? Couldn't I suppress all other information? Indeed, couldn't I get something out of the Romans which I could use to help my fellow countrymen? Certainly it was a shabby trick, a game of deceit and pretence. Could I take part in it? Was cheating allowed in emergencies?

What about Abraham? Hadn't he passed off his wife as his sister so that Pharaoh wouldn't kill him because he was her husband?[6] That had been a lie. Hadn't Jacob obtained the blessing by trickery and deceit – and yet he was the one who was blessed![7] Didn't David serve the Philistines as a mercenary[8] – and yet he had become the great king of the Jews! Didn't the history of my people show that not only those who did noble acts could be the vehicles of the blessing, but also the little people, the persecuted, those who fought less for honour than for survival. Was there not something about my fate which had always been the lot of my people: having to renounce lofty ideals in order to be able to survive and escape? Wasn't I, Andreas, also Abraham the fugitive, Jacob the persecuted one and David the bandit leader?

Putting my fortunes like this in the context of my people brought me great peace. All at once I felt certain that if I agreed to Pilate's blackmail I was not betraying my people. For the fate of my people was once again being played out in me.

I lay awake for a long time. When finally I fell asleep I had a dream. Before me was Pilate in his purple-striped toga. He kept saying, 'I'm not inhuman, I'm not a beast.' His features turned into a caricature. Great teeth sprouted in his mouth. His hands were clenched. Where the ring gleamed on his finger I could see claws. His body swelled up until a giant animal, a spitting monster, stood in front of me, which arrogantly threatened the whole world with its paws and kept hissing, 'I'm not inhuman, I'm not a beast.'

I wanted to run away, but my legs wouldn't move. I couldn't budge. Instead, the monster got nearer, and now it was snapping at my feet. Its paws touched my knees, and then it reared up to seize me by the throat. But suddenly it winced, cringed and grew small; it whimpered and writhed in the dust. All its pride and glory had disappeared, as though it were prostrate before an invisible power standing behind me.

I turned round. Behind me was a man. People surrounded him. They brought books. In them were written the crimes of the beast, not only the misdeeds of Pilate but those of the whole Roman empire. One crime after another was read out – and each time the beast whimpered and writhed in the dust. Finally the verdict was given: the beast was removed and killed. The man and his entourage took over its rule.

I woke up. Had I not read about a similar dream in books? Now I remembered. It was Daniel's dream of the four beasts from the abyss.[9] But in my dream I had seen only the last beast. I paused. For the four beasts were usually interpreted in terms of the four world empires of the Babylonians, the Medes, the Persians and the Greeks. The dream said that none of these bestial kingdoms would stand. All would be destroyed by the kingdom of the man – by a mysterious figure who came from heaven and looked like a man.

Some people interpreted this to mean that the dream had been fulfilled. After the collapse of the Hellenistic empire the Roman empire had come. It had brought peace where formerly war and destruction had prevailed. It was a human kingdom.

My dream revealed the opposite. The Roman empire was the last monster. This kingdom, too, was bestial. A really human kingdom had still to come.

I was still in the power of the beast. But I knew now that this beast could be conquered. There was something stronger. Now the beast still ruled over me. It had power over my body, which lay in fetters. But it had lost power over the person within – over that kingdom from which dreams come. Was it not my task to overthrow this kingdom by deceit?

When day came I sent a message to Pilate that I accepted his offer provided that Timon was immediately set free.

Dear Dr Kratzinger,

Thank you for your kind letter. I shall gladly adopt the changes of detail in the text which you suggest. I've thought about your suggestion that the narrative as a whole should not be written in the first person. The limitations of this style can be felt when the chief character is in prison: narrator and reader are shut up together. An omniscient narrator speaking in the third person could have been present everywhere. He would have been like a historian.

Nevertheless I would like to keep to the first person. Certainly this makes the narrative fundamentally different from a historical account. But doesn't the historian forget all too quickly that anything which he investigates is what is done by and to individuals between birth and the grave? All history is experienced and shaped by human beings from a limited perspective. To put it another way. There is no such thing as history per se; only history perceived from a perspective. The historian's view is one perspective alongside others, in which one side of history, which can be told only in the first person, does not perhaps get its due.

Against your advice I shall continue in the first person. Nevertheless I found your comments very valuable. May I also send you the fourth chapter?

With warmest good wishes,
Yours,
Gerd Theissen

4

The Commission

At last I was free. They had let me out one day but kept Timon. The last days of my imprisonment had been tolerable. True, I had had to go back to my dark cell, but I could wash, I was given the same food as the soldiers and even new clothes before my release. But it took the step into freedom to make a ragged prisoner into a human being again, whom I could recognize as myself. I went through the narrow streets of Jerusalem, enjoyed the familiar noises and smells of the market, watched the people thronging the alleyways with me: that mixture of pilgrims, merchants, farmers, priests and soldiers which gives the picture of the city its unique stamp.

How good it was to see the sun again! I could feel the light all over my body. It streamed over my face and hands. It flickered through space in the form of colour and shadow. It trickled down to the earth as warmth. There seemed to me to be a mute joy in all things, waiting for someone to give expression to it. So I murmured under my breath, almost involuntarily:

Lord our God,
the heavens reflect your beauty
and the earth is your echo,
every speck of dust your dwelling
and every day your festival.
You make all things beautiful;
your language is wordless.
All things praise you with an inaudible voice.
The sun comes forth,
loves the earth in a splendour of colours,

surrounded by planets.
Nothing is hidden from it.[1]

But on the very next day reality caught up with me. I had let myself in for a risky enterprise in order to see the sun again. That came home to me at the latest when I stood in front of the officer who had interrogated me the first time. His name was Metilius.

'Andreas, I'm glad that you're working with us,' he began. 'Let's get to the point straight away. We want information about some strange people. They call themselves Essenes and live in the wilderness.' He unrolled a map on the table and pointed to the north-eastern corner of the Dead Sea.

'Do you know this area?'

I became rather vague. I had lived for a year with Bannus not far from the Dead Sea, but I chose to play ignorant. Perhaps I could later sell things that I already knew as information which I had taken great pains to discover. So I just said:

'I've only a general knowledge of the area.'

'There's an oasis here where the Essenes have their centre. The accounts we have at present come from Roman tourists. According to them the Essenes live there without women, without offspring, without private property, surrounded by palms, on the shore of the Dead Sea. They are said to be constantly joined by people who are disgusted with normal life, or whose courage has been broken by blows of fate.[2] Take a look at these holy people. They are said to be peaceable, to use no weapons, to swear no oaths, to reject slavery and to observe all the religious commandments strictly.[3] What we are interested in is what sort of people have turned their backs on normal life. What moved them to go into the wilderness? Are they victims of fate? Are they tired of life? Or are some people hiding there to keep out of our way because they have committed some crime? Can one believe the reports that these people are pacifists in principle? You're to collect information about all that.'

'That's almost impossible. The Essenes don't give any information to outsiders. They've sworn an oath to keep anything to do with their community a secret.[4] That's well known. Even we Jews don't know much about them.'

'So it's all the more important for us to get material about them. Who knows what they keep secret? Possibly more than religious secrets.'

'It will be difficult to approach them.'

'We know that in addition to people by the Dead Sea there are Essenes who live dispersed through the land. Perhaps we can learn something from them.'[5]

'I'll try. But you must remember that the Essenes living outside the community may not have been initiated into all their secrets.'

'We'll certainly get something out of them. Even we have some information. Jerusalem priests have told us that the Essenes reject the present temple cult and the priests who officiate there. They say happened like this: about two hundred years ago a high priest from house of Zadok was forced out of office by a renegade. Out of protest he went into the wilderness, where he found some outsiders from whom he formed the Essene community – as a replacement for the temple in which he could no longer function.[6] This point interests us. How strong is this opposition to the temple and the priesthood established there? Does it have support among the populace? Can one play off the Essenes against the high priests? Or in the case of conflict will they take the side of the priestly aristocracy?

We also know that the Essenes supported Herod. An Essene prophet named Menahem prophesied even before there was a king that Herod would reign.[7] Herod kept quoting this prophecy. He was not descended from the royal house. The prophecy legitimated his kingdom.

I now ask myself whether the Essenes supported Herod because he had curtailed the power of the high priests – the power of their opponents. What is their view of the Herodian princes? Must we suppose that they are encouraging one of the present Herodians with prophecies that he will become king? We need information about all that.

The word "prophet" brings me to a second complex of questions. We want information about a prophet who might be connected with the Essenes. Like them, he lives in the wilderness – only a few miles north of them.'

A deadly fear came upon me. Did the Romans want to put me on to Bannus? I asked carefully,

'What interest do you have in him?'

We're interested in him because he is not only fundamentally opposed to society but also opposed to Antipas.'

Could that be Bannus? Opposition to society – that fitted. But what had he to do with Antipas? Cautiously, I went on to ask,

'What do you have against Antipas?'

Metilius waved his hand as if to say, 'That's a long story,' and bubbled on:

'Perhaps you know that relations between Pilate and Herod Antipas, the ruler of Galilee and Peraea, are less than good.[8] After the death of Herod the Great, Palestine was divided among three sons; Archelaus got the largest part, Judaea and Samaria. He was deposed after ten years and replaced by a Roman prefect. Of course Herod's other two sons, Antipas and Philip, had hoped to take over Archelaus's legacy. Antipas, who at one time had had his eye on the whole inheritance, was disappointed. Since then he has used every opportunity to show that the Roman prefects are ruling the land badly and that he could do it much better, since he is familiar with Jewish customs and sensibilities. He passes on to the emperor any news detrimental to Pilate.

Pilate has already got wind of this. You're sure to have heard about the conflict over the shields with the emperor's initials engraved on them. Pilate had them brought to Jerusalem and hung up in the Antonia fortress, where the cohorts are stationed. It's hard to see how this could violate the prohibition against images or represent divine worship of the emperor. Nevertheless there were protests – instigated by Herod Antipas, who played the role of defender of the Jewish faith. People had the audacity to claim that the affair was a blatant violation of the Jewish law. It showed once again how little Pilate understood about the Jewish religion. Antipas made a formal accusation to the emperor. Pilate was given orders from above to remove the shields.[9] He has never forgiven Antipas that, especially since in the meantime you have indicated that Antipas does not observe the law particularly strictly himself, when one thinks of his animal statues in Tiberias. And there's more to come. He married his brother's wife while his brother was still alive. That was another offence against your law. There was criticism. So what did Antipas do? He imprisoned the critic, a man called John, a holy man, a prophet, who was working in the wilderness by the Jordan. Even we Romans haven't gone that far yet. It's said that this John has a large following among the people. But in our reports there is only a very generalized description of him. Let me read it to you:

> John, called the Baptist, is an exemplary person. His teaching is that the Jews must learn to do good, namely to act justly towards other people and to worship God. On that basis they are to come together to be baptized. According to his teaching this baptism has value in the sight of God only if those who undergo it have already been purified within by the practice of righteousness. Baptism serves only to hallow the body, not to forgive all possible sins.[10]

To be honest, such a vague description isn't much good to us. Any of that could be said of many holy men. We need more detail. We've discovered that Herod Antipas imprisoned John because he feared a revolt among the people.[11] Our question is, "How can a harmless holy man provoke a rebellion?" I'm certain that the description I read out to you passes over the most important points. It leaves open three questions:

First, why did John work in the wilderness? Why this retreat from the normal world, as with the Essenes? Why this scorn for humanity? Above all, is there any link with the Nabataeans, your southern neighbours?

Secondly, what has become of John's supporters since their leader was imprisoned? Does he have an organized following? Have they transferred their activity to Judaea because things have got too hot for them in the realm of Herod Antipas? Should we worry about the unrest that they might cause?

Thirdly, what is Herod Antipas's attitude? Will he keep John in prison indefinitely? Does the opposition which John has provoked endanger his rule? Of course we're interested in any material that could incriminate Antipas. He blackens us to Rome on every possible occasion. We must look for some kind of counterbalance. Perhaps we could use the story about the holy man he's imprisoned. Herod

Antipas keeps priding himself on his great skill in dealing with complicated religious questions relating to the Jews.

So that's it. As a grain merchant you can travel all over the place. When you've got the first results, send them to us by the Roman army mail. Otherwise we'll expect you for a report in Jerusalem in about two months.'

I was just about to go when Metilius started up another conversation.

'Since we first talked together I've been thinking a lot about your religion. When I was collecting material about the Essenes, I had a thought. Might not this group be expressing a typical characteristic of your people? They withdraw from the rest of society and go into the wilderness, just as the whole people once left Egypt for the wilderness. Doesn't that express contempt for humanity, rejection of foreigners and others, indeed rejection of people generally?'

Metilius's words hit me hard. It was sad to hear him repeating prejudices about us Jews. For Metilius was a competent Roman official, perhaps with an important career ahead of him. He seemed not unsympathetic, he was well read, and anxious to understand our religion. Nevertheless he was tactless enough to play off our holiest traditions against us. I said bitterly,

'That charge of misanthropy is an evil slander. Our law teaches us to look for God's image in everything.'

Metilius justified himself,

'But why does one of our best historians say that you stick together and are very ready to help one another, but are bitterly hostile to everyone else?[12] What could have given him this impression? That's what I'm trying to understand. So I'm asking whether it has anything to do with your expulsion from Egypt. Perhaps that left behind a deep sickness in you,[13] a fear that you might be made outlaws everywhere and driven out?'

Metilius rolled up the map and put it in a leather case. His gesture was a picture of despair. I explained:

'The exodus from Egypt left a deep mark on us. It represents liberation from slavery and oppression. We remind ourselves of it not to keep aloof from others but to avoid doing to others the injustice we had to suffer in Egypt.'

'What does that add up to in practical terms?' he asked, tying up the open end of the case with a leather thong.

'That we treat foreigners in our land like brothers. That's what Moses commanded us: "When a stranger dwells with you in your land, you must not do him wrong. Let the stranger be like one of yourselves, and love him as yourself, for you were strangers in Egypt."'[14]

'But why is there so much hatred against us Romans in this country?'

We were talking at cross-purposes.

'The law says, "You must not do wrong to the stranger." Are we doing wrong to the Romans? Who is doing wrong to whom?'

My aggressive tone had irritated him. He raised his head and looked at me:

'We are not doing wrong; we're making peace. Your lawgiver Moses isn't far from our view. We too think that the position of foreigners in our empire should be safeguarded by law.'

I looked at Metilius sceptically. He was just about to put the map-case in a container on the wall. That produced a pause. Then he came over to me, put his hand on my shoulder, and said,

'Since we first talked I've been reading up about Moses. I found another account of your exodus from Egypt.[15] Moses is said to have been an Egyptian priest who emigrated to Judaea with his followers because he was dissatisfied with Egyptian religion. He is said to have criticized the Egyptians for depicting their gods in animal form, and the Greeks for depicting their gods as men and women. The God who embraces all things, land and sea, heaven and earth and all being, was invisible and not to be compared with anything visible. No images were to be made of him. So Moses established a religion without images in Jerusalem, and taught how God was to be worshipped. But his successors were superstitious priests who encouraged the people to set themselves apart from other peoples – by food tabus and circumcision. Moses' great idea of worship without images was obscured by these customs. I found this account fascinating. I think that Jews and Greeks could agree over worshipping a God who could not be depicted by any image. Some Greek philosophers also claim that it is ridiculous to portray God in the form of animals or human beings. What do you think?'

'Have these philosophers taught the Greeks, say, to give up their statues of gods? Have they dissuaded anyone from worshipping many gods side by side? No – they don't have the courage to set the idea of the one and only God over against popular religion. Only Moses had that courage. We Jews have simply drawn the consequences of his insights.'[16]

Metilius took a step backwards. His voice rang out passionately. 'But that's the problem, Andreas! Put yourself in other people's shoes. Think what your religion must seem like to them. You worship one God who is all alone. He has no father, no mother, no children among the other gods. He has no relations, no family! He is as isolated among the gods as you are among the nations. If the gods of the nations do not form a family, how can the nations grow together into a family? How can peace prevail among the nations?'

I protested: 'Your gods aren't a peaceful family. They fight and scheme among themselves. Only if all people revere the one and only God will there be peace on earth.'

'Really? Don't those who reject other gods, as you do, also reject the people who worship them? Don't those who proclaim a monopoly for their god also seek a monopoly for themselves? Can't you understand others feel threatened by this?'

'If the invisible God isn't on the side of the rulers, but on the side of losers and the weak, to whom is he a threat?'

'The Jews weren't always weak. They built mighty empires.'

'But now our people have been conquered. Whom do we threaten? For whom am I a danger, since I am in your hands?'

Metilius winced.

'Yes, you're a subject people. But the aim of Roman policy is to turn subjects into friends. I want to contribute towards that in this country. That's why I study your religion. I've learned a lot about it today. I understand why many people say that the Jews are a race of philosophers.[17] Philosophers have a difficult time. They're soon regarded as atheists and trouble-makers. Anaxagoras was hounded out, Socrates forced to drink the cup of hemlock. Why? They had new and different ideas. You Jews also have a new and different idea: belief in the one and only God, who helps the weak. It's a great idea. But bound up with it is a great burden: that of being different from other people.'

'It's often a burden. But it's a great vocation to be a witness to the living God until all peoples recognize him.'

Before we parted, I asked after Timon. Metilius said that he would be released the next day. I insisted that he should be given his freedom immediately. Metilius hesitated. But I pressed him as Moses pressed Pharaoh: 'Let us go. We can begin work today.' He finally agreed.

Dear Dr Kratzinger,

After reading the last chapter you ask me ironically whether it might not be better to call this book Dispute about Judaism *rather than* The Shadow of the Galilean. *But the point is that when Christian theology is arguing about the historical Jesus it has to contend with its Jewish origins. Where it is uninterested in the historical Jesus it tends to suppress these origins.*

We do indeed need an introduction to Jewish faith if we are to make the proclamation of Jesus comprehensible today. We are indebted to Judaism for belief in the one and only God. This was taken for granted for a long time. Now it's a minority cause. We must make it accessible again – since it is the most important historical and material presupposition of the proclamation of Jesus.

Here the Jewish origin of this faith is a help. Christian faith in God is often thoroughly compromised by being entangled with power and domination. As a persecuted minority Jews have for centuries given credible testimony that the God of the Bible is not on the side of the powerful and the rulers.

You hint in your letter that my assessment of Judaism is coloured by distress following the holocaust. Of course you're right! Of course I have a 'particular perspective', as you say. But isn't sympathy better than hostility and hatred? Perhaps we should argue less over our 'perspectives' than over what we see in them. Perhaps these perspectives will also show us something new about the historical Jesus.

The following chapter is also meant to bring to life the world of the Judaism of Jesus' time. I'm eager to hear what you think of it.

All good wishes,
Yours,
Gerd Theissen

5

The Wilderness Community

The three of us were together again. The very evening that Timon was released we began to look for Malchus. We found him with friends in Jerusalem. Now we were riding through the Jordanian wilderness in the direction of the Dead Sea. We were heading for the Essenes. It was an open question whether we would reach them. For how could we get at them? How could we overcome their distrust of outsiders? I brooded on that all the way.

Should we attempt a gift? Money opens many doors. Why should the people in Qumran be an exception? But they were supposed to despise money and private possessions. Everything belonged to the community. And I had been told that the community was well-to-do. The Essenes worked as farmers, potters and scribes. They farmed fish, and sold salt and asphalt from the Dead Sea.[1] They had an income of their own. That made them immune to money.

Should I pretend that I wanted to enter their community? Wouldn't they then have to tell me about all their secrets? But I guessed that they would probably collect more material about me than I collected about them. At least I knew that the process of admission took several years.[2] It would take a long time to gain their trust.

Perhaps I could find a way to them through Bannus. They would have to accept a wilderness ascetic as a kindred spirit. But how should I persuade Bannus to travel to Qumran with me? And I would have to find him first. Even then I would not have overcome all the obstacles. Wouldn't Bannus see me as an apostate?

It was almost impossible to get at the Essenes.

The road led through a landscape as dead as the Dead Sea: desolate sand dunes which allowed one to see little more than a few hundred yards ahead. No trees or bushes anywhere. There were stretches of dense wood only right next to the Jordan. I had spent my time with Bannus in a landscape like this, between the Jordan and the wilderness. But that had been much further up, in the north of the Jordan valley.

We trotted slowly through the dead area. Then – what was that? A person? Or had the dim light deceived us? But now there was no mistaking it. A dark figure was moving somewhere in the distance. Had he lost his way? He had neither horse nor ass.

As we approached, we noticed that the figure was moving very slowly. Then it sank to the ground. We rode faster. Perhaps we could help.

But why was the man raising his hands? Did he want to signal to us? It looked more as though he were fending us off. Now we were near enough to make him out. An exhausted figure was squatting on the ground. He certainly needed help. Nevertheless he was raising his hands to push us away!

Did he see us as enemies? Robbers who would plunder and ill-treat him? I got off my horse and left the others. In my hand I held up a water bottle to demonstrate my good intentions. And then I approached carefully.

The man still gestured me away. I could hear him calling out to me, 'No, no!'

I became uncertain. Was he already having hallucinations? Or was he some poor possessed person whom his demon had driven into the wilderness? Such people met a sorry end here unless they were brought near to inhabited places where they could live by begging.

As I approached, the stranger tried to run away. He staggered to his feet. He was at the end of his tether. I soon caught him up.

'Shalom,' I said. 'I am Andreas son of John.'

The man remained silent.

'Don't you want something to eat and drink?'

He shook his head. 'I may not,' he whispered.

I looked at him uncomprehendingly. 'You seem in urgent need of food and drink.'

'No, I may not. I'm bound by an oath. It's forbidden.'

'I don't understand.'

'No one will understand. Please go away. Leave me to my fate. Go away. It's better for us all.'

I felt very uneasy. Was he possessed? Was there a demon in him driving him on inexorably to destroy himself? Or was he one of those who fasted to excess so as to have visions on the borderline of consciousness and gain insights into heavenly mysteries? One thing was certain. He was hungry and thirsty. Why wouldn't he allow himself to be helped? I changed my tactics.

'We're lost,' I said pleadingly. 'Can't you help us?'

The stranger stopped. I had found the right note. Many sensitive people only allow themselves to be helped when one lets them play the helper.

'Where do you want to go?', asked the stranger.

'To the Essenes.'

He started.

'Can you take us to them?'

He shook his head. But then he said: 'I'll show you the way. But I won't come. Let me ask you just one thing. Can you take a message to the Essenes?'

'Of course. What shall we tell them?'

'Say to the Essenes that I, Baruch son of Berechiah, wish peace to all my brethren. I beg you, take me back. I am at the end of my strength and will not last long.'[3]

'So you're an Essene! Have they thrown you out? Driven you into the wilderness?'

'Yes.'

'But in that case why are you wandering through this dead landscape instead of going to Jericho or Jerusalem?'

'Anyone who is cast out of the community may not make contact with others. He may not accept food from them or drink a cup of water from them. Otherwise he has no chance of being received back again.'

'But that's inhuman!' I cried. 'What crime have you committed for them to treat you like this?'

'When we entered the community we swore an oath which binds us to silence.'[4]

Was Baruch a criminal? No, that was impossible. Would a criminal feel himself bound by an oath? Would he have scruples in extreme distress? What kind of uncanny power did this community exercise over this young man for him to prefer to end his life in torment rather than part from them? This power dominated him like a demon, so that the only alternative he knew was either to return to the community or to die in the wilderness. If only I knew how I could give him a new appetite for life!

An idea came to me.

'Suppose a wilderness ascetic came past, waiting for God in the wilderness like you – might he help you?'

Baruch shook his head. 'All those who do not belong to the community are children of darkness.'

I seemed helpless in the face of the spirit of this community. But I still didn't give up.

'All right. You may not accept food and drink from human hands. But will you also reject God's hand? He makes fruit and plants grow without human intervention. Will you not eat his food?'

'But nothing grows here.'

'Come,' I said, 'I will take you where you can get food which has not been sullied by any human hand.' Bannus had shown me how to live on plants, locusts and wild honey. He had learnt this from the Bedouins.[5]

I saw from Baruch's reaction that I had succeeded. We took turns in having him on our horses and rode in the direction of the Jordan. Soon we approached the green stretch which runs through the dead wilderness like a recollection of indestructible life. We brought Baruch to the bank. He knelt down and put his face into the Jordan. The water flowed into his mouth. He gulped it down. Meanwhile Timon, Malchus and I searched the neighbourhood for food: we gathered vegetables, fruit and locusts, which taste marvellous when roasted on the fire. And Baruch ate. He ate all this that nature had provided of its own accord. He ate and drank. It was a delight to watch him. It was as though life had conquered death.

We camped in the shade of some trees. Before us lay the wilderness, like the ruins of some prehistoric catastrophe, and behind us was the Jordan valley. What a miracle for plants, bushes and trees to spring up in this landscape. Just a little water managed to change a graveyard into a garden. It occurred to me that all life flourishes on the frontier of death. Forest turns into wilderness, living water into the Dead Sea, light into paralysing heat.

It was clear that we could not leave Baruch in this wilderness. He would perish. But what should happen next? Should we deliver his message? Should we help him to return to his community? Everything in me militated against this. This community exercised an uncanny power, a power which drove people to their deaths. Perhaps it was a power which contained hidden life. But how soon it turned to destruction and annihilation!

I also asked myself whether the community would take him back? What had he done? Perhaps something really horrific! But even if he had – at all events Baruch could be useful to me. He could give me all the information about the Essenes I needed – all the more openly the more he had fallen out with his community. But what had he done? I had to get that out of him.

His answer to my question was evasive: 'I can't say anything about it; it would involve divulging secrets which are among the best-kept secrets in the community.'

I didn't give up easily: 'Why do you cast this veil of secrecy over everything?'

'Anyone who comes to us has left normal life for ever. He sees all humanity rushing ignorantly to destruction – and may no longer have fellowship with them. They would lead him astray and make him leave the path he has chosen. He must burn all bridges, end all contacts. On entering the community he swears to love only the members of his own community and to hate all children of darkness – and not to divulge anything about the community to outsiders.'[6]

'So you swore hatred against all others?'

'Yes.'

Timon and Malchus had been following the conversation attentively while trying out the fruit we had collected. They particularly liked some cactus fruit, but left the roasted locusts untouched. Now Timon intervened. 'Do you really hate us?'

Baruch shook his head.

'I hate the children of darkness who transgress God's commandment,' he muttered.

Now Malchus also intervened: 'Do you really want to go back to your people?'

'What else can I do?'

'Couldn't you go back to your home village?'

'I've left everything. I've sold my inheritance. I gave all the proceeds to my community. I'm utterly dependent on them.'

'Don't you have parents still? Relations?'

'I've broken with my family. There's no way back. Either I return to the community or I must go on living in the wilderness.'

He hung his head and kept silent. So did Timon and Malchus. Our silence was caught up into the silence of the wilderness. Finally I said:

'Baruch, like you I once left normal life. I went to an ascetic in the wilderness. I was in search of the true life. I came back. I recognized that you don't escape the conflicts of life even in the wilderness. Let me make a suggestion. Join us. You can live with us. We'll help you make a new start.'

Baruch protested, 'We may not trust anyone outside our community.'

'But Baruch,' I retorted, 'you already have.'

In confusion he said: 'Perhaps you're right.'

I continued to press him: 'And do you really trust the Essenes?'

'That was the trouble,' he exclaimed. 'I wanted a community that you can trust.'

And suddenly it all came pouring out. He told us how he came to be thrown out. Often in unfinished sentences. Excitement kept making him pause. But gradually we began to understand.

Anyone who goes into the community surrenders all his possessions. So the members of the community call themselves 'The poor in spirit'. Riches are regarded as a step towards destruction. But during their novitiate, under the strictest secrecy members are told of mysterious copper plates to which only the overseer has access.[7] On these copper plates are engraved details of unimaginable treasures, exact information about where to dig to find them, details of quantities and types of metal. No one has ever seen this treasure. But everyone believes that it exists.

Baruch thought that the community should be consistent in

renouncing riches. How could people call themselves the 'poor' if they had far greater possessions than all the income of Judaea, Galilee and Palestine put together? The treasure should be used to support the poor.

There had been a great debate. In the course of the discussion Baruch had been carried away with the idea that perhaps the treasure didn't exist. Perhaps the novices were told about it only in order to make it easier for them to give up their possessions. They were meant to be confident that their material needs would be well looked after. But he did not want their common life to be built on illusions. Either it should be demonstrated to them that the treasure really existed or people should stop talking about it.

This suspicion of deceit embittered the majority. Baruch was expelled – indefinitely – as a threat to the peace of the community.

I asked about details of the rules for expulsions. Baruch gave some instances.

'For giving false information about possessions on entering the community the punishment is a year's exclusion and having rations cut by a quarter for life. The punishment for lying, anger at a community member or going around naked is six months. People are given one month for lack of discipline in community meetings, for example being absent without permission, spitting in the assembly or laughing loudly. Ten days' expulsion for going to sleep during a meeting or waving one's left hand around.'[8]

'Drastic punishments,' I said. 'Do you really want to go back to this community? Why are you so attached to it? Why did you enter it?'

'The first thing that I heard about the Essenes was that they reject slavery. They reject it because it is an offence against human equality: they argue that it goes against the law of nature, which bore and brought up all men. All are children of nature. All men are brothers. Riches led them astray, turned trust into mistrust, friendship into enmity.[9] I was fascinated. Where else is there a community which rejects slavery? Nowhere.'

'But haven't you exchanged human slavery for slavery to harsh laws?'

'Our community goes against the usual life-style. Any community which is so different must keep itself quite distinct from the world. Our laws have to be harsh.'

And after a pause he added.

'You see only the harsh side of our life. You don't see the other. What a joy it is to have escaped from a world in which people oppress, exploit and torment one another. We are waiting for a miraculous transformation of the world. And we are now already living as people will live in this new world.

We sing marvellous songs about it, which the founder of our community has left behind.[10]

I praise you, God,
for snatching my life from death.
You have freed me from hell,
I belong to a new world.
I will live in harmony with your new world.
I know that there is hope for me
although I am formed from dust.
For you free me from all my mistakes,
so that I can enter the community of holy men.

We sometimes sing such songs at our meals.[11] We particularly look forward to them. All are washed clean. They come straight from a bath and have set aside their working clothes. The baker brings the bread and the cook provides everyone with food. The priest blesses the food. All is quiet. An outsider wouldn't notice much. But we see these common meals as an anticipation of future meals. In the new world the Messiah will sit at table with us. But as I said, it's impossible to describe that to those who haven't been initiated. Only a member of the community can feel this joy.'

I interrupted him: 'I too will feel this joy if you eat with us.'

Baruch looked at me in amazement. I slowly took some dates from our baggage and offered them to him. Timon, Malchus and I looked at him tensely. Would he take them? He hesitated. No one said a word. Complete silence. The tension vibrated in the air between us. I kept holding the dates in front of him. Finally Baruch reached forward.

'Thanks,' he said, took the dates and shared them round. We laughed. We ate. Baruch was one of us.

The same day we returned from the wilderness to life: to Jericho.

Baruch stayed with us. In long conversations I learned all about the Essenes; more than I had hoped. I was fascinated by this community, even if it still seemed uncanny to me. In the inn in Jericho I sketched out a first report about them on papyrus. I had found a quiet place to do it. The guests, mostly merchants with small caravans, were camping in the shadow of the inn. I sat in a small room and wrote:

The Essenes

The Essenes are a very disciplined community who concentrate on religious matters. They have gone out into the wilderness because they think that they cannot fulfil God's commandments in everyday life. They differ from other Jews above all by their own calendar: they celebrate their festivals in accordance with the solar calendar, whereas all others follow the lunar calendar. So they cannot take part in the temple cult. When there are sacred festivals there, they are leading their ordinary life. When they hold festivals, others are having a normal day.[12]

Their relationship with the Jerusalem priesthood is not as tense as it used to be. True, they do not take part in the sacrificial cult, but they do send gifts to the temple.

They represent no danger to the state. On entering the community all members must swear that they will not be involved in robbery (and that includes attacks on the Romans). They have no secret stocks of weapons. Rather, each one is content with a sword as protection against attack.'[13]

The Essenes interpret our marriage laws very strictly. They reject all polygamy and say that God has made humanity as man and woman – and therefore not as man and two women. They argue that the marriage laws apply to both husband and wife. If a wife may have only one husband, the husband may have only one wife. Similarly they say that if a man may not marry his aunt, a woman may not marry her uncle. They also reject divorce.[14] Given this interpretation of the marriage laws they inevitably criticize the family life of our Herodian rulers. Herod the Great had many wives. His sons often married their own nieces. It's certain that the Essenes reject the marriage of Herod Antipas to his sister-in-law.

However, I did not write that the Essenes hated the Romans. They indeed repudiated armed rebellion in the present, dreaming instead of a great war at the end of time. Then, along with all the children of light, they would conquer and destroy the children of darkness. The only question was when they would come to feel that the last days were upon them. Then they could be dangerous.'[15]

Nor did I report the radical criticism of power and riches which had taken form in their community. Anyone who, like them, was living proof that life was possible without private property had to be rejected by all those in power and represented a danger to them.

I also kept quiet about their ardent expectation of an imminent change in affairs, about the coming of a new messianic high priest. Prophecies about changing everything were always regarded as dangerous by politicians. There were emperors who had forbidden all prophecies.

I was deep in thought about the Essenes when there was a noise in the inn. Something had happened. I listened. I could only hear fragments. Someone had been killed somewhere. Excited voices could be heard, then laments, then a muted murmuring. I was about to rush out when Baruch came in.

'Have you heard the news? They've killed him!'

'Killed who?'

'The prophet John.'

Dear Dr Kratzinger,

The Essenes remind you of the modern religious youth movements. Certainly. When writing the last chapter I kept the specific experiences of members of sects in mind. But does that mean that I have projected experiences from the present back on to the past?

First, a matter of principle. If we found only what matched our own experience in the past we would lose interest in it. If we found only what went against that experience, the past would remain incomprehensible. It is what is alien that is interesting. It becomes comprehensible when we relate it to what is familiar.

Now to the previous chapter. The Essenes are not a modern youth movement. They do not provide authoritarian support in a climate of 'liberal' uncertainty over which way to go. Despite their separation from society they have their roots in a general consensus: that in the Torah God has given valid instructions for life. The interpretation of the Torah may be disputed, but there is no dispute over its validity. However, it must be defended against the incursion of Hellenistic pagan culture.

At that time the question was whether one was fitting properly into a pre-existing framework. Following a pagan Hellenistic life-style was a real alternative only for a few. By contrast, young people today are asking where they can take their bearings at all. Although the Essenes remind us of a modern youth religion, they are rather different.

What makes historical research valuable in human terms is this clarification of the past by the present and vice versa. What we learn about past life always sheds light on us.

Finally, let me assure you how important your critical comments are. I hope that you will find time to give me your opinion on the next chapter as well.

All good wishes,
Yours sincerely,
Gerd Theissen

6

Analysis of a Murder

Baruch was out of breath. 'Herod Antipas has had John the Baptist executed. The whole city is buzzing with rumours.'

I was overwhelmed. Another horror. I had to learn more about it. That was something for Pilate. Now he had a triumph against Antipas in his grasp. Antipas had even had a holy man executed.

A crowd had gathered in the square in front of the inn. The young man who had brought the terrible news was standing in the middle of it and answering the rush of questions as best he could. I forced my way forward until I could hear everything properly. The young man was gesticulating with both hands: 'Herodias his new wife is behind it. She was intent on marrying him, although that goes against all our laws. For first she had to get divorced from Antipas' half-brother.[1] This woman isn't afraid of anything. She's guilty of the death of the prophet. She wanted to silence criticism of her new marriage.'

There were shouts of assent from the crowd. Someone else intervened. 'Herodias has been skilful. Antipas is much too easy-going. He is said to have had nothing against the Baptist. He had to order the execution against his will. Once when he was in a good mood he allowed his wife to lure him into a promise to grant her a wish – and then she asked for the head of John the Baptist.'

'A woman can't manage that sort of thing all by herself' called out another person. 'It needed two of them: Herodias and her daughter Salome. The nobs of Galilee and Peraea had come together for a banquet. The party was well under way. Antipas had already had some drinks. Then Salome began to dance in front of them. The company went wild. Antipas promised to fulfil any wish – even give her half his kingdom. Probably he had expected a harmless wish, the kind that girls have these days. But Salome let her mother tell her what to ask for: she wanted the head of John the Baptist.'

It was clear to me that this was court gossip.[2] If it went on like that people would end up telling how Salome had seduced her uncle Antipas. All these stories followed the usual pattern: for a court intrigue you need a couple of sophisticated women, a generous ruler, a victim, a rash promise, and so on. That couldn't be the whole truth. I turned to the person who had spoken first. His story had been least exaggerated.

'Where did you get the news from?'

'Some of Antipas' officials had a meeting in Jericho.'

'Are they still there?'

'They've quarters in Herod's winter palace.'[3]

'Do you know their names?'

'I think one's called Chuza. He's one of Antipas' stewards.'

That was good news. I knew Chuza well. He had been my business partner in many purchases of grain. No one knew more about the goings-on in Antipas' house than he did. I lost no time in sending Timon to Herod's palace with a message that I was in Jerusalem. Could I speak to him? Chuza answered by return that he very much looked forward to seeing me again. He was on the way back to Tiberias. Would I like to have supper with him and his wife?

Chuza and his wife Joanna received me in a luxurious tricilinium: three couches were set round a small table, as in a Roman villa. The floor was decorated with a beautifully designed mosaic, with plants as motifs.[4] On the walls pink and blue marble made a definite pattern. Or was the marble only painted on? We sat down to eat. Slaves brought the food: salad, ham, eggs, ground rice with honey, along with olives, mangoes, gherkins and onions.[5] A splendid wine went with it. I hadn't had such a good meal since I had gone to prison. It tasted marvellous. I had to restrain myself so as not to seem greedy. On one of the cups from which we drank was engraved in Greek script:[6]

Why are you here?
Be happy.

This cup suited Chuza: one of his favourite sayings came from

Ecclesiastes: 'Go eat your bread with joy and drink your wine with a joyful heart.'[7] He was very fond of all the writings of Solomon: his proverbs, his songs, his wisdom. Chuza was a Sadducee[8] – a tradition of belief among our upper classes. His motto was 'Enjoy life.' And he did – along with his young wife.

Our conversation first revolved round unimportant things. Of course we both wanted to get down to the topic of the day. First of all, though, we talked about other things. Chuza was well informed.

'Pilate's had problems in Jerusalem again. Do you know the details?' I started. Did he also already know that I had been caught up in events? Should I tell him anything about it? He would certainly hear about it some time. So I said: 'In a demonstration against him five people were killed by his police. I was in the neighbourhood and was temporarily imprisoned.' Then I told him the whole story. I saw how eagerly Chuza took it in. As a supporter of Antipas he was interested in bad news about Pilate. I was in a quandary. How far could I blacken Pilate without endangering myself? Pilate might learn what I was saying about him. So I urged Chuza,

'For God's sake don't tell anyone else that you got the story from me. Pilate can be brutal. He must never learn what I told you.'

Chuza nodded and went on, 'Besides, he's on to new atrocities. I've just heard that he killed some Galilean pilgrims – and their sacrificial animals.'[9]

'What, does he want to have the whole country against him?'

'The climate's ripe. Little things lead to exaggerated reactions. At any rate, these were Galileans, and Antipas is responsible for them. We shall protest.'

Here Joanna intervened. 'Don't pretend it isn't all very convenient for you! Antipas had a prophet executed, Pilate a few Galileans. The incidents balance each other out. Neither side will be in a position to blacken the other before the emperor or the Syrian legate. One crow pecks the other's eye out.'

Chuza retorted, 'Granted. It's to our advantage for Pilate to have difficulties. This story about John the Baptist is going to cause us more trouble.'

'Did you know him?' I asked.

'Of course. A weird type. His clothing alone! A leather girdle and camel skin – that was all. Otherwise long hair, a beard, vegetarian food.'

'Some of these weird types aren't so bad.' I was thinking of Bannus. 'There's sometimes a good man behind an off-putting exterior. What did you make of John? Did he appeal to you?'

'A bit, I suppose. As a Sadducee I can't make out these prophets who announce the end of the world. First, there are too many of them. Secondly, the world isn't ending. But there was one good thing. You know that I'm very broad-minded in religious questions. So our senior religious figures don't like me, and I like them still less. In their eyes we're second-class Jews. John was impressive on this very point. He preached that God does not distinguish between the more pious and the less pious. The pious are a brood of snakes and adders if they hope to escape the judgment. All must change their behaviour radically, pious and impious alike. All are threatened by inexorable judgment!'

'Why did Antipas have him killed? What's really behind it? The people are saying that it's Herodias' fault.'

Here Joanna protested, 'Of course women are always blamed for everything.'

Chuza laughed: 'My wife is very sensitive on this point,' he said. 'You know that Antipas was married to a Nabataean princess, the daughter of King Aretas IV. Diplomatically that was a good move. Aretas is our southern neighbour who has an unpleasant way of reaching out northwards. The marriage was intended to hold him in check: he wouldn't wage war on a son-in-law and claim land from him. So the Romans agreed to the marriage, although usually they mistrust any contact between their client princes and independent kings. And then the Herodias business got in the way!'

'Was that love at first sight?'

'Love certainly came into it,' Joanna replied. 'Would Antipas otherwise have taken on all the political disadvantages which arose from this marriage?'

Chuza added: 'It wasn't just love; there were political reasons as well. The two got on together so well because they had the same political ambition. You know that Herod changed his will many times. Each time someone different was set to inherit everything. At one time

Antipas too had been heir to it all, but he lost out when the inheritance was divided and just became tetrarch. Herodias was married to another former heir to everything, Antipas' brother, who came off even worse when the heritage was finally divided. He got nothing at all. Now Herodias is descended from the Hasmonaean royal family through her mother Mariamne. She's a real princess. By contrast the Herodians are only upstarts. And what does a real princess want to be? Queen, of course. That was impossible for her while she was married to her first husband, but it might come about if she were married to a prince. The two happened to fall in love at the very time when Antipas was setting off on a journey to Rome – rumour has it in the hope of becoming king of Judaea and Samaria in succession to the prefect Valerius Gratus. They both had high ambitions.'

'But in political terms the marriage was a fiasco for Antipas,' Joanna interjected.

Chuza explained: 'There was a snag. First, Antipas had taken his brother's wife. That's an offence against our laws. Secondly, the initiative came from Herodias. She was the driving force. That goes against Jewish custom.[10] Thirdly, Herodias wanted Antipas to get rid of his first wife – although according to Jewish law he could have lived with several wives. All these offences against the law caused unrest among the people. John the Baptist made himself the opposition spokesman on the home front.'

At this point Joanna livened up: 'You can also look at things in a different way. Herodias claimed for herself the rights that any woman has in the Roman empire. In Rome the wife can get a divorce, whereas among us so far only the husband can get rid of his wife. That's unjust. If there is to be divorce, both must have the same rights. That's all that Herodias claimed for herself. The same goes for the last point. In Rome a husband may not have several wives. I think that's a step forward. It's the only way of making clear that the wife has the same worth as the husband. Herodias was right to refuse to become Antipas' second wife alongside the first. Herodias was trying to bring some progress to our backward country. And what happens? A backwoods-prophet gets in the way of progress. I don't see John as the great saint people make him out to be.'

Chuza nodded thoughtfully, 'Whatever the morals of the affair, in

political terms Antipas has underestimated
people.'

I agreed. 'At this point the people are remen
stories, like that of Elijah, who opposed the paga.
Jezebel. John the Baptist had the same sort of effect, whe.
Herodias. Rumour has it that he's Elijah come back a₅
wrong-foots Antipas completely.'

Chuza continued: 'The consequences abroad were also disastrous.
Antipas' Nabataean wife got wind of her imminent rejection and fled
to her father before it happened.[11] Since then we've got a powerful
enemy in the south. Antipas' situation is precarious. He'll have a
foreign war on his hands, because his former father-in-law will never
forgive him for the humiliating expulsion of his daughter, especially
as our law didn't call for it. And at home there's powerful opposition,
backed by the unrestrained force of religious fanaticism.'

'But can this opposition cause trouble for him at home? What can
an individual prophet achieve?'

'Just think of what happened to Archelaus.[12] Almost twenty-five
years ago he lost his throne. For many reasons, but one of them was
certainly his unfortunate marriage to Glaphyra. In many ways it's
reminiscent of Antipas' marriage to Herodias. Archelaus, too, had to
get a divorce from his first wife to marry Glaphyra. Even more
important: in her first marriage Glaphyra had been married to
Alexander, a half-brother of Archelaus – one of those sons of Herod
whom Herod the Great had had executed. So this was a case of
marrying one's brother-in-law, which our law allows in only one
instance, namely if after a brother's death there are no children of the
marriage.[13] But that wasn't the case. Glaphyra had children by
Alexander. Archelaus wasn't allowed to marry her. This illegal
marriage did him a great deal of harm. His reputation among the
people plummeted. His opponents successfully accused him before
Caesar. He was deposed. It's all well known. Now if Antipas enters
into a similar marriage to his brother – that's a challenge to his
domestic political opponents to work to depose him.'

'But did you seriously fear that John the Baptist himself might have
instigated a violent rebellion or have collaborated with a foreign
enemy?'[14]

...here was never that danger. But there could have been an unholy alliance between the opposition at home and a foreign enemy, without necessarily involving a conspiracy. One of John's favourite sayings comes from the book of the prophet Isaiah:[15]

> *The voice of one crying in the wilderness:*
> *make ready the way of the Lord!*
> *Make his path straight!*

Just imagine Aretas coming out of the wilderness with an army, to the accompaniment of John's proclamation "Prepare the way of the Lord." Of course John means God. His way is to be prepared in the wilderness. But think how quickly our superstitious populace could associate the slogan with Aretas. See him as divine judgment upon Antipas. This slogan would demoralize any Jewish army. There would be deserters. We would suffer an annihilating defeat.'[16]

'But isn't that danger still there? Antipas has got new enemies by executing John the Baptist.'

Chuza agreed: 'The situation's still tense. Antipas is banking on the criticism of his marriage dying down.'

'Do you think he'll succeed?'

Chuza shrugged his shoulders. 'Perhaps; perhaps not.'

Antipas' fears were justified. His marriage to Herodias brought disaster on him. His former father-in-law soon laid claim to territory on the southern frontier. There was a war. Antipas suffered an annihilating defeat. Some of his soldiers had deserted. All the people then said that the defeat was divine punishment for the murder of John the Baptist. The Romans had to intervene to protect the frontier against the Nabataeans.[17] But Antipas began to stockpile weapons in secret, to be better prepared for a new war.

That, too, was to prove a disaster. Prompted by Herodias he asked the emperor to allow him to bear the title king, whereupon his enemies (in particular his nephew) started rumours in Rome about his secret arsenals. Antipas could not deny them. The emperor suspected a conspiracy against him. Antipas was deposed and exiled to Gaul. Herodias had the choice of following him into exile or returning to Galilee. She chose exile, and in so doing showed more character and love than malicious gossip had given her credit for. All this was to happen almost a decade later.[18] But now we were sitting in Jericho. Joanna once again took the side of Herodias.

'Let me make one thing clear. Herodias is not at fault for the execution of John the Baptist. Antipas himself is responsible for that. He ordered the execution on political grounds – in an emergency which the fanatical John had brought upon him. Believe me, Antipas himself often talked with John the Baptist, even in prison, in an attempt to persuade him to turn a blind eye to his marriage. But it was all in vain. And now the blame is being foisted on Herodias.'

'Perhaps the whole story will now be forgotten,' I interrupted. 'But that depends on John's followers. Are there disciples?'

Joanna nodded her head. 'I've got to know one of them. I was discussing with him whether it was right that among us a man can get rid of his wife but not a woman her husband. Do you know what he replied?

Whoever divorces his wife and marries another commits adultery against her; and if she divorces her husband and marries another, she commits adultery.[19]

I liked that. Here at least the two sides have equal rights.'

Chuza looked at his wife in some amazement. 'But that's even more radical than John the Baptist. He insisted only on observing the traditional laws. But his disciples want to change these laws, and in an unrealistic direction at that. It's totally unrealistic to forbid divorces.'

Joanna defended herself: 'No divorce is good. It's always sad when two people split up.'

Chuza objected yet again. 'I think that this disciple of John's is another lunatic, and we've enough of those.'

I saw Joanna wince. Just at that moment I had been wondering whether the two of them were having problems. I'd better keep off the question of divorce. So I asked,

'What's the name of this disciple of John the Baptist?'

'Jesus of Nazareth, I think.'

'And where does he live?'

'He travels around in Galilee.'

Chuza sighed: 'Just where we live. Couldn't he spread his new ideas in Judaea? Then Pilate would have to deal with him.'

'If he has no fixed abode, perhaps he'll come to Judaea.'

Chuza had an idea: 'How would it be if we made things a bit hot for him? Spread the rumour that Antipas wanted to execute him? And at the same time gave a discreet sign that he might like to cross the border?[20] That would get rid of him. How about your taking a hand in the matter?' He turned to me. 'Nazareth is only six miles from Sepphoris. You know the area.'

I was horrified. There was a trap here. If Pilate learned that I was saddling him with a prophet . . . that wouldn't work. I objected:

'This Jesus needs a tip-off from people whom he can trust that he should disappear. Nazareth's a small village. We city people don't have much to do with countryfolk. For them we're just the rich, those with a Greek education, who collaborate with Herodians and Romans.'

Chuza pondered: 'We ought to get some pious people. Perhaps a couple of Pharisees. Jesus would certainly listen to a warning from them.'

I had another objection, 'Can't he cause more trouble for Antipas in Judaea than in Galilee? Just think: Pilate would play him off against Antipas. What could be more convenient for him than for the whole Jewish public to learn that Antipas was forsaking traditional customs?'

Chuza laughed: 'Why shouldn't someone who kills Galilean pilgrims also kill a Galilean prophet? Besides, prophets don't need help from the Romans in doing us down. You don't know our prophets!'

We talked for a long time further, drank and ate. Finally Chuza picked up his zither and sang his favourite songs: the songs of Solomon. He sang them as songs for Joanna:

You are beautiful, my love,
you are beautiful.
Your eyes are doves
behind your veil . . .[21]

Joanna was certainly a very beautiful woman.

Dear Dr Kratzinger,

You say that as chance would have it, this very semester you're holding a seminar on John the Baptist and that you were tempted to read the last chapter with your students. But you were afraid that my story – which by-passes laborious analysis of the sources – suggests historical knowledge where there is only poetic fiction.

I don't share your fears. It dawned on me while writing that the conversations in this book reflect scholarly discussion more accurately than learned articles. In articles, after a great many pros and cons, the author arrives at a result which is presented as plausibly as possible – and which becomes far more plausible than it really is on its way from thought to print. By contrast, a narrative dialogue can remain open. No one has to have the last word. Which of the participants is expressing the truth may be left vague.

This open-endedness matches the actual process of scholarly research. For what is historical scholarship, if not an ongoing conversation about the past in which no one has the last word. In contrast to dialogue in stories, academic conversation follows strict rules which we call historical method. This represents an agreement, based on long experience, as to what kind of arguments are permissible and what are not. For example, value judgments don't count as arguments in the reconstruction of historical situations. I may like a variant text, but that doesn't mean that it is original.

By portraying events in a series of conversations, Andreas is reflecting the process of historical research without having to submit to the rules of its method. Thinking about his dialogues has given me many ideas about academic work and I've gathered material for new articles.

Perhaps you will still read the chapter to your students before the end of your seminar.

All good wishes,
Yours sincerely,
Gerd Theissen

7

Jesus – A Security Risk?

I returned to Jerusalem to report to Metilius. As John the Baptist was dead, I regarded my mission as completed. Soon, I hoped, I would be travelling through Palestine again with Malchus and Timon as a simple grain dealer.

The road to Jerusalem leads steeply upwards into the hills. Coming from the fertile oasis of Jericho one enters a desolate mountain wilderness. Crumbling rocks limit the view. The heat makes any movement difficult. As one gets close to the summit, signs of life increase. The greenery in the gullies increases. Footpaths wind through the landscape, traces of human activity. A light breeze takes the edge off the heat. Expectations reach beyond the horizon: one suspects another country beyond the heights.

And that is what ultimately happens. You can see the city. The temple towers above the dark maze of alleyways and houses. Gleaming sunlight reflects from its stones. A great platform heaves up its buildings. Colonnades frame the platform, surrounding a giant square, the 'Courtyard of the Gentiles', which is open to everyone. In its midst is the inner temple precinct, which only Jews may enter. The temple proper is there, and only priests have access to it. But even they are excluded from the Holy of Holies, which only the high priest may enter, once a year, to reconcile the people with God. And yet many thoughts are directed to it every day. For God is present there. A power emanates from it, the force of which directs the heart towards an unknown centre which one can never see, hear, experience or feel.

I stopped. Whenever I see Jerusalem I seem to be coming home. I hummed a song which our ancestors wrote in exile. Their Babylon is our Rome, and their exile is now oppression in our own land.[1]

By the waters of Babylon
we sit and weep
when we think of Zion.
We have hanged our zithers
on the willow trees.
Those who oppress us
want us to sing them beautiful songs;
but how can we sing beautiful songs
when we are in exile?
If I forget you,
Jerusalem,
may my tongue wither away,
if you, Jerusalem, were not more dear to me
than all joys and festivals!
O Babylon,
oppressor!
Happy is the one who visits you
for what you have done to us!
Happy is the one who seizes your children
and shatters them on the rocks.

As long as the Romans determined my fate I was a prisoner in my own land. But I was confident. Soon all the complications would be at an end. After all, I had carried out my commission well. Thanks to Baruch and Chuza I had learned more about the Essenes and the followers of John the Baptist than ever I could have hoped. It was entirely up to me what I handed on to the Romans. I was confident that I would be able to make the right choice. Nothing, but nothing to the detriment of our land would pass my lips. That was the mood in which I went to Metilius.

Metilius had already received news of the death of John the Baptist. He seemed to me more tense than during our last conversation.

'Andreas, just at the right moment! The situation's bad. Herod Antipas has officially informed us that he has avoided a revolt by executing John the Baptist.'

I told Metilius something of what I had learned about the background to this execution. He listened attentively. Then he said:

'What worries us is that the execution of John the Baptist coincides with events which indicate increased activity on the part of the resistance fighters.

Not long ago there was this unfortunate demonstration against Pilate during which you were arrested. During your absence there has been a second incident in the vicinity of Jerusalem. A detachment of Roman soldiers had searched a group of Galilean pilgrims for weapons. It turned out that some pilgrims were armed; presumably they were terrorists. There was a fight. Several pilgrims were killed – probably innocent people who had no idea who was travelling in their midst. Now the people are in an uproar about us Romans – not about the terrorists.'[2]

Metilius paced up and down. He continued, 'To fill our cup of misfortunes to overflowing, a slave of the emperor, travelling on important business, was attacked by terrorists on the road between Caesarea and Jerusalem and robbed.[3] The slave and his companions managed to escape but a large amount of money fell into the hands of the terrorists. We immediately sent a cohort into the area. But the terrorists had vanished off the face of the earth. We couldn't get anything out of the population. No one had seen anything, no one had known of the attack. Our soldiers got nervous and burnt all the villages in the vicinity of the attack as a deterrent. This was to be a sign to the population that in future terrorist attacks they had the choice of either handing over the terrorists or . . .'

Metilius did not finish the sentence. It was clear how unpalatable he found the Roman reprisals. They were unworthy of perceptive government. He cleared his throat and summed up:

'All these reports indicate that the terrorists are planning something. They're getting money by robbery, moving weapons around, and could use the present unrest to set off later actions. We're very worried.'

Metilius was on the right lines. Under the surface the land was seething.

'In this difficult situation it's imperative for us to know how to assess possible supporters of John the Baptist: will they make common cause with the terrorists. Or will they scatter and get lost?'

The Romans were evidently worried that various groups would

join forces against them with popular support. They couldn't weigh up the situation. Their anxiety might lead them to even more drastic measures – and that could goad on resistance further. So I tried to calm things down:

'As far as the Essenes and John the Baptist's followers are concerned, I'm certain that they won't make common cause with the terrorists. These are religious movements whose aim is for men to live in accordance with God's commandments. They're not working towards political change.'

'But don't they cherish the expectation that a great change is about to come?' Metilius interjected.

'They'll never try to bring about this change themselves. They're waiting for God to make the great change.'

'But what if someone came forward and said that God was bringing about the great change now – wouldn't everyone believe that the days of Roman rule were over?'

Metilius was right. But I had to distract him from this true insight. I had to attempt to reassure him. I spent a long time explaining all the factors which made the Essenes and the followers of John the Baptist seem innocuous groups. Metilius remained sceptical. He had his own information.

'Another thing makes me suspicious. Why do these people withdraw into the wilderness? Since we last met I've been reading your sacred writings.' When I looked questioningly at him he added, 'Not in the original Hebrew, but in the Greek translation, the Septuagint.[4] There the wilderness has quite a definite significance: God led your ancestors through the wilderness into this land and drove out all enemies before you. Before David became king he lived as a bandit leader in the wilderness and made things difficult for King Saul. Pious Israelites waged war from the wilderness against the rule of the Syrian kings and succeeded in driving out the Syrians. In short, anyone who wanted to offer radical opposition went back to the wilderness and waited for God to come from the wilderness to drive his enemies out of the land. One can even say that your God is a wilderness God. He dwells on Sinai.'

I objected: 'There's an old prophetic oracle that says, "The Lord prepares the way in the wilderness." Both John's disciples and the

Essenes refer to it. The Essenes understand preparing the way to refer to the study of the Law. John the Baptist said that one prepares the way for God by confessing one's sins, being baptized in the Jordan and improving one's life.[5] Such movements pose no danger to the Romans.'[6]

Metilius was stubborn. He still didn't trust John the Baptist and asked,

'Wasn't Antipas right to have the wilderness preacher John executed as a dangerous rebel?'

'Antipas will always justify his oppression to the Romans as a means of preventing revolt. But the decisive reason for the execution of John the Baptist is a private one, arising out of Antipas' marriage. The followers of John the Baptist also put the stress there. One of them regards divorce as a concession to human imperfection, but rejects it in principle.'

'Have you spoken to this disciple?'

'No, but I've heard of him from reliable sources.'

'What's his name?'

'Jesus of Nazareth.'

Metilius reflected.

'Never heard the name. Where is Nazareth?'

'In Galilee, not far from Sepphoris.'

'Galilee.' Metilius leapt up. 'We've good reason to suspect that terrorists hole up in Galilee and use it as a base.'

'Terrorists aren't interested in marriage laws. This Jesus seems to be quite a normal Jewish teacher. Our rabbis discuss all kinds of questions to do with human social life.'

'You're wrong. At present the terrorists could have an interest in marriage questions. If they're preparing a rebellion against Antipas and us, they have to make Antipas unpopular among the people. What easier way of doing this than by attacking his marriage?'

'But precisely for that reason Jesus cannot be a terrorist.'

'Of course not. But the fact that he comes from Galilee could suggest it. Just think, only recently terrorists concealed themselves in a group of pilgrims coming from Galilee.'

'But if all the Galileans were suspected of being terrorists, would it not be unwise to choose Galileans to hide among?'

Metilius ignored my objection.

'The first revolt against the Romans was led by Judas the Galilean.[7] You'll have heard of him. You know where he made his first appearance? In Sepphoris! And now this Jesus, the disciple of a prophet executed for rebellion, comes from a little village near Sepphoris.' He paused briefly. Then he turned to me. 'I'm giving you a new commission, starting now. You're to discover whether Jesus is a security risk for the state and whether he has any connection with the resistance fighters.'

I was shattered. I had hoped to be able to return to my normal work. What was happening to me now was much more unpleasant than discovering about Essenes and John the Baptist. Now it involved armed resistance fighters. I objected:

'In Galilee my family is regarded as pro-Roman. How am I going to win the confidence of anti-Roman resistance fighters?'

'That shouldn't be a great problem. We've made it known that you were arrested at an anti-Roman demonstration.'

'They'll mistrust anyone from the propertied upper classes.'

'On the contrary. The younger generation of the well-to-do are the main supporters of the resistance fighters. We know that some of their own leaders come from these groups.'[8]

How right he was, I thought: Barabbas came from a poor family, but basically he was of my class. Now I was to spy on him and his people. That could imperil my life. When a peasant in debt took to the hills, his reasons for doing so were clear; but if members of the upper class went to the resistance fighters, they had to be regarded as either enemies or potential leaders – or as traitors. They would be bound to be extremely suspicious of me unless I openly took their side, and I couldn't do that. I had an idea. 'How would it be if I gave the terrorists information about an impending action against them? Then I would be able to convince them that I sympathized with them.'

'But we couldn't betray our plans.'

'That's not necessary. It could be a pseudo-action, for example tighter controls between Ptolemais and Galilee. I could warn them in advance. And if that actually happened, they would trust me.'

'Not a bad idea,' thought Metilius. 'How would it be if we implemented these controls in three weeks?'

'Fine, but before that I must have made contact with the resistance fighters. That won't be easy, since they live in inaccessible caves. How about these pseudo-controls in about six weeks?'

'Certainly not. The first action is enough. If it takes place as announced and is deliberately a failure, the terrorists will be over-confident and reckless. That would suit us well.'

I had heard enough. If Metilius spoke of a first action, a second must be on the way. And this second action would take place in six weeks.

Meanwhile Metilius had got up to fetch a papyrus sheet with notes on it: 'I must tell you about the most important information I found in our records about the terrorists:

When Archelaus the son of Herod was deposed about twenty-four years ago, Judaea and Samaria came under direct Roman administration. This transition to Roman administration included an assessment of the whole population for taxation purposes, the kind that we carry out in all provinces. The task was entrusted to Quirinius, legate of Syria. It is our experience that such assessments and censuses often lead to unrest, as e.g. in Lusitania and Dalmatia. The same thing happened in Judaea. The main trouble-maker was Judas the Galilean,[9] who had already caused unrest in Sepphoris right at the beginning of Archelaus' rule. He came from a bandit family with a long tradition. His father Hezekiah, a promi-nent bandit, had already made things difficult for King Herod. He allied himself with a Jewish scribe called Zadok and propagated the doctrine that payments of tax to the Romans contravened the first commandment of the Jewish religion. Anyone who paid tax to the emperor recognized another as ruler alongside God. The land belonged to God alone. Only God had the right claim offerings of the produce of the land, in the form of offerings to the temple. These resistance groups sometimes also call themselves Zealots. They are zealous for God and the Jewish laws, which they interpret in quite an extreme way. Their rebellion was put down with much bloodshed. Judas was probably killed at that time.[10] Presumably his sons are still carrying on the resistance in secret.'[11]

Metilius was still holding his notes in his hand. He mused: 'We've now been governing this country for a quarter of a century and there is still no real peace in the land. Under the surface it's still seething. We're doing something wrong. But what? Andreas, what is Pilate really not doing right?'

I wasn't ready for this question. Did Metilius want to humiliate me by asking me for suggestions about how to do a better job of suppressing my people? Did he want to discover my views about Pilate? To test my loyalty towards the Roman prefect? Or did he doubt the correctness of the policy that he, too, had to implement? I had to be careful.

'I think that Pilate is on the right lines, but sometimes he chooses the wrong methods.'

'What do you mean by that?'

'Well, take his policy on coins. All the prefects before him refrained from having pagan symbols on their coins. They were content with ears of corn or palms or other harmless things. But right at the beginning of his term of office Pilate had coins minted with a libation vessel and an augur's staff on them.'

'But didn't the Herodian prince Philip have a pagan temple on his coins? And yet he enjoyed high esteem.'

'We know where we are with the Herodians. But we didn't know Pilate. There was a suspicion that he was deliberately following a programme of introducing pagan customs and symbols into our country.'

'He just wanted pagan customs and non-Jewish symbols also to be tolerated in this land – nothing more.'

'Then why did he act in such a provocative way? Why did he have imperial standards brought to Jerusalem secretly by night – images into the city of the God who has no image? All right, he had to withdraw them when we protested. Did he learn anything from that? No. He tried the same trick once again with shields with the name of the emperor engraved on them. Why did he do that? Why does he violate something that is so valuable to us?' Metilius seemed to understand my arguments. But he was stubborn. 'But why were there those protests against the plan to use temple money for an aqueduct? What did we do wrong there?'

'In normal circumstances the aqueduct business would have gone down well. But now there was mistrust. It's strengthened every day by the coins which pass through our hands. This mistrust must be removed. That's the most important task.'

I didn't dare to say that there was probably only one way of doing that, to recall Pilate. He had destroyed too much trust. But I had to leave the final conclusion to Metilius himself. Metilius posed the problem yet again from another angle.

'If I see things rightly, our problems are bound up with the temple. In the eyes of many Jews we're violating its holiness. But try to see things from our point of view. We want to respect the temple – as we respect all temples in the world. Our way of doing that is that the governor of a particular land always makes a point of sacrificing publicly to its god. He takes part in the cult. He is included in the circle of the worshippers of the god. Why can we do so little with you? Why do you only allow Jews into the temple? All the other gods are only too happy to see strangers offering sacrifices on their altars. Only your God is so inhospitable.'[12]

'Our God wants more than sacrifices and consecrated gifts. Only those who take his commandments seriously throughout their lives may offer him sacrifice. Our religion is closely bound up with our whole way of life. And that does not happen anywhere else. The gods of the nations do not require people to live the whole of their lives in accordance with their particular commandments. They accept sacrifices from everyone.'

'But I see that you yourself cannot fulfil the commands of your God consistently. You've got that little idol at home.'

'We know that we never fulfil the commandments perfectly. That's why the temple is so important to us. Once a year the high priest goes into the holiest of holies to receive grace for all the ways in which our people have transgressed the commandments. And not only the people as a whole, but each individual can make good his transgressions, in the sanctuary by expiatory offerings. Precisely because we take God's commandments so seriously we are drawn to the temple. Without it there would be no reconciliation.'

'Do all your scholars teach that?'

'Every Jew would agree with me.'

'Including John the Baptist? Didn't you tell me before that he calls on men and women to be baptized in the Jordan to receive forgiveness of sins? Doesn't that put all your religion in question? What about the temple, if one can achieve atonement independently of it? And what about your Essenes? They make a point of not taking part in temple worship.'

I had to compliment Metilius. He was right. There was a contradiction here.

Metilius was now in full flood: 'So on the one hand there are people among you who undermine the position of the temple. You call them holy. On the other hand we Romans attack the holiness of the temple by some clumsy actions. But we are represented as evildoers.'

I objected: 'None of our holy men will ever want to bring a pagan symbol anywhere near the temple. That's the difference.'

'That's as may be,' said Metilius. He again paced up and down the room in excitement. Finally he exclaimed, 'Now I know why our policy always comes to grief on the holiness of the temple. You argue about the temple among yourselves. Because you yourselves argue about it, you react hysterically when outsiders mention it. The fanaticism with which you defend the temple against our alleged attacks is really directed towards your own people.'

Metilius said this emphatically, as though he had made a great discovery. In my view he underestimated the role of the Romans.

'We may argue over the temple, but we argue because it's of infinite value to us. Precisely because our God is invisible and wills to be worshipped without images, our heart is fixed on the one visible place in the world where he has promised to be near.'

We talked on for a long time about the religious and political situation in the country. Metilius was an intelligent man. He soon understood what our religion was all about. On one point I believed him completely. He wanted to maintain law and order in the land with as little oppression and bloodshed as possible. He had good intentions. And yet he served a system which I had seen in a dream as a bestial creature, and which still kept hold of me in its merciless claws. Today I had again felt something of this mercilessness. At the very moment when I had hoped to have escaped, it had caught me again. Again it wanted me to betray my own people – this time possibly even those who were close to me. And all of it in the name of peace and order! Was that a humane peace?

In my dream a 'man' had appeared who conquered the monster and had freed me from a nightmare. But now I could feel nothing of that. I was glad to be back with Timon and Malchus in our lodgings and to be able to distract myself with inconsequential conversation. My thoughts kept turning to Barabbas, whom I knew, and to Jesus, whom I did not know and about whom I was to collect material over the next few weeks. What kind of a man was he? An ascetic like Bannus? A prophet like John the Baptist? A lunatic? A terrorist?

Dear Dr Kratzinger,

Once again you've raised a matter of principle: two centuries of historical-critical exegesis have made us sceptical about the possibility of any historical evaluation of our sources. We know that these sources are tendentious and one-sided, and contain more of a religious message than historical information. You say that my story passes over this scepticism. Your particular question is, 'What do we really know about Pilate?'

Granted, all sources come from fallible human beings. But if they are incapable of communicating historical truth without falsification, they are equally incapable of reshaping the sources in such a way that historical truth gets completely lost. With imperfect human beings there are limits in both directions.

May I invite you to speculate for a moment? Suppose that in the Palestine of the first century AD *there was a Committee for Misleading Later Historians, which had conspired to leave behind for us an inaccurate historical picture of the events of the time – even the most powerful committee would not be powerful enough to control and refashion all the sources. Suppose that it really had persuaded very different writers or their copyists to insert information about Pilate into their work, the notes that we now find in Philo, Josephus, Tacitus and the Gospels? Did the Committee go through Palestine hiding copper coins minted by Pilate at random sites? Did it even commission an inscription according to which Pilate dedicated a 'Tiberieum' to his emperor and which later was preserved for posterity in a modest way as a step in the theatre at Caesarea? That's impossible!*

The chance distribution of remains and sources about Pilate convince us that Pilate lived. What the Gospels write about him does not contradict the other sources, but cannot be derived from them. In the case of Pilate there is no doubt that the Gospels have a 'historical background'. One could argue in a similar way for Herod Antipas. For here, too, we an test early Christian statements by sources outside the New Testament. In that case should we not conclude by analogy that the Jesus traditions contained in the Gospels also have a historical background. That does not mean that they are identical with historical truth. You see that I'm not as sceptical as you are. That's why I would not want to be without your critical judgment.

Until next time,
Yours,
Gerd Theissen

8

Researches in Nazareth

At last I was back home again in Sepphoris. My family had heard of my imprisonment and was overjoyed to see me again. I kept quiet about the price for my release. Discretion and shame kept my mouth shut on that. How much I wished it were all a mistake, a bad dream that one shakes off on awakening! But it wasn't a dream; it wasn't a mistake; it was reality.

We made an arrangement with Baruch that he should join our business. He was intelligent, and could write and count. Above all he had learned from the Essenes how to run a warehouse. He was a good steward.

But I want to get straight to the main point: to my researches into Jesus. The most obvious thing to do first was to visit his home town. I felt that there must be members of his family there or people who knew him. In any case we often bought olives in Nazareth. We made olive oil out of them in Sepphoris and sold the oil at a great profit to Jews in the cities of Syria. They preferred to buy Galilean oil because it had the reputation of being pure and had not come into contact with Gentiles; in fact they would pay much more for our 'pure' oil than for the oil of our Gentile competitors.[1] That was fine for us. Our business flourished.

So I went with Timon and Malchus to Nazareth. We usually bought our olives from one of the larger farmsteads, but this time I was interested in getting to know ordinary people. It wasn't difficult. A farmer called Tholomaeus was ready to sell me his crop straight away. He lived with his wife Susanna in a poor house. They were about fifty years old and lived by themselves. Perhaps they were childless? Perhaps the children had already grown up? We took a long time haggling over the purchase price. I didn't force Tholomaeus down too far because I wanted to keep him in a good mood in order to learn as much as possible from him. After business was over we had a chat. We sat in front of his house with his wife and talked about the weather, the harvest and the olive business, while Timon and Malchus were loading the olives we had bought on to our ass.

Tholomaeus and Susanna seemed oppressed. 'Now we've to do everything ourselves,' they complained.

I looked enquiringly at them. Tholomaeus explained.

'We had three strong sons. And now they're no more.'

'How terrible – are they dead?'

'No, they're alive. But they've run away, just up and gone, and left us alone.'

'Was there a quarrel?'

'Not at all. We got on well. But so many people run away these days.'

'One can hardly blame the young people,' Susanna interjected. 'The first person to vanish in the village was our neighbour Eleazar. Suddenly he had gone – along with his wife and children.'

'But why do people disappear?'

'Eleazar was a smallholder who got a miserable living from his land. A few years ago we had one bad harvest after another over a period. Eleazar had to eat his seed grain in order to avoid starvation. New seed was dear because of the general scarcity of grain. Anyone who had any grain left did well, but the poor fared worse than ever. Eleazar got into debt. He couldn't pay it back. What was he to do? Was he to sell his children on the slave market in Tyre, as others had? Never. Was he to sell himself and his family to a richer Jew, to ensure his freedom at most after seven years?[2] Should he wait until his creditors took him before the judge to have him imprisoned for debt? And then watch his wife going downhill? Eleazar was a proud man. He rebelled against the threat of disaster. He and his family vanished into the hills.'

I knew what that meant. Barabbas had disappeared there on leaving Bannus. Eleazar had joined the Zealots. Everyone in Galilee knew what that meant. So I said,

'It's a good thing that Eleazar took his family with him when he disappeared. That means that no one can put pressure on them on his account. I recently heard of a similar case in Egypt.[3] A poor man was behind with his payments and ran away for fear of punishment. Thereupon the tax collector to whom he owed the money carried off his wife, children, parents and kinsfolk by force. He beat and maltreated them to make them betray the fugitive or pay back his debts. But they couldn't do either. They didn't know where he was, and they were as poor as he. However, the tax collector did not let them go, but tortured them and killed them in a terrible way. He attached cords to a basket filled with sand, hung this heavy burden round their necks and put them up for sale in the market in the open air. Wind and sunburn, the public shame and the burdens that they bore broke their hearts. It was meant to be a deterrent to those who were forced to be spectators. In fact some of those in debt have stabbed, poisoned or hanged themselves, since death without torture seemed to them to be the lesser of two evils. Those who had not killed themselves would be taken, one after the other, as in cases of disputes over wills: first the closest relatives, then the relatives at second and third remove, down to the most distant ones; and when no more relatives were left, they went on to the neighbours. In this way whole villages and towns have lost their inhabitants, because everyone went into hiding.'

The couple had been listening to me intently: 'If things go on like that with us, the villages here will soon also be empty – as in some areas of Egypt. Even more will disappear like Eleazar.'

I ventured another question, 'Did your sons disappear for that reason?'

'The reasons were different,' Tholomaeus explained. 'We're poor, but so far we've got by. Our sons could have stayed. But our neighbour Eleazar set an example. He showed everyone in the village that there's a way out when you're at your wits' end.'

Susanna added, 'Without Eleazar's example, perhaps our sons would have put up with a good deal. But from that point on they were aware that they didn't have to swallow everything.'

Tholomaeus continued, 'The first to disappear was our oldest son Philip. Along with others from our village he had a leasing arrangement with a large landowner: they had to give half the produce of the land they leased to the owner, and the other half was their property. They could just about get along on that. I should mention that the owner lives a long way away in Ptolemais, on the Mediterranean, and has his property looked after by an overseer. Every year a representative comes from Ptolemais to take away half the harvest. There's often an argument over it. The owner doesn't care how big the harvest is; the main thing is that he earns money from it. If he chooses a favourable opportunity and sells early, he can sometimes earn more than if he lets the grain ripen and sells when the whole market is flooded with grain products. The prices for an early harvest are much higher. The tenants, by contrast, are interested in the biggest possible harvest, for they have to live on it. They want to harvest late. So on this occasion they sent the first representative back with empty pockets. The owner sent two others with threats: if they didn't hand over his share of the harvest soon, he would bring them to court and ruin them. Philip and his fellow tenant were furious. They beat the two representatives and drove them out of our village.[4] That made them even more liable to prosecution. What were they to do? The court in Ptolemais would have found for the owner, especially since this would be the case of a city dweller seeking redress from country people. There was only one possibility. They disappeared into the hills.'

'I too have friends who disappeared into the hills,' I said. I was thinking of Barabbas who had become a Zealot – but out of conviction rather than need.

Tholomaeus looked at me gratefully because I did not condemn his son. 'Many people think that the people in the hills are bandits. But they're just people in desperation who knew of no other way. Eleazar and Philip are good men.'

His wife took over: 'Not everyone goes to the hills. With our second son Jason it was different. In order to exist we have to take on odd jobs as well as look after our land – as seasonal workers and day labourers. Jason often went to the market where those in search of work gather.[5] There the rich farmers and stewards hire the people they need. Sometimes there was terribly long waiting, and often he stood around the whole day without finding work – and then he was called an idler. There's nothing he would have liked better than work. When he stood with the other unemployed they talked about the big cities, in which there were more possibilities. The less work they found here, the more they dreamed of them. And Jason saw no prospects here. He knew that one day he would inherit part of our land – but that would be far too little to feed a family. So one day he set off for Alexandria. Last year he wrote that things were going well. If he came into money, he would visit us. But that wouldn't be yet.'

Tholomaeus nodded: 'The young people tend to daydream; they keep talking about those who've got rich and famous abroad. They don't hear about the many others.'

Susanna continued: 'Nevertheless, it's better to go abroad than to go crazy here. When you leave our village you will meet a few beggars who are out of their minds. Once they, too, had a home. When they got into difficulties they lost their reason. They're possessed. A demon's entered into them. Now they hang around, in graves and on the roads. That sort usually die soon. Until then they eke out a wretched existence on what their old friends in the village give them. Thank God that none of our sons has gone crazy. But I almost went mad when our last son left us.'

The woman was standing with tears in her eyes. I looked questioningly at Tholomaeus. He explained:

'The worst thing was that Bartholomaeus also left us. My wife still can't understand that.'

'But why? After the two others had gone away, he could well have fed a small family on your land.'

'That's why it's all so incomprehensible,' said Susanna. 'The others went because they had to. They were in a desperate situation. But the last one could have stayed. At least one of them should have stayed with his parents.'

Tholomaeus said gently: 'He'll come back. He's already paid us a visit. It's true: he didn't go out of sheer necessity. But he, too, was driven by some kind of need. Bartholomaeus was a sensitive young man. He was friendly with our neighbour's children, the sons of Eleazar. He could never understand why they had to become "bandits". That hurt him. It was a second shock for him when his brothers left us. He despaired of this world because it's run so badly. He knew that things couldn't go on like this. The rich cannot always oppress the poor, the judges cannot always favour the great, foreigners cannot always oppress the land. Things must change one day. The injustice on earth cries out to heaven. God sees and hears everything. He will not let things go on like this. He will bring about a change and see that everyone has his fill, that young people have a place in this world, that the rich have to give up their possessions and the oppressors to lose power. God himself will take control.'

'Many people are expecting the kingdom of God,' I said, 'but that doesn't mean that they leave their parents.'

'Quite so,' said Tholomaeus. 'And he didn't do it of his own accord. Someone from our village persuaded him. He went through the land proclaiming that the kingdom of God was already beginning now. We did not have to wait until distant times for everything to be different. The great change was already taking place. It was the most important thing in the world – more important than work and family, more important than father and mother. Bartholomaeus quoted some words of Jesus to me when he visited us. They're good:

> Blessed are you poor, for yours is the kingdom of God.
> Blessed are you who hunger now, for you will be filled.
> Blessed are you who weep now, for you will laugh.[6]

Jesus went through the land saying these words and told some young people who could not bear things here any longer, "Follow me. Things will change. The poor will no longer be poor, the hungry will no longer hunger and those who weep will no longer weep."'

Then Susanna interrupted. She was clearly distraught: 'This Jesus is bad and leads people astray. He corrupts the young people. It all sounds fine: Blessed are you who weep, for you will laugh. But what does he actually do? He makes parents weep over their lost sons. He promises that everything will change. But what actually changes? Families are destroyed because children run away from their parents.'

Tholomaeus defended his son: 'Isn't it better for him to run after this Jesus than to disappear into the hills? Isn't it better for him to live with a new hope than to lose his mind? And isn't it better for him to stay in Galilee than to go abroad? He can come back at any time. I haven't lost hope.'

Susanna retorted: 'Why won't he stay with us?' Tholomaeus looked away. He didn't want to discuss that in the presence of a stranger. But Susanna was in full swing. In great agitation she cried out, 'When he was here I didn't make things easy for him. I said to him, What you're doing is immoral. We're getting old. We've brought up you children. And now you leave us in the lurch. Do you know what he said to me? Someone once came to his master wanting to follow him, but first he had to bury his dead father. Jesus said, "Let the dead bury their dead"[7] and told the man to follow him immediately. Isn't that inhuman? Aren't parents worth anything any more? Are we parents worth no more than animal corpses, that one need not bury?

Then he quoted another saying of Jesus which is just as offensive:

If anyone comes to me
and does not hate his father and his mother,
his wife and his children,
his brothers and his sisters
and his own life also,
he cannot be my disciple![8]

How can life be worth living if you can't rely on members of your family? It's a sad thing that these young people leave us in the lurch; it's terrible that they justify it with such sayings.'

'This Jesus comes from your village. So what do members of his family think of such teaching?' I asked.

Susanna laughed. 'They think he's crazy. They once wanted to bring him back home by force. But they couldn't. He had too much of an audience. So they sent a message to him: Your mother and brothers are here and want to speak to you. What did he say in reply? "Who are my mother and my brothers?" he asked. Then he pointed to his audience and added, "Anyone who does the will of God is my brother, my sister and my mother!"'[9]

Susanna broke down and sobbed. Tholomaeus put his arm round her and stroked her hair gently. He too had tears in his eyes.

By now Timon and Malchus were ready and said that it was time to go. We wanted to be back in Sepphoris before sunset. So we made our farewells.

This Jesus did have unattractive qualities! Some things about him were reminiscent of the Essenes. In both instances there was the uncanny power over young people, the radical break with the world around, contempt for riches. In both cases there was hope for a great change! And yet there was a great difference. Behind Jesus there was no well-organized community with hidden treasure. He offered no home, no security. He offered nothing at all. He didn't even go into the wilderness but wandered around. He seemed to spend most of his time near Lake Gennesaret, between Capernaum and Bethsaida. As we left, Susanna had told me that if I met Bartholomaeus, I was to give him greetings.

I could not judge whether Jesus was a security risk for the state – but he was certainly a risk for the families of Nazareth. I thought of an old prophetic oracle about the end time: 'The son will despise the father and the daughter will oppose the mother, the daughter-in-law the mother-in-law, and a man's enemies will be those of his own household.'[10] Was this saying about divisions in the family now being fulfilled?

Dear Dr Kratzinger,

Once again you counter my argument that Jesus belonged among the lower classes with basic historical scepticism. You say that we know too little about Jesus to say anything about his social status. In contrast to Pilate there are no sources outside the Bible; only a few notes in ancient authors which in the view of most scholars say nothing significant about him.

We are agreed that the long section about Jesus in Josephus (Antt.18, 63f. = XVIII, 3,3) is a Christian revision of the text, perhaps an interpolation. I regard Josephus' account of the execution of James the brother of the Lord in AD 62 (Antt.20, 197–203 = XX, 9,1), where Josephus speaks of 'Jesus who was called Christ', as being above suspicion. The same thing goes for the passage in Tacitus about the 'Chrestiani' whom Nero blamed for burning Rome in AD 64. Tacitus derives their name from 'Christus' and reports that 'he was executed in the reign of Tiberius on the orders of the procurator Pontius Pilate' (Annals XV, 44,3).

We can infer from these notices that Jesus came into conflict with ruling circles. A Roman procurator was responsible for his death. Later the Jewish aristocracy persecuted his followers. Suetonius (Claudius, 25) and Pliny the Younger (Epistles X, 96) mention Jesus in connection with conflicts between his followers and the authorities.

Do these sources really tell us nothing of significance? They say that in all probability Jesus was not a member of the upper classes and that it was not 'the Jews' but a Roman official who was responsible for his execution. The history of Christianity would look different if these two things had always been kept in mind. These few ancient sources say a good deal about Jesus – and also a good deal about the historical-critical exegetes to whom they mean so little!

The question of the social position of Jesus will be important for the further course of our narrative. I wonder if I still have a chance of winning you over to my view of things?

All good wishes,
Yours,
Gerd Theissen

9

In the Caves of Arbela

I took the earliest opportunity to make a business trip from Sepphoris to Bethsaida Julias. Along with Timon and Malchus I went through the plain of Asochis in the direction of Lake Gennesaret. I wanted to visit Joanna and Chuza in Tiberias on the way back.

I hoped that I would meet Jesus, or at least find traces of him, somewhere on the north shore of the lake. But I was in no way eager to get to know him. We would probably not get on with each other. We came from different worlds: I from a well-to-do family living in the most modern city in Galilee, he from modest circumstances in an insignificant village. His abrupt and uncompromising sayings, reported to me by Tholomaeus, still rang in my ears:

> *It is easier for a camel to go through the eye of a needle*
> *than for a rich man to enter the kingdom of God.*[1]

> *No one can serve two masters;*
> *for either he will hate the one*
> *and love the other,*
> *or he will be devoted to the one*
> *and despise the other.*
> *You cannot serve God and your possessions at the same time.*[2]

> *Woe to you that are rich,*
> *for you have received your consolation.*[3]

Didn't such sayings express the contempt of the poor inhabitants of the land for the rich city-dwellers? And if you were rich yourself, you had mixed feelings about such sayings. Was Jesus one of those who exploited the needs of simple people in order to cause unrest? One of those who nurtured hatred against the rich? Those who aroused unrealistic hopes that everything would change if the rich were deprived of their riches and the powerful stripped of their power? It was understandable that the young people should run to him to escape oppressive circumstances.

So I trotted along the road from Sepphoris to Bethsaida sunk in though. It was a beautiful day. The green landscape shone in the sunlight. On the hills the terraces shimmered as a pattern of parallel stripes. Fruit trees added spots of shadow in the brightness. Galilee was a marvellous land – a land in which everyone could have enough to eat.[4] Shouldn't this land be there for everyone? Couldn't one indeed come to think here that distress and misery should not be part of creation?

> *Creator of the world,*
> *you are infinitely great,*
> *surrounded by beauty*
> *and bathed in light.*
> *You can be traced in the riddle of time*
> *and the mystery of space.*
> *You are manifest in the wonders of the world*
> *and hidden in the suffering of your creatures.*
> *You sleep in the stone*
> *and dream in the flower.*
> *You arouse yourself in the animal*
> *and speak to men and women.*
> *You change light into life*
> *and rain into growth.*
> *You make corn and wine grow*
> *for all,*
> *for poor and rich,*
> *black and white.*
> *Lord, yours is the earth,*
> *your garden which you gave us.*[5]

It really was a glorious day. And it would have remained a glorious day had not a loud shout suddenly distracted me from my thoughts. It all happened amazingly quickly. A horde of armed men stormed around us. About fifteen against the three of us. We hadn't a chance. Before we could even think of resisting we had been overpowered, thrown from our asses, and driven up a mountain path with hands tied and eyes bound.

My anxiety returned. My heart beat fit to burst. Cold sweat burst out of every pore and my muscles got cramp. What did these bandits want with us? Were they ordinary robbers? In that case why didn't they take all our money and let us go? They conversed only in brief shouts. There was nothing to disclose the purpose and aim of their ambush. I tried to speak to them, but they didn't react.

We went through the hills for three hours. I felt that we were getting to the summit. The path became stonier. Suddenly we stopped. Someone said, 'You must now go down a narrow stairway and some ladders. Be careful! A false step can cost you your life! We're climbing along a sheer cliff.' Even now they didn't let us take off our blindfolds. We were to have no chance to see where we were. The way up had partly been hewn in the stone and partly made by portable ladders. We slowly inched our way forward. In difficult places our companions told us where to put our feet. In the meantime the thought ran through my mind, 'If they wanted to get rid of me, they would only need to give me a push.'

At last we had firm ground under our feet again. We had to bend down to creep through a narrow opening. We were separated. I heard Timon, Malchus and an escort going away in another direction. I was spun round and round until I had lost all sense of direction. Then the blindfolds were taken off. I was standing in a dark room, dimly lit by a little oil lamp. The walls were rock. Noises indicated that there were other people elsewhere. But first of all I was left alone – though not until someone had tied up my feet.

An idea occurred to me: the caves of Arbela! I could be there. Resistance fighters had long made this their hideout. My father had often told me how the great King Herod had fought against them. It was a sorry story. I could hear his voice in my mind, telling it to me:[6]

'The caves of Arbela were on almost vertical slopes and there was no access to them from any direction except by winding, steep and very narrow paths. The cliff in which the entrances were stretched right down ravines of immense depth. So for a long time Herod did not know what to do because of the extreme difficulty of the terrain. Finally, however, he came up with a very dangerous idea. He ordered the toughest of his men to be lowered down the cliff in baskets on ropes. This gave them access to the caves. They threw firebrands at anyone who resisted and subdued them and their families. Herod wanted to save some of them and invited them to come up to him. However, no one surrendered voluntarily. Many preferred death to captivity. Among the resistance fighters was an old man with seven sons. His wife and sons begged him for permission to leave the caves because they had been promised a pardon. He killed them in the following way: he ordered them come out one by one while he stood at the entrance to the cave and cast down each of his sons as he emerged. Herod, looking on from afar, was seized with compassion, held out his right hand to the old man and begged him to spare his sons. But these words made no impression on him; on the contrary, he sneered at Herod for his lowly origin, killed not only his sons but his wife, flung the bodies into the abyss and then leapt down himself.'

And now I was sitting in these caves of Arbela. We had fallen into the hands of fanatics. Anyone prepared to kill his own children would kill anyone if his convictions called on him to do so. Could not this fanatical old man also have uttered Jesus' saying, 'Anyone who does not hate his father and mother, his wife and children, cannot be my disciple'? Might this Jesus not be a Zealot? Except that he did not hide in caves but taught publicly and therefore did not put forward his rebellious message so clearly.

I heard footsteps. A dim light cast blurred shadows on the rocky wall. A man came up to me. He was carrying an oil lamp which he held in front of him so that I couldn't recognize his face. He declared:

'You're our prisoner until your family pays a ransom for you. We've searched your baggage. You're rich people. We want half a talent of silver – payable within thirty days. We shall send your two slaves to your house with a message. You must now write a letter with our demands.'

I dared to object: 'And if my family doesn't pay? Half a talent of silver is a lot of money.'

He replied quietly, 'That will be expensive for your family too. Burials cost a lot of money. We'll provide the corpses.'

'And if I don't write the letter?'

'Then there will be three funerals.'

'Would you really kill us for money?'

'I've orders not to discuss anything with you. Write the letter. It's up to you for everything to end well.'

The words cut me like whiplashes. I could do only one thing: counter the icy coldness of my abductors with my hatred. At this moment, as far as I was concerned they had ceased to be human. They turned into devils and animals. Only my recollection of the story of the old man and his seven sons provided a weak counterbalance. Once I had admired this man as a hero. Were our kidnappers stamped with the same pitiless heroism? The idea led me to try again to begin a conversation:

'Why do you do all this?'

But the other snapped back, 'Shut up. Write.'

Without a word he loosened the fetters on my hands. I was given a papyrus sheet, pen, ink and a small desk. While I was getting ready to write I thought fast. Should I ask after Barabbas? I knew that the Zealots often split into rival groups. What if Barabbas belonged to another group? What if he had already left the Zealots and was regarded as a traitor? No, I could go from the frying pan into the fire if I played the few cards in my hands too early. So I wrote the letter:

Andreas to his father and mother, greetings.

I hope all goes well with you. I'm constantly thinking of you. Unfortunately I've had a great misfortune. Today I was kidnapped by robbers. They want half a talent of silver as ransom and give you thirty days to pay it in. They have threatened to kill me and the others. But be confident: I got out of the Roman prison so I shall get out of this one too.

Greetings to Baruch!

Timon and Malchus will bring this letter.

Peace be to you all.

I thought that my kidnappers would certainly read the letter before they sent it. Once they knew that I had recently been imprisoned by Pilate they must surely be more welcoming. I gave the papyrus sheet to my guard, who was sitting there darkly. He took the letter without looking at it. Could he read? I was disappointed. Before he went away he bound my hands. Then I heard him disappearing into the labyrinth of passages. I was alone.

I pondered: were these the young people who had disappeared from the Galilean villages? Were they people like Eleazar and Philip, who had once suffered injustice? And who were themselves now practising injustice? What had happened to them that they could cold-bloodedly threaten innocent people with murder – on orders from above, with a quiet voice, as though it were the most natural thing in the world?

A few days earlier, when I had been with Tholomaeus, I had felt understanding and sympathy for the Zealots. Anyone who rebelled against a hopeless situation deserves our recognition. But now I noticed how recognition and sympathy had crumbled away. When one was sitting in their caves bound hand and foot and with an uncertain fate in prospect, all admiration for the heroic courage of the resistance fighters disappeared. It gave place to contempt – contempt as for Pilate. There was anxiety at being delivered helpless into the hands of someone who had the power of life and death. There was bitterness at the shameless exploitation of dependency: had not Pilate blackmailed and threatened in just the same way, but in a rather more skilful, rather more refined manner? Had he not exploited his power in just the same way? Where was the difference?

I closed my eyes: once again pictures of Galilee emerged before me: the miraculous clarity of the valleys and hills – the sun in the clear sky. How beautiful it had all been! But how abhorrent were the things that happened under the sun – the way in which people exploited and oppressed, blackmailed, ill-treated and threatened. And the sun rose and set over it all as though it didn't care. Old words came to mind:

Again I saw all the oppressions that are practised under the sun. And behold, the tears of the oppressed, and they had no one to comfort them! On the side of their oppressors there was power, and there was no one to

comfort them. And I thought the dead who are already dead more
fortunate than the living who are still alive, but better than both is he
who has not yet been, and has not seen the evil deeds that are done under
the sun.[7]

I imagined seeing the sun. How marvellous it would be if I were really
allowed to see it again!

I don't know how long I stared into the weak light of the oil lamp.
The ceramic style was foreign, from Tyre. It had probably been made
by a Phoenician craftsman and brought by a Galilean merchant to
Palestine. Perhaps he had been kidnapped? Now the oil lamp was
burning in the caves of Arbela – and my hope was mingled with the
small but steady light.

Again footsteps approached. I was freed from my fetters and taken
into a room. A number of men were sitting in a circle. I couldn't make
out their faces. The room was dimly lit. It looked like a trial. Was I
going to be interrogated? In front of me was someone sitting on a
raised seat, probably the president. He addressed me:

'Andreas, son of John, is it true that the Romans arrested you?'

My calculation had paid off. I was relieved. They had read the
letter and bitten. Now I told them in detail about the demonstration
against Pilate and ended with the thought that this demonstration
hadn't really been about Pilate's aqueduct. The money was the
important thing: the Romans were unjustly draining the land of its
resources through taxation. Now they were even going so far as to
claim for themselves the only legitimate offerings – the offerings to
the temple. They had to be resisted.

The president turned to someone sitting nearby: 'You were at the
demonstration. Can you confirm what he says?'

'Yes,' said the person addressed. He had not seen me at the
demonstration, but he had heard that two young men from Sepphoris
had been wrongfully imprisoned. Not because there was anything
against them but because they were known to be enemies of the
Romans.

The president spoke again:

'Because you're against the Romans we'll forget the ransom. But
we need proof that you're on our side. The Romans wrongfully take

taxes from us Jews. We require you and your family to pay to us each year a contribution equivalent to the tax you pay to the Romans. In return, in future we shall let your trade caravans and messengers pass through unharmed. That's a fair offer.'

In reality it was extortion. But what was I to do? There were rumours throughout Galilee about such arrangements. Robbers and Zealots regularly took tolls from merchants. That was the only way in which the number of attacks could be kept down. To that extent the offer was 'trade practice'. But the price was shamelessly high. I began to haggle:

'Only Jews are wrongfully taxed by Rome, not Gentiles. In Sepphoris we have some Gentile slaves. They don't count.'

I refrained from saying that Timon was a semi-Gentile slave. He was one of those people whom we call godfearers: they believe in one God and observe the ten commandments, and take part in synagogue worship – but they are not circumcised. As long as Timon was in the power of these people that had to be kept quiet. The Zealots were said to give anyone they suspected of being at all Jewish a choice: death or circumcision!

To my surprise the Zealots accepted my argument. The one or two Gentile slaves were not to be counted. I kept going:

'In Galilee we don't pay tax direct to the Romans but to Herod Antipas, who passes on part of it to the Romans. There must be a discount for that. Herod Antipas is a Jew. He's our legitimate ruler.'

'He's an Idumaean,' came the reply. 'The Herods have usurped power.'

After some toing and froing I achieved another small reduction by promising to provide information now and then. In this way I was able to sell all my pseudo-information about imminent controls in the border country between Ptolemais and Galilee at a good price. I noticed how I was becoming more confident during the negotiation. Once people begin to do business you can work them out. A villainous trader is easier to deal with than a fanatical terrorist.

Finally the president said with satisfaction:

'That was a good deal – a deal based on mutual self-interest.'

I added, 'And on the fact that you dragged me into these caves.'

The president laughed: 'Believe me, Andreas: in a long life I've learned that it's very difficult to persuade people to do useful things of their own accord. Sometimes they have to be helped along.'

Just what Pilate had said.

He broke off and then became more serious: 'One more thing. If you don't keep to the agreement we shall tell people in Caesarea and elsewhere that you're suspected of having dealings with terrorists. That won't do your business much good. OK?' Then he laughed, 'Now let's have something to eat and drink.'

The atmosphere became more jovial. Timon and Malchus were brought. Many oil lamps now lit the room, so that I could see faces. Most of them were about my age. Only the leader was clearly more than thirty. But who was that over there? I couldn't believe my eyes. Wasn't that Barabbas? Yes it was. I wanted to fling my arms round him. But he turned away as if he didn't know me. Was I wrong? I waited until I could get another look at the stranger. No, there could be no doubt about it. That was Barabbas. Again he turned his back on me. It dawned on me: he didn't want anyone to know that we were acquainted. Perhaps I wasn't out of the wood yet? I was confused. But I didn't show anything of this when he innocently asked me:

'Where were you born? What does your father do? How many brothers and sisters do you have?'

Now I was certain. He wanted to give the impression that he didn't know me. He must have had reasons. I played along with him. When our eyes met for a moment, he winked, as though he wanted to confirm that he was my friend. A pleasant warmth stole over my body. How good it felt to have a friend in the midst of this band. Surely nothing could go wrong now.

It was agreed that we should spend the night in the cave. We were to set off next morning, very early. Then everyone went to sleep. I was given a separate room, with Timon and Malchus. Soon I heard the steady breathing of the two young men.

Dear Dr Kratzinger,

It worries you that I have made a rich merchant the main figure in my story when in fact I want to see Jesus in 'a perspective from below'. The reason is simple: in that way we can identify ourselves with Andreas. He is somewhat removed from the social world of Jesus. He is not completely at home in his religious traditions. He has never met Jesus directly (so far). He is a 'researcher' following the traces of Jesus – very like someone engaged in historical-critical research.

Andreas has to reconstruct a picture of Jesus on the basis of various traditions. He has to combine sayings and evaluate them critically. History writing begins when people no longer just affirm 'It was like that', but say, 'On the basis of this source or that – for want of better insights – I would outline the following picture of events.'

Andreas is trying to illuminate the renewal movement associated with Jesus by historical analogies – just as historians do. He constantly reflects on what Jesus, the Zealots and other religious movements in the Palestine of his time have in common.

He discovers connections which are not immediately evident, e.g. those between economic distress, religious unrest and political resistance. Like a historian he uncovers a web of conditions and reciprocal effects.

Criticism, analogy and correlation are the basic categories of historical understanding. They even come into Andreas' research. That doesn't make him a scholar. If he were, he would have to give an account of his method (what I am doing in these letters). But all in all he is an embodiment of the adventure of historical-critical research. That also applies to detachment from and proximity to the object of his investigations. For him an unpleasant chore of research turns into an existential encounter. The researcher is drawn into his subject-matter.

I'll reply to the political questions that you touch on next time. The following chapter will provide new perspectives.

Warmest greetings,
Yours,
Gerd Theissen

10

Terror and Love of One's Enemy

I gradually dozed off. I don't know whether I was dreaming or day-dreaming. Pictures of the previous day whirled around in confusion. At one moment I was before the Zealot tribunal and at another before Pilate. At one moment I was going through the sunny landscape of Galilee and then it got dark again, and I didn't know whether I was in prison in Jerusalem or in the caves of Arbela. Faces appeared out of the darkness: the Zealot leader was grinning at me. Then Pilate appeared. He grinned too. Their faces kept changing. I heard again the growling of the wild beast, saw giant teeth, claws which sought to destroy me. I could feel them on my face . . .

And I woke up in terror. Someone had touched me. The thought went through my mind that they planned to kill me secretly, in the night. But a familiar voice whispered, 'Ssshh. Follow me quietly.' It was Barabbas.

We crept carefully along a passage which led into the open air. Outside we clambered along the rock until we came to a small hollow.

'We're safe here,' whispered Barabbas. 'I'm on night watch.'

'Barabbas!' I threw my arms around his neck.

We sat and looked into the night. There was a clear starry sky over Galilee. The moon shed a pale light on the rocks. Its reflection shone the still surface of Lake Gennesaret. We squatted in the shadows. No one took any notice of us here. Barabbas whispered:

'I ought to tell you that I denied you today. They mustn't know that we're acquainted. Otherwise they would have attempted to win you over – also using pressure and blackmail. And if you'd said no, I don't know what would have happened.'

I remained silent.

'It was my idea to change the ransom demand into a long-term agreement.'

'Thanks very much! But tell me, would they have killed me if I'd said no to everything?'

Barabbas didn't reply. I asked him again: 'Would they have killed me?'

He sighed: 'I suppose you think that we're cold-blooded murderers. I grant you, I have killed people. The first was a Roman soldier who was pursuing me. I had to kill him, or he would have killed me. The second was a rich landowner whom we had condemned to death. He had driven a family to suicide. They were in debt, but they preferred death to prison.'

'But I haven't threatened anyone, pursued anyone, oppressed anyone, and you threatened to kill me. Why? Just because I come from a rich family. That's my only crime,' I protested.

Barabbas put a finger to his lips and made a gesture to silence me. We had to be careful. A stone fell some way away and clattered into the depths. I held my breath. But everything remained quiet. We were alone.

'We haven't killed you. We only wanted your money. Perhaps you call that robbery, but we're only taking from you rich what you've taken from the poor, often without breaking a single law. We're making sure that the good things of this earth find their true owners. Look at all the men here. Most of them have been driven out of house and home. They came to us because they saw no other way out. We're their final stop, their last hope.'

'But you had other possibilities. Your family isn't doing too badly.'

'I'm an exception. That's why I stay here. I've a lot to do. My idea is that we should punish all the rich, all the judges and officials who act unjustly. The state ought really to do that, but it doesn't. Indeed it's increasing injustice by making laws which are to the detriment of the poor. We must take its place. We must see that justice is done. Once people realize that their evil deeds will no longer go un-punished, in future they will think before they exploit little people. So I must remain here. I'm making sure that these desperate men don't just plunder and murder, but carry out an idea.'

'Do you call it justice to threaten to murder two young slaves?

Whom have Timon and Malchus wronged? Whom are they oppressing?'

Barabbas was silent. I kept on at him:

'Is it so easy to get at the real culprits? Any rich landowner will live in his house with servants and slaves, old people and children. If you set fire to the house by night you risk killing innocent people – not the rich, not the oppressors, not the bloodsuckers, but those who are themselves oppressed, drained dry, exploited! If you kill a rich person you have to attack the slaves with him and kill them as well. If you destroy his harvest you destroy the staple diet of all those who work and slave on his property. I'm disgusted with the way many people of our class behave. But what improvement is it on that for you to terrorize us?'

Again we kept quiet for a while. Then Barabbas said, 'Someone left us recently. He spoke like you do. I was friendly with him.'

'What's he doing now?'

'He's following a remarkable prophet whom he once got to know catching fish for us in the Sea of Galilee.'

'Tell me, is the prophet called Jesus?'

'You know him?'

'I've never seen him. But I've heard of him. I thought he was a Zealot himself. What he says about the rich sounds almost like you.'

'Andreas, you're wrong. This Jesus is crazy. I've never met anyone who has such mad ideas.'

'But doesn't he say, just like you, that a great turning point is coming? That God will no longer put up with injustice? That his kingdom is finally on the way?'

'But there's a great difference. We too want God alone to rule, not the Romans who oppress our land. But we're convinced that God only helps those who take their destiny into their own hands.[1] He helps only those who are ready for rebellion and for violence against the enemy. But do you know what this Jesus says? Simon told me one of his parables.

The kingdom of God is as if a man should scatter seed upon the ground, and should sleep and rise night and day, and the seed should sprout and grow, he knows not how. The earth produces of itself, first the blade,

then the ear, then the full grain in the ear. But when the grain is ripe,
at once he puts in the sickle, because the harvest has come.[2]

He makes it all seem so innocuous. The kingdom of God comes by
itself, as gently and softly as plants from the ground. Indeed he
sometimes speaks in mysterious words about it, as if it is already
there, though anyone can see that the Romans are still ruling our
land. He's crazy. So is Simon.'
   'Who?'
   'Simon is my friend, the one who left us. Among the followers of
Jesus he's known as Simon the Zealot.[3] Simon once asked Jesus
whether one shouldn't resist injustice. Do you know what Jesus
replied? He said,

> *You have heard that it was said,*
> *An eye for an eye and a tooth for a tooth.*
> *But I say to you,*
> *Do not resist one who is evil.*
> *But if any one strikes you on the right cheek,*
> *turn to him the other also;*
> *and if any one would sue you and take your coat,*
> *let him have your cloak as well;*
> *and if any one forces you to go one mile,*
> *go with him two miles.*[4]

Andreas, anyone who says that sort of thing is crazy. We say, If
anyone hits you, hit back! If anyone takes your coat, burn down
his house! If anyone puts pressure on you, take away his children
and put pressure on him! That's the only way of stopping
injustice.'
   'But Simon the Zealot approves of these eccentric ideas that Jesus
is spreading.'
   '"Eccentric" is putting it mildly. At a pinch one can imagine
someone preferring to suffer injustice from a friend rather than do
injustice to him – but when it comes to enemies! Isn't it our duty to
help friends and harm enemies? When Simon asked Jesus about this,
he replied:

You have heard that it was said,
You shall love your neighbour and hate your enemy.
But I say to you,
Love your enemies
and pray for those who persecute you,
so that you may be sons of your father who is in heaven;
for he makes his sun rise on the evil and on the good,
and sends rain on the just and on the unjust.[5]

Who can allow himself to be so generous to his enemies? Only someone who is strong and independent enough for his enemies not to be able to get at him. That's possible only for the great victors, the kings and emperors. But this Jesus goes through our oppressed land and wants to inculcate in ordinary people an attitude which only the uppermost class can allow themselves as a luxury, and which gets in the way of the only thing that can bring change: the solidarity of the oppressed in the face of those who hurt them and their hatred of the great.'

'But does he teach that one should simply give in to the great? Sharp words of his against the rich are going the rounds.'

'Yes, that's true. He expresses the displeasure of the people towards the great. For example he says,

You know
that those who are supposed to rule over the Gentiles lord it over them,
and their great men exercise authority over them.
But it shall not be so among you:
but whoever would be great among you must be your servant,
and whoever would be first among you
must be slave of all.[6]

The people like to hear that. They think that it's possible to get rid of oppression and exploitation without violence. But what does this oppression actually consist of? People have to pay tax and don't know where they are to get the money from to pay their debts, so they lose their possessions.[7]

Oppression means that the rulers appropriate for themselves so much of the produce of the land that the people are constantly on the verge of starvation. Such oppression has to keep going for its own sake. The burden of taxation and offerings is inevitably always so high that the population falls into two groups: on the one hand those who are interested in maintaining the *status quo* and on the other the large number who are worried sick over keeping alive. That kind of worry saps their courage to try to change things on a large scale. And the meagre possibilities of keeping alive suggest to them that even with things as they are it's possible to get by with hard work and a bit of good luck. Anyone who goes under either has himself to blame or has extraordinary bad luck. That's the kind of oppression prevalent here. You can see how vital the question of taxation is.

We asked Jesus what he would do about this oppression. We asked whether it was lawful to pay tax to the emperor or not. He had a denarius brought to him and asked, "Whose portrait is on the coin? Whom does the inscription mention?" And when we replied, "The emperor", he said,

> Then give to the emperor what is the emperor's
> and to God what is God's.[8]

He always gets evasive when it comes to specific questions. He wants to take the gentle way.'

'Is it really so innocuous for him to say that the rulers oppress their people everywhere and that things must be different for his followers? Many people say that it's an illusion to want to practise politics without oppression. But Jesus said, "Even if all other peoples and societies cannot get by without oppression, you must be different. It is your task to overcome the division of the people into oppressed and oppressors."'

'Jesus expressed something which has been our distinguishing mark since earliest days. All our neighbours have formed states in which kings and their people possessed the land and the farmers working on the land were little better than slaves. But from the beginning we've guarded against living in such conditions. And we shall go on fighting for that.'

'But didn't God allow us to be brought under the rule of other peoples? How could we rebel against that?'

'God allowed us to be made slaves in Egypt. But he revealed his real will when he freed us from this slavery. When we came into this land we lived for two hundred years without a central government, as free farmers who supported one another against their enemies. We showed that a people can live with a minimum of government.'

'But then we too had to accept rulers! We too experienced the way in which a ruling class expanded under the monarchy.'

'Without kings we would have become dependent on other peoples. But from the beginning we took precautions against our kings ruling like Pharaohs. Under the monarchy prophets emerged. They criticized our rulers in the name of God when their power became too strong. And when the kings came to grief, our prophets saw this as a punishment for their misuse of power, both at home and abroad. God again showed that he was not on the side of the rulers.'

'But then we became dependent on the Babylonians, Persians and Greeks.'

'God sent us new prophets when we were in exile in Babylon. He promised a new exodus from Egypt. He used the Persian king Cyrus, who conquered the Babylonians and set us free.'

'But the Persians remained our rulers! And God willed it.'

'The Persians allowed us to organize our life in accordance with the divine commandments. When the people were in danger of falling apart into two classes as a result of poverty and debt, the Persian governor Nehemiah carried through a great reform in the name of God. All debts were remitted. All Israelites became free.'[9]

'Doesn't Nehemiah's reform show that there is another way than that of violence?'

'In favourable circumstances, yes. But the circumstances are seldom favourable. They changed under the Greeks and the Syrians. Our Greek conquerors were amazed at the many free smallholders among us.[10] But they didn't respect our traditions. They regarded all conquered land as their property and everything living on it as their possessions. Only in their cities did they give freedom to a small group of citizens. They wanted to establish the same conditions in our country. Some rich Jews allowed them to found a free Greek city in Jerusalem. With the adoption of a Greek life-style they were to fuse their religion with Greek belief. At that time our temple was dedicated to Zeus. There was a rebellion against that in the country. Belief in God was the basis of everyone's freedom: so any threat to it put the freedom and livelihood of many smallholders at stake.[11] Since then we've come to know that if we gave up belief in God we would no longer have any means of guarding against the servitude under which all our neighbours live. Only respect for our religious traditions prevents the Romans even now from doing away with all our freedom. That's why we guard so fanatically against any attack on our faith.'

'But may there not again be times which call for a reform? As under Nehemiah?'

'I think that's an illusion! Without the pressure of force nothing will change in this land. See how the Romans are more and more intent on incorporating our country into their empire. At first they still allowed us to be governed by our own rulers. Then they replaced our princes with the Herodians, who owed all their power to the Romans. Finally, in Judaea and Samaria they took over the government themselves. They respected our religious traditions for twenty years. But now they're trying to question the special status of the temple. They're having pagan coins minted. They're bringing effigies of the emperor to Jerusalem. Step by step they're blurring everything that separates us from other peoples. Soon no one will be able to say: "Rulers are oppressing their peoples everywhere but it mustn't be like that among you." Rather, they'll be saying: "The Romans rule everywhere as benefactors of the peoples. And it will be just the same for you." Then oppression will no longer be called oppression nor exploitation exploitation. So now is the time for violent resistance. Now is not the time of Nehemiah. Now is not the time for Jesus of Nazareth.'

'But Jesus also wants things to change.'

'That's true. He raises hopes that things might change without resistance and bloodshed. He's worse than those who say that you must reconcile yourself to everything. He wants change and peace at the same time, and that's an illusion. A dangerous illusion.'

'But don't you have illusions, too? Has Simon perhaps recognized that your methods are no better? Did he follow Jesus because it seemed the only way of getting out of these caves?'

'Simon is a problem. If his example catches on many more will leave us. So some have suggested that we should execute him as a traitor.'

'For God's sake!'

'I stopped it.'

Barabbas said that quietly. But it moved me very deeply. Gratitude and sympathy overcame the indifference of the night. Everything seemed to be looking at us as if the universe had an interest in saving a life. Wasn't it also looking to me to get Barabbas out of here?

'Barabbas – I beg you. Give up this life in the caves. You needn't go Simon's way. There are others.'

'It's not so easy. If I leave here there's nothing to stop so-called traitors being killed. In other words, they will attempt to kill me. They don't even need to do it themselves. They need only betray to the authorities that I've killed a Roman soldier and a landowner. I have to stay here.'

We had to break off to get back before dawn. Before we got into the cave I whispered to Barabbas: 'No matter what, I'll help you. You can vanish into the diaspora. You can rely on me. I'll always help you. I promise you.'

We clambered carefully back without being noticed. I lay down, but couldn't get to sleep. Confused and disconnected pictures again whirled through my sleepless mind. But they gradually fell into shape. My dilemma became increasingly clear.

There I was, travelling through the land for the Romans. I had no personal loyalty to them; I meant to put the destiny of my people above Roman interests. Now here I found a group which was wholly identified with the interests of our people – and which treated me as badly as the Romans had. How different were they from Pilate? I saw only blackmail and counter-blackmail, oppression and counter-pressure, terrorism from above and terrorism from below.

There were understanding people on both sides. Metilius was not inhuman. Couldn't Roman officials like him make peace? Couldn't they at least organize oppression in such a way as to avoid unnecessary suffering? Could politics achieve more? Was Metilius an exception?

And wasn't Barabbas an exception, too? Was he isolated in his thinking? He too wanted a minimum of counter-violence, a minimum of terrorism – and yet he couldn't avoid the ominous consequences of the course he had embarked on.

I had to press forward in no man's land. I wasn't at home in either camp. Then I spoke to God:[12]

Lord my God,
how can I remain true to myself?
Wherever I go
I find myself on rugged ways.
If I could speak like others
I would feel no grief.
They claim that the world is organized in such a way
that only violence and oppression bring results.
And they have success.
They attain riches!
They attain respect!
They attain power!
Is it not senseless
for me to attempt to live without guilt?
For me not to howl with the wolves.
That is why I am torn apart,
and constantly in pain.
If I talked like everyone else –
it would seem as though I were betraying everything that I have become.
Nevertheless I am always in your presence.
You lead me where I do not want to go,
you restore my honour,
you give me back respect.

I again thought back to our ancestors, to Abraham who deceived the Egyptians, Jacob who tricked his brother, David who served the enemies of the land. They too had gone on crooked ways. They too had wandered around in no man's land. Could not the devious ways I was treading perhaps lead to a good end? Could God bring everything to a good ending?

This thought lulled me to sleep for a while. But I was soon woken up. It was still dark. Two Zealots led Timon, Malchus and myself blindfold from the cave. I had seen the steep cliffs in the night. They were really dangerous. Again we went along precipitous paths and over ladders down the rocks. I was glad when we were on the ridges. There we were given our asses back. I noticed how our guides deliberately led us a roundabout way so that we lost all sense of direction. Finally, after two hours, we were allowed to take off our blindfolds.

We were standing on the slope of a hill. Before us lay the Sea of Galilee. The morning sun, which had risen in the east over the Golan heights, was shining on it. Everything was still, as though spellbound, with colours playing on the water.

Finally one of the Zealots turned to me: 'My name's Mattathias son Matthias. Can you do me a favour?' He pointed to the north end of the sea: 'There in the mist lies Capernaum. My parents live there with my family. Take them this letter and this money. They couldn't survive without my support. I couldn't bear their being so poor any longer. That's why I joined the Zealots.'

I promised to do as he asked. I looked for a long time in the direction he had shown me: somewhere in the morning mist were these men's homes. There they slaved away, suffered, complained and despaired. But the sun rose on them heedlessly, as though it wasn't concerned with 'all the injustice that happened under it'.[13]

I looked back. Timon and Malchus were saying good-bye to our escort. The morning light seemed to transform everyone's face. Even the two Zealots looked different. As they stood there by Timon and Malchus, all of a sudden they seemed to be much younger. In their weathered faces I detected the soft features of children. There we were together: terrorists, innocents and myself. Was it just through indifference to human suffering that the sun shone on us all? Wasn't it an expression of incomprehensible goodness that it did not distinguish between these bandits and ourselves?

And I praised God for making his sun rise anew every day, on good and bad, on righteous and unrighteous. The thought struck me that if the sun shines on Romans and Zealots, poor and rich, masters and slaves, if it is on both sides – was I not justified in swinging to and fro between Romans and Jews, authorities and Zealots, rich and poor? Surely it must be possible to ignore all these boundaries without coming to grief on them. I gained new courage.

Dear Dr Kratzinger,

You didn't like the last chapter. You criticized the 'politicizing' of the preaching of Jesus. You said that the saying about the leaders who were to be the servants of all did not refer to power relationships in politics, but to inter-personal relationships within the community. However, my understanding of the saying is supported by the fact that Jesus draws a distinction between his view and the policy among 'Gentiles'. The counterpart to 'Gentiles' is 'Israel'. 'It must not be like this among you' means that in Israel things are not to be as they are among other peoples. Here he is addressing the disciples, who repre-sent all Israel. He chose the Twelve as representatives of the twelve tribes.

Here we come up against a basic problem of interpretation: Jesus did not want to found a Christian community; he wanted to renew Israel. Anyone who refers his words only to the church fails to see that they were addressed to the whole of Jewish and Palestinian society.

He expected a miraculous change in this society: the poor, the children, the meek and the foreigners would come into their own in it. That would be the king-dom of God. It is not a purely spiritual entity. People can eat and drink in it. It is in Palestine. People stream to it from all sides. There is a new temple in it.

Jesus expected radically changed political circumstances, but did not expect that they would be brought about through political change. His aim was 'political', but it was to come about without politics. God would realize this aim. And that meant that people were not to achieve this aim by treating others violently. Nor, however, were they to be completely passive.

I often ask myself why Jesus counts so little among great theologians. Certainly the difficulty of establishing his role, of establishing a historically presentable picture of him, has something to do with it. But could it not be that there has always been a suspicion that once one admits the historical Jesus one admits a proclamation aimed at changes not only in the church but also throughout society?

Perhaps we can return to this question later.

With warmest greetings,
Yours,
Gerd Theissen

11

Conflict in Capernaum

Capernaum was on the way to Bethsaida Julias, about seven miles from Arbela. From there it was another three miles to our destination. We wanted to be in Bethsaida before the evening so that we could rest on the sabbath.[1]

We hurried there in order to settle our business in Capernaum as quickly as possible. Mattathias and his family lived in a small fisherman's house by the lake. The father was fishing. His wife Hannah had stayed at home instead of working in the fields. One of their daughters was sick. She was called Miriam and she was perhaps twelve years old. She lay in a corner of the hut, pale and with feverish eyes. Her older sisters moved quietly round the house. Everything was stuffy and still. I knew this atmosphere. It was the atmosphere of a family frightened of death. No one dared say as much. But everyone knew it. As soon as you entered the house you felt the shadow of death – and the stubborn hope for deliverance.

Nevertheless they brightened a bit when I handed over the letter and the money. I didn't need to give any long explanations.

'A stranger in Arbela gave me this for you. He sends his greetings.'

The family understood. I was warmly welcomed and had to sit down in the room. Timon and Malchus kept watch on our donkey.

Miriam looked at me with big eyes. I noticed that she wanted to ask me something and smiled at her. Then she said:

'Are you the Messiah?'

For God's sake, I thought, she's sick and fantasizing in her fever. I answered in a friendly way:

'I'm Andreas, a merchant from Sepphoris.'

'Do you know when the Messiah is coming?' she asked, with disappointment all over her face.

I gave the usual answer that you give children:

'He's coming at the end of time.'

'No, he's already here.'

I looked questioningly at Hannah. She explained: 'She means a prophet whom some hold to be the Messiah. He heals the sick and drives out demons. Many people in the village believe in him. Some young people follow him. She hopes that he will come and heal her.'

'Do you mean Jesus?'

Miriam nodded. 'Have you seen him?'

'No,' I said, 'But I would love to. Everyone's talking about him. He's said to be in this neighbourhood often.'

'He's never long in one place,' said Hannah.

'Why isn't he here?' Miriam murmured. 'Why doesn't he make me better?'

Miriam's mother sat by her on the floor and lovingly stroked her hair: 'He said,

The blind see and the lame walk,
the lepers are cleansed and the deaf hear,
the dead are raised
and the poor hear good news.
Happy is he who takes no offence in me.'[2]

'If only he would come,' whispered the child.

Hannah wrapped her daughter in a blanket and put her on her lap.

'I can't go and get him. Believe me, I just can't. But I can tell you a story about him. Would you like that?'

Miriam nodded and Hannah began:[3]

There was a woman who had had a flow of blood for twelve years, and who had suffered much under physicians, and had spent all that she had, and was no better but rather grew worse. She had heard the reports about Jesus, and came up behind him in the crowd and touched his garments. For she said, 'If I touch his garments, I shall be made well.' And immediately the haemorrhage ceased; and she felt in her body that she was healed of her disease. And Jesus, perceiving in himself that power had gone forth from him, immediately turned about in the crowd

and said, 'Who touched my garments?' And his disciples said to him,
'You see the crowd pressing around you, and yet you say, "Who touched
me?"' And he looked around to see who had done it. But the woman,
knowing what had been done to her, came in fear and trembling and fell
down before him, and told him the truth. And he said to her, 'Daughter,
your faith has made you well; go in peace, and be healed of your disease.'

Miriam had been listening eagerly as though it were all said to her.
But now she could no longer contain herself. She cried:

'Why doesn't he come? Why can't I touch him like the woman, so
that I become well? Why not?' And she began to weep.

Then I had an idea: I went to her, put my hand on her brow and
said:

'Miriam, you're like the woman in the story. You believe that
touching makes people better. Didn't you listen to what Jesus said at
the end? He said, "Your faith has made you well." He didn't say,
"Touching me has made you well."'

I grant that this was a desperate idea. I myself wasn't convinced
that what I was doing was right. I wanted to say something kind to the
girl who was frightened of dying.

Miriam looked at me gratefully. She grew calmer. She asked for
more stories and Hannah told them. She told about a woman who had
asked Jesus to heal her small daughter – and Jesus healed her at a
distance, without going to her.[4] Hannah added:

'Why does he have to come to our house? Can't he heal from a
distance?'

And then she told of blind people who saw again, of lepers who
were healed, of lame men who could walk again. The stories got more
and more miraculous and more and more improbable. Miriam lapped
them all up. They were her stories. She was blind and could see again.
She was lame and could walk again. She was sick and got better. And
she drew new hope from every word.

I too listened spellbound. Some things in these stories repelled me.
They sounded superstitious and primitive. But on the whole I was
just as entranced with them as Miriam. I noted that these poor people
pinned all their hopes on such stories. In them I heard their rebellion
against suffering and death. I felt that as long as these stories were

told, people would not be content for men and women to hunger and thirst, be crippled and paralysed, be sick and helpless. As long as they had these stories they would have hope.

I asked myself whether Hannah had heard all the stories about Jesus which she had told to Miriam. Had she perhaps invented some of them to comfort little Miriam? I believe that if she had run out of stories, I myself would have added some and invented some. I know that telling stories alone does not cure people. But I had the feeling that without these stories Miriam would not be healed.

In the meantime her father had come back from catching fish. He had steeled himself for bad news. His face lit up when he found Miriam peaceful and that he had a letter and money from his son.

Meanwhile I had devised a plan to help Miriam. In Tiberias I knew a doctor called Hippocrates, a Greek, as was obvious from his name. By boat you could get to Tiberias in four hours. If one of Mattathias' older sons crossed over that evening with Timon and Malchus and spent the night on the beach there, the next day they could go and get Hippocrates and return to Capernaum.

Mattathias objected to my plan: 'We've too little money to pay a doctor. We need that bit of money to live, and to pay the taxes.'

I reassured him. I would pay the money. Immediately I wrote a letter to Hippocrates and asked him urgently to come to help. I would see to his fee and expenses. In addition I sent a message to Chuza and Joanna that I would visit them the next week in Tiberias.

There was another hour before sunset. The young people went down to the shore. The setting sun cast a golden glow on the lake, into which the boat disappeared as a black speck. We lit the sabbath lights, said the blessing and ate.

It was not long before there was a knock on the door. Two people wanted to speak to Mattathias. The older one was called Gamaliel, the younger one Daniel. Mattathias invited them in. Both of them sat down.

Gamaliel began: 'Your son has gone fishing on the sabbath with a couple of strangers. Don't you know that it's forbidden to work on the sabbath?'

Mattathias reassured him. 'They're not going fishing. They wanted to go to Tiberias to get a doctor for Miriam. No one has broken the sabbath.'

Daniel objected: 'Couldn't you wait until the sabbath was over?'

I intervened: 'I sent them. Miriam needs help. When a healing is involved it's permissible to break the sabbath regulations.'

'No,' objected Daniel. 'Only if there is no alternative.'

I got cross. In Sepphoris it was taken for granted that you could get the doctor on the sabbath. How narrow-minded these country people were! But perhaps they were both only justifying themselves for having disturbed our meal.

Gamaliel said thoughtfully: 'Some cases are allowed. If a sheep falls into a well on the sabbath, it can be got out again.'

Daniel protested: 'I think differently. If God wants the sheep to survive, it will survive. You can only see to it after the sabbath.'[5]

Gamaliel objected. 'How can it survive? It will drown. Do you want to make God do miracles? You Essenes are stricter than we Pharisees. We want practicable solutions. Most scribes agree with me that it is permissible to rescue an animal on the sabbath. Arguing from the lesser to the greater I come to the conclusion that if it is permissible to rescue an animal it is all the more permissible to cure a human being.'

Miriam had been following the discussion. She interrupted it by exclaiming: 'Jesus also healed someone on the sabbath. Mama, tell us the story.'

Hannah clearly found it difficult to talk about Jesus in front of the two visitors. But what mother in this situation would have refused her child's request? So she said:

Jesus went into the synagogue on the sabbath, and a man was there who had a withered hand. And they watched him, to see whether he would heal him on the sabbath, so that they might accuse him. And he said to the man who had the withered hand, 'Come here.' And he said to them, 'Is it lawful on the sabbath to do good or to do harm, to save life or to kill?' But they were silent. And he looked around at them with anger, grieved at their hardness of heart, and said to the man, 'Stretch out your hand.' He stretched it out, and his hand was restored.[6]

Everyone had listened to her attentively. Gamaliel said in a kind way: 'Miriam, isn't that rather different from our sheep in the well?

The sheep would drown if someone didn't get it out. But couldn't the man with the withered hand wait a day? It's not a matter of doing good or evil, healing or killing! It's a matter of doing good today or tomorrow.'

Daniel interjected: 'You see what happens when people make concessions. They're exploited. This Jesus is well aware that all scribes agree with him that you can help someone else on the sabbath. But he takes it to extremes. His view is that anyone can decide when he has to observe the sabbath rules and when not, when he is obliged to help and when not.'

Hannah listened impatiently. 'I don't understand this hair-splitting, but it's clear that you can help on the sabbath. The sabbath was made for man and not man for the sabbath. Human life is worth more than the sabbath.'[7]

Gamaliel defended himself. 'What does "help" mean here? Anyone could say "I want to help my neighbour with the harvest, so I may break the sabbath rules." No, it's important for us to have detailed rules for individual instances.'

I tried to mediate: 'So let's at least agree in this instance that it's permissible to send for a doctor on the sabbath. We did nothing wrong in sending for Hippocrates.'

I shouldn't have said that. Daniel attacked me immediately. 'Hippocrates? A pagan doctor? A foreigner? Aren't there Jewish doctors in Tiberias? That's really going too far. First breaking the sabbath and then transgressing the laws of purity. Don't you know that foreigners and Jews may not make physical contact? They're to be kept separate, like what is clean and what is unclean. And you want to have a Jewish girl treated by a Gentile doctor? Do you want to bring him into this house?'

'Hippocrates treats Jews in Tiberias,' I stubbornly retorted. 'Why not in Capernaum?'

Mattathias pointedly turned his back on us, got himself a stool and sat by Hannah, who was still holding the feverish child in her lap.

Gamaliel said earnestly, 'People in Tiberias aren't so strict about the rules of purity. When Herod Antipas founded the city, he knew that the settlement offended against our laws. For Tiberias was built on a great many graves.[8] Our law says that such settlements are unclean. But no one takes any notice of that. This Tiberias is an unclean city.'

Daniel supported him: 'Carelessness is now spreading all over the country. The followers of Jesus neglect the difference between clean and unclean. They don't wash their hands before eating.[9] They go through the fields and pluck ears of corn on the sabbath.[10] They don't keep aloof from foreigners. Now they even bring pagan doctors into Jewish homes.'

At that point I got cross. 'I'm not a supporter of Jesus! I've never seen Jesus! And I would always get a Gentile doctor, no matter what Jesus or you said. But what has Jesus said about the laws of purity?'

Gamaliel explained. 'I heard him discussing them. He swept away all our reflections with the argument:

> It's not what goes into a man from outside
> that defiles a man,
> but what comes out from a man,
> that defiles the man.'[11]

'Does he mean that there is no difference between clean and unclean?' I asked.

'Yes. If he's right, there would be no unclean food any more, no unclean people, no unclean places. Everything would be clean. You could buy anything from Gentiles and sell anything to Gentiles.'

I pricked up my ears: 'You could also buy olive oil from Gentiles?'

Gamaliel nodded: 'That would follow.'

I began to think about possible consequences for our trade in olives, but then Mattathias joined in the discussion:

'I couldn't care less about this discussion on clean and unclean, on your sabbath rules! Aren't you breaking the sabbath yourselves when you bother people with your learned discussions instead of leaving us and our sick child in peace? Don't you see how sick she is? Don't you see that we have quite different worries? And there you are discussing helping and not helping, what is allowed and what is not allowed, instead of actually being helpful. You can't even keep quiet. Jesus has quite different things to say about you:[12]

Woe to you, scribes and Pharisees, hypocrites!
For you cleanse the outside of the cup and of the plate,
but inside they are full of extortion and rapacity.
Woe to you, scribes and Pharisees, hypocrites!
For you are like whitewashed tombs,
which outwardly appear beautiful,
but within you are full of hypocrisy and iniquity.

He's right!'

There was no doubt about it. That finished it. Our two scribes got up to go. Gamaliel said,

'You're unfair, Mattathias. It's clear you're worried about your child. I hope she gets better.' Then the two hurried out.

I was tempted to follow them. I wanted to say something conciliatory. But now it was more important to calm Miriam. I sat down beside her and told her harmless stories, not miracle stories but fables and fairy stories. Soon she fell asleep. And we too lay down to sleep.

On the sabbath I went to the morning service. The solemn stillness transformed the village. The people who had been slaving for six days emerged from their huts standing upright. They all gathered at the synagogue. Gamaliel read the scripture and interpreted it. He began with his blessing:

Blessed are you, Lord, our God,
king of the universe,
who forms light
and creates darkness,
who makes peace
and brings all things into being.
Who gives light to the earth
and those who dwell on it,
and in your goodness
renews every day
the work of creation.[13]

Then he read from the book of Exodus. It was the story of God's revelation on Sinai. His exposition concentrated on one sentence:

> *For all the earth is mine, and you shall be to me a kingdom of priests and a holy nation.*[14]

Gamaliel said:

'How could God speak of priests in the wilderness? There was no temple there! No sacrifice! But the whole world is God's temple. He said, "All the earth is mine." So we should behave everywhere as though we were in the temple where everything is holy, sun and light, day and night, mountains and rivers, sea and land, plants and animals. We must treat them all with reverence.

Perhaps you will argue that only priests go into the temple, that God requires special attention to the holiness of the temple only from them. But God wants all of us to become a holy people. There are not to be two classes, priests with special holiness and others outside. Before him all are alike!

Perhaps some of you may wonder whether it is not enough for us to appear before God on the sabbath. But if the world is the temple of God, then we stand before God every moment, even when we are not aware of it. But on the sabbath we remind one another of God. Otherwise we would forget him. We might think all sorts of things more important than thinking about God – if strict regulations did not keep us from working every seventh day.'

After the service Gamaliel came up to me. He asked after Miriam and said,

'I was very unhappy yesterday because our conversation broke up like that. Today I shall go back to Mattathias and have a word with him.'

I reassured Gamaliel. Mattathias was a good-natured man. Miriam had soon gone to sleep and had looked better the next morning. I, too, would have like to continue the conversation the previous day. It had become clear to me that the scribes attached more importance to helping other people than to keeping the sabbath. But why had the exceptions to be laid down so carefully? Why wasn't every individual trusted to decide for himself what could be done on the sabbath and what not? Gamaliel nodded as I spoke and replied:

'See how other people live. They don't have a sabbath. They have only sacrificial festivals to the gods. Count the number of those in a year. Perhaps twenty days, perhaps thirty, but no more. Ordinary people work on most days of the year. Only rarely can they enjoy the rest which landowners and the powerful take for granted. But it's different for us Jews. We celebrate the sabbath fifty-two times a year. Not only do the nobility and the rich celebrate it; so do ordinary people. Even servants and slaves. And in addition to these fifty-two sabbaths there are festivals.

There are the great autumn festivals: Rosh Hashanah, the New Year Festival; Yom Kippur, the Day of Atonement; and Sukkoth, the Feast of Tabernacles. Then there are the festivals in spring and early summer: Passover and the Feast of Weeks. Even the ordinary person has about sixty days' rest a year. No wonder that other people suspect us of being lazy.'[15]

'None of us wants to do away with these many days of rest. But why all the rules about matters of detail? Why the agitation when they aren't all observed?'

'No one wants to do away with them. But many rich people would like their slaves, their servants, their tenants to work for them on the sabbath. Then they could earn even more. Especially when they see how their Gentile competitors and business partners exploit their people and make them work on the sabbath as well. They certainly don't want to abolish the sabbath, but they do want to undermine it. They would allow a thousand exceptions. When money is involved you have to produce very clear regulations, otherwise money and riches prevail.'

'Are you afraid, then, that people like Jesus undermine the sabbath in this way?'

'He doesn't do it deliberately. On the contrary! The rich and powerful find little support from him. But he doesn't think enough. His example could become popular. It could become the fashion to treat the prohibition against working on the sabbath lightly. Others could exploit it for their own ends.'

'In your view, is what Jesus does against the law?'

'You can't say that. Any one of us could put forward all Jesus' teaching about the sabbath and about the laws of purity. Certainly he takes a radical view. But many people among us put forward radical views.'

'But why are there always arguments about his teaching?'

'He thinks too little of the consequences. He doesn't see that any breach of the sabbath regulations could in due course lead to our living like Gentiles. And this thoughtlessness is a regular feature of his. He goes around in dubious company; with drunkards, prostitutes, cheats. That's not forbidden. We have respect for anyone who brings a sinner back on the right way. We know that God's mercy is extended to those who fail. We rejoice over the conversion of those who are wicked. But he eats with them without making sure that they have turned from their previous way of life. He makes no demands on them. He hopes that they will come to repent of their own accord! I call that carelessness. Perhaps he helps some people in that way, but what sort of effect will it have on many others? Won't they ask why they have to strive to do good? If Jesus is right, God is already happy with me as I am.'

Gamaliel had got very intense. He became more vociferous.

'Yes,' he said, 'This Jesus could be my pupil. He could put forward all his views. But I would compel him to think through the consequences for our people and for everyday life. Let me mention another instance. One day a Gentile centurion living here in Capernaum came to him.[16] He asked him to heal his orderly. Of course you have to help Gentiles. But why this one? Everyone knows that most of these Gentile officers are homosexual. Their orderlies are their lovers. But Jesus isn't interested in that sort of thing. He didn't ask anything about the orderly. He healed him – and the thought didn't occur to him that later someone might think of appealing to him in support of the view that homosexuality was permissible.'

'Are you certain that the centurion was homosexual?'

'Of course not, but everyone must have their suspicions. Jesus wasn't at all bothered. At this point I would advise more caution.'

'All right, perhaps it was ill-advised. But was it forbidden?'

'No, I couldn't say that. God wants all people to be helped.'

'Including toll collectors and prostitutes?'

'Including them.'

'But why was Jesus criticized for eating with them?'

'If just anyone did it we would keep quiet. But this Jesus is an influential man. He's a teacher. He's one of us. We only criticize him because he's near to us.'

'And what is there to criticize in Jewish teachers dealing with toll collectors? We merchants often have dealings with them.'

'Think of the consequences. We have nothing against individual publicans. They're human like anyone else. But they represent the Romans in our land. What they collect largely goes abroad. We mustn't give the impression that Jewish teachers have come to terms with foreign rule. The Romans mustn't receive an aura of divine legitimation from us.'

'Are you afraid that Jesus could give them this aura?'

'No, but the crowd which follows him could get false impressions. Anyone whom the people believe to be teaching the will of God shouldn't blatantly help foreign soldiers. He shouldn't converse openly with toll collectors. Jesus doesn't know how much is at stake when we mix with Gentiles, when we behave as they do. I criticize the openness with which he does it. It looks as if he were standing in a kind of no man's land.'

Suddenly it struck me: I too was in a kind of no man's land. And in Gamaliel's eyes I too must be a problematical figure. Would Gamaliel ever be able to understand me? When I went on to ask more questions I was asking about myself.

'How does Jesus justify his behaviour?'

'Let me stress once again: the views which Jesus puts forward could be put forward by us Pharisees and scribes. We are accustomed to discussing a variety of opinions. But Jesus stands aloof from our usual methods of discussion. He doesn't express his view as one among others. He doesn't discuss it with reasons for or against. He acts as though God himself were speaking through him. This contempt for our forms – that's what causes offence.'

We went on talking about Jesus for a long time. I felt how much this figure attracted me. I too was hovering in no man's land. Wasn't I like a toll collector, except that I collected information rather than money to hand on to the Romans? Wouldn't Jesus understand my position?

I accompanied Gamaliel to Mattathias's hut. Gamaliel took some fruit to give to Miriam. 'On the sabbath there should be peace among us,' he said. And Mattathias replied: 'Shalom. Peace be with you.'

Yesterday's row was over.

Soon the young men came with Hippocrates from Tiberias. He examined Miriam and expressed his opinion: 'I think that the worst is over.'

Then light returned to the small hut, as though life were beginning all over again.

Dear Dr Kratzinger,

I'm glad that we agree in our estimation of the Pharisees. I'm aware that research is far from over. We have become more careful about using later texts about the Pharisees in connection with circumstances before AD 70.

Independently of this, scholars have a great duty to restore the reputation of the Pharisees. All too often they have transgressed the most elementary principles of historical scholarship by accepting polemic against the Pharisees as valid comment. The discovery of the Qumran texts was the first development to lead to corrections: in comparison with the radical Essenes, the Pharisees appeared to be a trend concerned for compromise and moderation. After the catastrophe of AD 70 *these Pharisees refounded Judaism. The new understanding of Judaism at the present time has necessarily also changed our historical assessment of them.*

In recent times theology has constantly been confronted with the task of distinguishing between outdated and valid aspects of the Christian religion. What was more natural than to make Judaism with a Pharisaic stamp responsible for anything from which one wanted to be dissociated; the Jewish legacy to Christianity was the one that was thought to be out of date. Freedom from dependence on the 'law' could be understood as an anticipation of the emancipation of people from external authorities in the modern world.

Consequently, many learned professors of theology developed their modern self-understanding apart from Judaism. And they found an echo among the Christian middle classes, who had an antipathy to Jews for quite different reasons. They felt threatened economically by modern developments and made Jews responsible for everything that they complained about: liberalism, capitalism, democracy, the collapse of religion.

There was an amazing coalition between liberal theologians who wanted to be modern and unsettled middle-class people who were anxious about the nature of progress into modern times. Both found their needs fulfilled in New Testament polemic against Pharisees (and against Jews generally).

Perhaps you can understand why I am glad that you, too, are in favour of a revision of our image of Pharisaic Judaism.

With warmest greetings,
Yours,
Gerd Theissen

12

Men on the Frontier

We went on from Capernaum to Bethsaida, two days late. Bethsaida is a small town on the north shore of the Sea of Galilee, across the frontier. It belongs in the territory of Herod Philip. Not so long ago Philip had wanted to develop the Jewish village into a small Hellenistic city. His new foundation was called Bethsaida Julias, in honour of Julia, the daughter of Emperor Augustus.[1] Basically it was still no more than a large village.

On the way to Bethsaida we had to go through the toll gate. The toll collector was well known to us: a cheerful man who, after the usual haggling over tariffs and bribes, would gladly accept an invitation to a drink of wine.

This time, however, we were surprised. Instead of Levi the toll collector, we met a stranger. He introduced himself.

'My name's Kostabar. I'm the new toll collector[2] at this post. What goods are you carrying?'

He comes straight to the point, I thought. I asked in reply,

'What's happened to Levi?'

'Levi's no longer a toll collector. In future you'll be dealing with me.'

'Has something happened to him?'

Kostabar shrugged his shoulders: 'Can't say. He didn't want to be a toll collector any more. He disappeared.'

Someone else who suddenly disappeared. I kept at him:

'Has he gone to join the bandits?'

'I don't know. I've not heard any more of him. Now I'm the toll collector. Once again: what goods do you have to declare?'

We showed him all that we were carrying. Kostabar asked me,

'Is that all?'

In fact it wasn't much. Incredibly little for a merchant like me. I explained:

'Surprisingly we found a taker for some of our goods in Galilee. That's all that is left.'

Our 'takers' had been the Zealots, who had confiscated much of our goods as payment for the annual tribute. Kostabar remained suspicious.

'And where have you hidden the rest?'

I grinned. Now came the trick I played on the toll collectors.

'Perhaps I've forgotten something.'

Kostabar felt around in our baggage. Then he found it. He brought a medium-size wineskin out from among the other things:

'What's that?'

'It's not for sale.'

'That doesn't matter. Duty must be paid.'

'I'm not paying.'

'Of course you're paying. Otherwise the goods will be confiscated.'

'Tax is payable only on goods which are imported into the country. So I'm not paying.'

'Do you want to pour the wine on the floor here?'

'Not on the floor.'

Kostabar looked at me in a puzzled way. Then I said with a smile:

'This wine is for us to drink together duty free. There's also fruit and bread.'

Kostabar shook his head. 'No drink in the toll house.'

I protested: 'A drink of wine is hardly a booze-up.'

'But that's how it begins.'

'What?'

'All the inefficiency that I've found here.'

I shook my head uncomprehendingly. 'You're the first toll collector to tell me that one drink in the toll house is inefficiency. Your predecessors were different.'

'Precisely.'

Kostabar remained stubborn. I made a mental note not to mention the name of his predecessor. Something had happened. At all events, I would never persuade this toll collector to have a drink. Kostabar was intent on sobriety. Of course he knew as well as I did that it is easier to mislead a drunken toll collector than one who is stone cold sober. We got back to business. Kostabar wanted ten per cent.

I protested: 'So far the duty here has always been only six per cent.'

'Precisely.'

'I don't understand.'

'Then why did my predecessor give up his job? Because he couldn't live on a paltry six per cent. Six per cent is too little.'

'But the tariffs are fixed.'

'Yes – and I agree that the tariff is six per cent. A toll collector could live on that if people didn't keep smuggling. The only alternative is for me to stick this four per cent on the tariff – as compensation for the earnings I lose.'

'That's unfair on those who pay properly for their goods.'

'And it's doubly unfair first to cheat us toll collectors – and then blame us because we soberly take our losses into account.'

I gave way: 'How about a two per cent increase – a special rate for honest merchants like me? And in addition a drink of wine to console you over what others keep back from Kostabar the toll collector.'

Kostabar seemed to be thinking it over. We came to an agreement. Business over, we sat in the shade in front of the toll house, ate bread and fruit and drank the wine that Kostabar had discovered. As we sat there I suddenly saw a remarkable procession approaching the toll house. First came someone whom even at a distance you could see to be a borderline case, on the verge of madness. Behind him hobbled a toothless old man, moving on crutches. After that a ragged figure tapped his way along the road. Clearly he was blind. A few beggars' children clad in rags surrounded the trio.

'For God's sake,' Kostabar shouted. 'They're coming back. That's what happens when you drink wine in the toll house.'

'How's that?' I asked. 'I've often drunk wine in toll houses.'

'They want to join in the eating and drinking,' said Kostabar in despair. 'They always come when they suspect someone's here. They're like leeches. I can't get rid of them.'

'How long have they been coming?'

'Since I arrived. Or more precisely, since Levi introduced these new customs here.'

Meanwhile we could hear from afar the voices of the approaching group. One of them cried out:

'Has Jesus come back?'

'What has Jesus got to do with it?' I asked Kostabar.

'My predecessor Levi was a follower of Jesus. He had got to know Jesus because he often comes by here. Jesus crosses the frontier regularly. He's always moving from one district to another.'

'Why?'

'I suspect that he doesn't feel safe in Galilee. Perhaps Antipas is after him. So he keeps disappearing over the frontier, often into the territory of Herod Philip. Either he comes past here or he crosses the lake by boat, sometimes by night so that no one notices. Sometimes he also withdraws into the territory of the neighbouring cities, Tyre and Sidon, Hippo and Gadara. Not into the cities themselves but into the surrounding areas, where many Jews live.'

'I come from Sepphoris. None of us can recall that Jesus was ever in Sepphoris, though he comes from a small place near by.'

'That fits. He avoids the cities. He goes to the villages to be among the little people.'[3]

'But what's that got to do with this crazy procession?'

I pointed to the group, which was slowly approaching the toll house.

'As I was saying, Levi got to know Jesus and was impressed by his teaching. He changed his behaviour completely under Jesus' influence. He began by providing food regularly for the poor. The word soon got around. They flocked to him from all sides. But that was only the beginning. One day when Jesus came by, Levi resolved to follow him. But first he wanted to have a big farewell party.[4] It must have been a remarkable affair. The poor people are still talking about it. Ever since, in our neighbourhood Jesus has been called a glutton and a winebibber, a friend of toll collectors and sinners.[5] In fact it really was a madhouse. These three human wrecks you can see were also there. It was the great event in their life. Now they're waiting for Jesus to come back. They know that he often crosses the frontier here. And they keep hoping that there will be another party like that – here in the toll house. Every time they ask me when I shall be giving my big party. As though I were Levi.'

In the meantime the group had come nearer. You could hear their voices more clearly. They called out to me, 'Are you Jesus?'

'I'm not Jesus,' I replied.

'Anyone who gives us food and drink is Jesus.'

I saw that you couldn't have a normal conversation with them. They had formed a circle round us and looked expectantly at our food. The ragged children played around among them.

'Can't you leave us in peace?' I said.

But the children giggled and shouted:

'Have you brought us anything?'

Kostabar whispered to me: 'For God's sake don't give them anything! Otherwise they'll come back again. It may not matter to you; you're going on. But I'll always have them round my neck. I can't get rid of them.'

'Shall we go into the toll house?' I suggested. 'Perhaps they'll go away then.'

When we had finished eating we did that, and withdrew inside the house. Timon and Malchus had to stay outside to look after the ass and the goods. Inside we sat on mats. It was pleasantly cool in the hut. Kostabar said:

'Don't think that these people are starving. We have a poor fund in Bethsaida.[6] I pay my share, too, though through an intermediary. We feed these poor people on that. But their great dream is that this Jesus will come past again and hold a big party. They come and besiege me every week.'

We had begun to eat and drink again. I didn't like the way things had turned out, but I had to maintain a good relationship with Kostabar. It was certainly not the last time that I should have to pay duty to him. But we were interrupted again. The toothless old man had crept up to the window. He stuck his head into the hut and began to croak:

When you give a dinner,
do not invite your friends or your brothers or your kinsmen
or rich neighbours,
lest they also invite you in return, and you be repaid.
But when you give a feast, invite the poor, the maimed,

> *the lame, the blind.*
> *and you will be blessed, because they cannot repay you.*
> *You will be repaid at the resurrection of the just.*[7]

Having croaked this message into the small room he withdrew his head again and Kostabar explained:

'That's a saying of Jesus that they regularly quote at me. Listen; the sequel will come in a moment.'

In fact we could now hear a chorus of voices. They chanted a verse like a slogan at a demonstration:

> *Come to me*
> *all you who are weary and heavy laden*
> *and I will give you rest.*
> *Come to me*
> *all you who are weary and heavy laden*
> *and I will give you rest.*[8]

They kept repeating it. There was no stopping them. Finally Kostabar got up and went outside. He lost his temper. I heard him roaring:

'Now I'll give you rest. Get lost! Run away! We want our rest now.'

The chorus fell silent. A child's voice could be heard asking, 'Will you invite us to a meal now?' Then we heard again the croaking voice of the old man: 'Kostabar, don't you know the parable of Jesus?'[9]

> *A man once gave a great banquet, and invited many; and at the time for the banquet he sent his servant to say to those who had been invited, 'Come, for all is now ready.' But they all alike began to make excuses. The first said to him, 'I have bought a field, and I must go out and see it; I pray you, have me excused.' And another said, 'I have bought five yoke of oxen, and I go to examine them; I pray you, have me excused.' And another said, 'I have married a wife, and therefore I cannot come.' So the servant came and reported this to his master. Then the householder in anger said to his servant, 'Go out quickly to the streets and lanes of the city, and bring in the poor and maimed and blind and lame.' And the servant said, 'Sir, what you commanded has been done,*

and still there is room.' And the master said to the servant, 'Go out to the highways and hedges, and compel people to come in, that my house may be filled. For I tell you, none of those men who were invited shall taste my banquet.'

I noticed how they all listened to the old man. Even Kostabar seemed to be listening to him. When he had finished Kostabar added:
'You haven't told the parable to the end. There's more of it.'

But when the host came in to look at the guests, he saw there a man who had no wedding garment; and he said to him, 'Friend, how did you get in here without a wedding garment?' And he was speechless. Then the king said to the attendants, 'Bind him hand and foot, and cast him out into the outer darkness; there men will weep and gnash their teeth.'[10]

Kostabar's voice became sharp and cold: 'So get lost, or I'll bring soldiers who will bind you hand and foot and cast you into prison.'
    A child protested: 'Jesus never told that ending. You've made it up. It's wrong! It's a lie.'
    Kostabar began to bluster: 'That's the real ending. You'll find out soon enough. Away with you, you unwashed lot. Go to the devil!'
    I sat in the hut like a cat on hot bricks. Should I go out and defuse the situation? The parable had moved me. The child was right. The conclusion added by Kostabar didn't fit. But I also understood Kostabar: to be visited regularly by these people was a punishment!
    At first Kostabar succeeded. I heard the group going away. He came in.
    'They're off. These people are a plague. They used to be happy if you gave them bread. Then they went away. But since people like Jesus and Levi have raised their hopes they've become more importunate. They're waiting for the great turning point, the kingdom of God. Then they'll sit at richly decked tables with Jesus, the halt and the lame, the wheezers and the derelicts. Then they'll have their turn at enjoying the good fortune which God has prepared for them and which their fellows refused them. Meanwhile they live with these fantastic hopes, with demands which no village, no town,

no one can fulfil. With demands which belong in another world, not in our land.'

'I'm sorry for the children,' I said. 'They can't help being born in poverty.'

'You're right,' said Kostabar. 'Do you think I find it easy to send them away? But what can I do? Once I start giving food for beggars and children here, they'll be coming to me from all over the country. That's what Levi did. He made the people feel that there was always food here. Sometimes I think that's why he disappeared. He couldn't stand it any longer. Perhaps he took himself off. How could he bear all these people all the time? Perhaps he faced the choice of either going bankrupt or giving up the business. Whatever it was, he's disappeared. He followed Jesus. Can you see why I don't want to get into his position? I want to feed myself and my family from this business. I can't just disappear. I can't ruin my business by benevolence, as Levi did. I can only do my bit in the welfare system. No more.'

It was already late. We had to set off if we were to get to Bethsaida in time. We trotted slowly along the shore on our asses. The Sea of Galilee glittered in the sunshine. The mountains rose up from it like pale shadows. It was a peaceful afternoon.

Suddenly the beggar children whom we had met at the toll gate emerged. They held out their hands and barred our way.

'What are you doing?', I asked.

'We're playing at toll collectors.'

'What frontier is this?'

'This is the beginning of the kingdom of God.'

I wanted to explode with anger, but I restrained myself. Why shouldn't I play their game? So I did.

'What must I do to enter into your kingdom?'

The children laughed. The oldest one said:

Unless you become like children again,
you will not enter the kingdom of God.[11]

'Who rules in your kingdom?'

'We rule in this kingdom. The children. The kingdom of God is ours.'[12]

'And what duty must I pay?'

'Give us something to eat.'

'Is that all?'

'There is no kingdom you can enter so easily. All you must do is give away what you possess. Then you belong to it.'

I didn't know whether it was a game or in real earnest. I said:

'All right. Here is the duty for your kingdom.'

And I gave them a couple of loaves of bread and some fruit. Their faces shone. They gave way. We were allowed to pass. We had crossed this frontier as well.

Dear Dr Kratzinger,

Of course I'm pleased that you liked the last chapter. However, your strict academic standards led you to ask whether the tradition about the banquet given by the toll collector (Mark 2.15–17) is not the expression of problems in the community. A story was needed in early Christianity in which Jesus ate together with toll collectors and sinners. This could provide justification for Gentile and Jewish Christians eating together, even if the Gentiles did not observe Jewish food laws. The problem became acute at the end of the forties in Antioch (cf. Gal.2.11f.). Did the story come into being in order to solve this problem?

The story presupposes a toll station by the Sea of Galilee (in Capernaum). That can only be a frontier station. In the time of Jesus a frontier ran between Capernaum and Bethsaida which disappeared in the course of the first century. It did not exist between AD 39 and 44 when Agrippa I united the areas east and west of the Jordan. Nor was it there under his son Agrippa II, from AD 54 to the end of the century. The ten years between 44 and 54 are hard to assess. Probably both parts of the country were still united in a Roman province. In other words, the story of the toll collector's party presupposes conditions which only existed in the time of Jesus, and no longer held after AD 39. This brings us to a time in which meals shared between Jews and Gentiles in the early Christian communities were still no problem. At any rate, the problem was not yet acute at the time of the Apostolic Council (in the forties).

So could it be that the tradition of the toll collector's party contains a historical reminiscence? There is no doubt that it was used later to solve problems about eating together in the community.

As ever,
Yours,
Gerd Theissen

13

A Woman Protests

Although we asked about Jesus everywhere, we never met him. We did not find him either on the road to Bethsaida or on the way back when we went along the Sea of Galilee to Tiberias. Everyone had heard about him and many people had seen him. He seemed to have been almost everywhere. If one was to believe the reports about where he had been at any one time one could have assumed that he moved incredibly quickly from place to place. No wonder that someone told us that he could walk on water![1] So he appeared at some places unexpectedly and then soon disappeared again. Another puzzle was how he could feed so many people who went through the country with him. The story was going the rounds that he could multiply loaves. At one place they talked about seven loaves for four thousand people and at another about five loaves for five thousand people.[2] Of course I didn't believe a word of it. Anything seemed possible for this Jesus. The people probably thought that if someone could make sick people well, then he could be trusted to do anything. All these miracle stories could only come into being because he already had the reputation of being a miracle worker.

I think I may have discovered an explanation for one of these miracles, but I'm not sure. When we got to Tiberias, we put our luggage in our offices there. Timon and Malchus stayed behind and I went to Chuza's house. It was a modern house in Graeco-Roman style: a number of rooms surrounding an atrium with pillars. There was a guest room on a second floor which had a splendid view over the Sea of Galilee. I sat there with Joanna and waited for Chuza, who was expected back any moment from Antipas' estates.

I soon turned the conversation towards Jesus. Joanna had been the first person to tell me of him. I couldn't believe my ears when I heard that she supported Jesus. She told me quite openly:

'I send him money and food.[3] My husband doesn't know. You mustn't tell him. When it's possible I look for Jesus in order to listen to him.'

All the followers of Jesus whom I had met so far were ordinary people. But Joanna was a member of the upper class. I asked,

'Do other well-to-do people support him?'

'A few. He gets support from everywhere. But that doesn't fit what people say. He is said to feed his followers by magic. I've heard quite improbable stories. He's said even to have multiplied loaves.'

'The people tell lots of stories. I can only tell you what I know. When I or others send him food, bread, fish and fruit and my people suddenly bring it out, the crowd thinks it's a miracle that there's so much to eat. These poor people have often never seen so much food all at once. If you like, it's indeed a miracle.'

'How?'

'Once the people believe that there's enough food for everyone they lose their fear of hunger. Then they get out the reserve supplies of bread that they've kept hidden so as not to have to share them with others. They share their own bread. They're no longer afraid of going short.'

'Do you think that this is an explanation of the story of the miraculous multiplication of the loaves?'

'Not directly. You can't say that it happened here or there. The people keep discovering the amazing way in which Jesus finds support without working, begging or organizing.'

'But in that case couldn't someone come to the conclusion that the bread should be distributed fairly all over the country?'

'Of course! That's what people hope for. Some wait expectantly for Jesus to come forward as Messiah. For him to produce justice, to see to fertility, to make everything come out right and to drive out the Romans.'[4]

'But in that case he's certainly dangerous!'

I couldn't go on. We heard Chuza coming. We greeted one another warmly. When he had sat down I came directly to the point.

'Everyone in Galilee is talking about Jesus. He's the great topic of conversation. What do you think about him? Is he a troublemaker, a rebel?'

Chuza replied: 'Herod Antipas is worried. He has a bad conscience about the execution of John the Baptist. None of his problems has got any less. He once expressed the crazy view that Jesus was John the Baptist risen from the dead, which is why miraculous powers were at work in him.[5] He's worried. He becomes almost superstitious and even believes in the resurrection of the dead!'

'But the Pharisees and many others believe in that.'

'We don't. Antipas and I go with the Sadducees in matters of belief.[6] We Sadducees believe that the soul perishes along with the body. We reject the expectation of a new and better world. Our teaching has only a few followers, mostly people in high places. By contrast the Pharisees have their following among the lower classes. They believe in the immortality of the soul and in reward and punishment in the hereafter depending on how people have lived. This Jesus and his people are closer to the Pharisees than to us.'

'But politically the Pharisees are not a danger. They're represented in the Sanhedrin.[7] They collaborate with the authorities. There are probably a few extremists among them who have joined the Zealots. But they're exceptions. Do you think that Jesus belongs to these extremists?'

'No, I think that Jesus is a harmless lunatic. You could forget him if there weren't so many people who regard him as a prophet or even the Messiah. These people are our problem – not Jesus. Especially those who support him. If there weren't always some credulous people who gave him money and food, this genteel movement would long since have collapsed. But in this way they sell their ideas successfully and can even live on them.'

Joanna had gone red. She winced, but was clearly anxious not to show anything. Her voice sounded more heated.

'But perhaps the ideas aren't too bad.'

Chuza now got even more into his stride. His voice became loud.

'Good ideas? What does this world's end prophet preach about? The kingdom of God! Everything is going to change. Eternal life is going to begin soon. Have you ever wondered why these ideas are so popular among ordinary people? Why do we Sadducees only find supporters for our doctrine among the upper classes? *For the fate of human beings and the fate of beasts is the same; as one dies so dies the other.*[8] We are the only ones who have no illusions about human beings and death. We are the only ones to give realistic advice about living: *Go, eat your bread with enjoyment, and drink your wine with a merry heart; for God has approved what you do.*[9] We are almost the only ones who do not believe in the resurrection or immortality.'

Joanna interrupted. 'But even Herod Antipas cannot really believe that John the Baptist is finally dead.'

'That's the scandal. How can he give way to such superstition?' exclaimed Chuza. 'The little people cling to this superstition. They have nothing to enjoy. They have only work, worry and drudgery. So they console themselves with the hope of a better world beyond, in which everyone has something to eat. These hopes are sick hopes. They come from a sick life. Jesus spins out these sick hopes. He gives the people their dreams. He calls out to them:

> *Come to me*
> *you who are weary and heavy laden,*
> *and I will give you rest.*[10]

We should leave him to the weary and heavy laden. Let him spread his crazy ideas there. There's no room for them in our life.'

Joanna jumped up. Her face was glowing with anger:

'See here, Chuza. I won't stand for that. Perhaps we women understand the dreams and hopes of the little people more than you do. What you say is wrong.'

Chuza dug his heels in. 'Isn't it the case that he consoles people with the kingdom of God? Like so many others before him?'

'Many people have longed for the kingdom of God,' Joanna retorted. 'But Jesus says that it's beginning now. You don't have to wait for a distant day. Someone once asked him when the kingdom of God was coming. He said:

> *The kingdom of God is not coming with signs to be observed,*
> *nor will they say "Lo, here it is" or "There",*
> *for behold the kingdom of God is in you.*[11]

Someone then doubted whether it could already be there if it could not be seen. He answered:

If I by the spirit of God cast out demons,
then the kingdom of God has already come among you.'[12]

Chuza wouldn't give up. 'That's precisely what I mean. How does he give hope? With miracles! With magic! The little people mistrust their own strength. So they long for great miracle workers who are expected to do things that the people think they themselves cannot do. That is why they invent stories about Jesus – stories about things he has never done. I recently heard a miracle story about him which I had already heard about a Syrian:[13] "You know this Syrian who collects people who bow down to the moon, roll their eyes and have their mouths full of foam. He raises them up and sends them away healthy, once he has been paid a great reward. It all goes like this: when he comes upon a person lying on the ground and asks where the demon has come from into the body, the sick person is silent. But the demon answers for him in Greek or some other foreign language, depending on the land from which he came before he had entered into the person. The Syrian then performs exorcisms. If the demon does not obey he utters strong threats against him and so drives him out." And then my conversation partner added with a wink: "I myself saw one going out; he was black and smoky."'

I had to laugh. And Joanna chuckled. But then she became serious.

'Have you heard the stories about Jesus? They sound similar. But Jesus does not want any reward for his cures. And what is even more important, he knows that the people have an exaggerated belief in miracles because they mistrust their own powers. So he often stresses that "Your faith has healed you."' He explicitly says: "I didn't do the miracle; the power to become whole lies in you yourself." He wants to cure these little people of their superstitious mistrust of themselves.'

Chuza replied: 'But doesn't he persuade them that life here is worthless and that the good life only begins later?'

Joanna protested again: 'Jesus says the opposite. The time is fulfilled now. Now is the time of joy. Therefore it is as impossible to fast now as it is at a wedding.[15] You can be happy now. He once exclaimed to the people:

> *Blessed are the eyes*
> *which see what you see!*
> *For I tell you*
> *that many prophets and kings desired*
> *to see what you see, and did not see it,*
> *and to hear what you hear, and did not hear it.*[16]

What is he saying if not that your life is worth more than that of kings and prophets? You are happier than they. Happier than the Queen of Sheba, who travelled from afar to hear the wisdom of Solomon.'[17]

Chuza was still not convinced: 'You're standing things on their head. This Jesus gives people delusions. They are poor drudges, but they imagine that they're worth more than kings. Nevertheless, in their daily life they have to go on being subservient. Doesn't this Jesus teach that you may not defend yourself? Doesn't he teach a morality typical of little people? A morality of people who have to put up with everything?'

Joanna didn't give up. She became even more impassioned.

'What irritates you about this Jesus is precisely the opposite of the limited morality of people. He gives little people attitudes which previously were your privilege.

Isn't it the privilege of the upper class to be able to live without care? But Jesus says that the privilege is there for everyone, including those who have nothing:

> *Do not be anxious about your life,*
> *what you shall eat or what you shall drink,*
> *nor about your body, what you shall put on.*
> *Is not life more than food,*
> *and the body more than clothing?*
> *Look at the birds of the air; they neither sow nor reap*
> *nor gather into barns,*
> *and yet your heavenly Father feeds them.*
> *Are you not of more value than they?*[18]

Is that the morality of little people? Jesus himself compares these carefree people with Solomon; if the lilies of the field are already clothed in more splendour than King Solomon, how much more are men and women!

And isn't it a privilege of the powerful not to have to fear their enemies? The powerful can be magnanimous, since they know that their enemies cannot harm them but must come to terms with them. But Jesus says to everyone, and not just to the powerful:

Love your enemies,
and pray for those who persecute you,
that you may be children of your Father in heaven![19]

All are to be sons of God. People used to call only the kings of Israel sons of God. But Jesus applies that term to anyone who is generous to his enemies. Everyone is then a king.

And is it not a privilege of the powerful to be able to give laws and repeal old ones? What does Jesus do? He defines new laws. He says:

You have heard that it was said to those of old time,
You shall not kill,
and whoever kills is worthy of judgment.
But I say to you,
Anyone who is angry with his brother deserves judgment.'[20]

Chuza had gone pale. He protested wearily:

'But why does he present his teaching only to the little people? Why doesn't he come to Tiberias? Why doesn't he teach Antipas? I can think of only one answer. He dreams the dreams of little people.'

Joanna agreed: 'Of course he dreams the dreams of little people. He's not addressing the rich and powerful. But what does he want to do? These little people are bent double by their toil. He wants them to walk upright. They're bowed down by cares. He wants them to be free from cares. They're people who feel insignificant. He gives them the feeling that their life has meaning. And you're all worried about that. All of you and Herod Antipas, you're worried that the little people might come to feel that they're not little people. So you've spread the rumour that you want to kill Jesus. So that he disappears over the frontier. So that he leaves you in peace. So that the little people don't hit on rebellious notions and become a danger to you.'

Chuza tried to change the subject: he turned to me with a smile.

'You asked me a moment ago whether this Jesus is a troublemaker and a rebel. One thing is certain. He's already made my wife rebellious.'

Joanna paused a moment and then said gently: 'No, you've made me rebellious.'

'I?' asked Chuza in amazement.

'When you brought up Jesus and his ideas to begin with, you hurt me.'

'I couldn't have known how important these ideas are to you.'

'Chuza, I was worried that you might despise me.'

'How?' Chuza still didn't understand his wife.

'Don't you despise eccentric women?'

'But I've never thought that you were eccentric? Not even dreamed of it,' Chuza said emphatically.

'But you mock eccentric people who send Jesus money and food.'

Chuza's mouth dropped open and he just stood there: 'Do you mean to say . . .'

Joanna nodded: 'I mean that I support Jesus.'

'How could I have guessed that?'

There was a pause. Then Joanna said gently: 'I did it secretly. I didn't dare tell you about it. I didn't want you to despise me.'

Chuza seemed very moved: 'You're not to think that of me. If you value him – I would rather change my views about Jesus than despise you.'

'But when I heard you mocking him . . .'

I breathed again. I had started the argument, but then followed it with the uncomfortable feeling of someone who really shouldn't be there. I said good-bye and left the two of them alone. Wherever I went there were disputes about Jesus. There was always a crisis between parents and children, husband and wife, friends and neighbours, even between toll collectors and businessmen. This travelling preacher was really setting people at odds.

I had a short walk on the shore of the lake. There was no wind to

ripple its surface. Everything was clearly reflected in it: the Golan
hills in the distance, strips of cloud motionless above, the evening
colouring of the sky. I saw my shadow in the lake. But otherwise none
of this tranquillity was reflected in me. It was alien to me. My
thoughts moved restlessly to and fro. I looked in the direction of
Capernaum. Jesus must be somewhere over there.

On my way back to my lodging I passed Chuza's house again. I
heard his voice in the distance. He was singing one of his favourite
songs, a song of Solomon. I softly joined in the words and the
melody.[21]

> *Set me as a seal upon your heart,*
> *as a seal upon your arm;*
> *for love is as strong as death,*
> *jealousy is cruel as the grave.*
> *Its flashes are flashes of fire,*
> *a most vehement flame.*
> *Many waters cannot quench love,*
> *neither can floods drown it.*
> *If a man offered for love*
> *all the wealth of his house,*
> *It would be utterly scorned.*

What a beautiful song it was! Was Chuza singing it to make things up
with Joanna? Or was he simply expressing his sorrows in the evening
air. One thing was certain: it was a message to Joanna, and I was sure
that she would respond.

It had got dark. The air was as warm as it was during the day. The
stillness grew. But I was still in a turmoil. I lay on my bed but couldn't
get to sleep. It was not the heat that kept me awake. It was the dispute
over Jesus. Many voices kept whirling through my mind. I heard the
voices of Joanna and Chuza, of the toll collector, the beggars, the
children, the voice of Barabbas. Strange voices took over my dreams
and thoughts. I tried to force them out and sink into the depths of
sleep. But I couldn't. For these were no longer strange voices. They
were my own inner voices, my own thoughts and feelings, my
anxieties and hopes. The dispute over Jesus was a dispute within me;

the controversy over him was a controversy with myself. There was something in me that was both repelled and attracted by him. There was something in me that mocked his ideas and yet was fascinated by him. I was afraid of the disturbances that he caused and yet longed for them, as though they contained hope. So his image wavered before me.

Towards morning I fell into a troubled sleep. When I woke up I had the vague feeling that something in my life had changed.

Dear Dr Kratzinger,

I think back with pleasure to our conversations at the last New Testament conference. It has become clear to me that you are not expressing radical scepticism, but see the Jesus tradition as historical in so far as it cannot be derived either from Judaism or from early Christianity and in so far as it provides a picture which does not clash with the historical traditions which have been discovered in this way. You refer here to the criterion for difference and coherence which is usual in the quest of the historical Jesus.

You recognize that the previous chapter outlines a coherent picture of the preaching of Jesus. Joanna keeps showing that Jesus claims for little people the attitudes and modes of behaviour of the upper classes, e.g. freedom from material care for those without possessions, wisdom for the unlearned. He brings about a revolution in values, a takeover of upper-class attitudes by the lower class.

You rightly object that the inner coherence of a picture of Jesus is no guarantee of its historicity. First of all one must have a firm starting point in historical facts before asking 'What fits them?'

The basic facts I want to use are only those traditions which cannot be derived from Judaism and earliest Christianity. Two of these, at any rate, are certain. Jesus began as a follower of John the Baptist who was later executed. And Jesus himself ended up on the cross. His preaching must find a place between these two basic facts.

And now let me ask you: does not the picture of Jesus sketched out in the previous chapter fit admirably into these basic facts? John the Baptist is an opponent of the aristocracy. His disciple wants to make what otherwise can only be found 'up there' accessible to the people. Like so many revolutionaries he ends up on the cross.

Does the inner coherence of this picture of Jesus rest on the fact that I have chosen what suits me from the tradition, on the basis of my evaluation? Is there any value in a picture of Jesus which leaves unexplained why John the Baptist and Jesus were executed by the ruling class? You have rightly recognized that I, too, argue for a modus vivendi *between the two classes. But it remains open whether in this respect Jesus claims me as his ally or I him.*

All good wishes,
Yours,
Gerd Theissen

14

Report on Jesus, or, Jesus in Disguise

I never met Jesus on my travels through Galilee. I just found traces of him everywhere: anecdotes and stories, traditions and rumours. He himself remained intangible. But everything that I heard of him fitted together. Even quite exaggerated stories about him had a charac-teristic stamp. They would not have been told about anyone else in this way.

My commission was to discover whether Jesus was a security risk. There was no doubt here. He was a risk. Anyone who follows his conscience rather than regulations and laws, anyone who does not regard the existing distribution of power and possessions as final, anyone who makes little people think that they are princes, is a security risk.

I wouldn't tell the Romans anything about this. I didn't feel obliged to carry out their commission. If it was up to us to decide whether or not to observe the commandment to rest on the sabbath – how much more must that apply to commissions from the Romans!

But how was I to disguise Jesus? How should I make a rebel into an innocuous travelling preacher? What I said about him had to fit. Metilius would certainly also get information about Jesus from other sources. Perhaps he would even meet him one day. I had to tell the truth – but it could only be half the truth, just enough to disguise the whole truth. I brooded on this problem for a long time.

Finally I had an idea. I had to portray Jesus in such a way that he became a familiar figure to the Romans, someone who fitted their ideas. When we are trying to help foreigners understand the religious trends in our country, we like to compare these trends to schools of philosophy: the Pharisees to Stoics, the Essenes to Pythagoreans, the Sadducees to Epicureans.[1] Why shouldn't I make Jesus into an itinerant philosopher of the Cynic school? Wasn't he indeed an itinerant philosopher?

I had to portray his teaching in such a way that it corresponded in as many points as possible to sayings by Greek and Roman writers. That sort of thing should prove reassuring. Perhaps I could also sell him as a poet? Didn't he tell a great many parables? It was clear to me that I had to find as many analogies to his sayings as possible.

I had a great deal of work ahead of me. I returned to Sepphoris, handed over the business to Baruch and instead read all the books I could lay my hands on. I looked everywhere for sayings which could be compared to the teaching of Jesus. When I had collected enough material, I began to write a short report for Metilius.

On Jesus as a Philosopher

Jesus is a philosopher comparable to the Cynic itinerant philosophers.[2] Like them he teaches the utmost modesty in needs; he travels round the country without a fixed abode; lives without a family, with neither profession nor possessions. He requires his disciples to get by without money, without shoes, without a bag for their journeys and with one coat.[3]

He teaches that to love God and to love one's fellow human beings are the two most important commandments and that these sum up all demands made on humanity. That agrees with Greek tradition: piety towards God and justice towards fellow men are regarded there as the most important virtues.[4]

For behaviour towards others his criterion is the 'golden rule': act towards others as you would have them act towards you. This rule is widespread throughout the world. Many sages advocate it.[5]

If one suffers injustice at the hands of others he says, 'If someone smites you on the cheek, offer him the other one.'[6] It is the view of Socrates that one should suffer injustice rather than perpetrate it.[7]

He also teaches that one should love one's enemies. For God makes his sun shine on good and evil alike. Seneca similarly writes: If you want to imitate the gods, show kindness even to the ungrateful, for the sun also rises on criminals and the seas are open to pirates.[8]

If one sees others acting unjustly one should not be too hasty to condemn them. No one is perfect. Anyone is in danger of seeing the speck in his brother's eye and missing the log in his own.[9]

On possessions he teaches that we should not only be ready to separate ourselves from them externally but that we should also be free from them inwardly by overcoming the concerns which bind us to them.[10] His teaching is reminiscent of Diogenes in the barrel, the philosopher who despised all possessions.

On aggressive actions he teaches that not only is someone who kills guilty, but even someone who hates another person. This recalls the teaching of the philosopher Cleanthes. Even someone who intends to steal and kill is a robber. Evil begins with intent.[11]

On adultery he teaches that one does not commit adultery just by sleeping with another woman but even by wanting to sleep with her. That, too, is reminiscent of Cleanthes: anyone who nurtures a desire will put it into action if given the opportunity.[12]

On honesty he teaches that each of our words must be as true as if we had sworn an oath. He rejects oaths. Epictetus' teaching is similar; one should avoid oaths as far as possible.[13]

On purity he says that there are no such things as pure and impure objects, but only inner attitudes which make something pure or impure.[14] In this connection a saying attributed to Phocylides should be recalled. It is not purification which makes a body clean, but the soul.[15]

On prayer he teaches that a multiplicity of words is superfluous. For God knows in advance what people need.[16]

On giving he teaches that one should not give to gain respect from others but as if the left hand did not know what the right was doing.[17]

On religious fasting he teaches that one should not observe fasts because this is what is expected, but should fast in secret, where only God sees.[18]

On the sabbath he teaches that one may break it if one can be of help or if there is an urgent reason.[19]

So far everything sounded innocuous. The Romans would have to be sympathetic to some of it. Perhaps they would like the readiness not to observe the sabbath rules strictly. On many points there were

similar views among Greeks and Romans. Jesus had been well dis-
guised. Too well! The picture of him was too innocuous. Metilius
would ask, 'So why are they getting stirred up about this gentle
itinerant philosopher? Why does he provoke such opposition?' In
order to seem credible I also had to report some of the provocative
features of his preaching.

Here I entered a difficult field: Jesus' demand for a radical change
in behaviour and attitudes, because with the kingdom of God
everything became different, was extremely provocative. How could
I make it clear to a Roman for whom the goal of history was not the
rule of God but the rule of Rome? Of course the Romans, too,
believed in the rule of the gods. Where Romans ruled, Roman gods
ruled. But it was a strange notion for them that the rule of a foreign
god would one day come to do away with all other rules. That was
revolt and rebellion. So I planned to write very vaguely about the
kingdom of God and continued:

Jesus teaches his commandments in order to subject people to the
rule of God. He thinks that the kingdom of God is present in
secret. It is spreading through human hearts. It leads to a new
assessment of one's fellow human beings which differs from the
usual judgments.

The current opinion is that children are less valuable than
adults. But Jesus says, 'Let the children come to me, for theirs is
the kingdom of God.' According to him adults enter it only when
they become like children again.[20]

The current opinion is that one has to despise toll collectors and
prostitutes. But Jesus says: 'Toll collectors and prostitutes will
enter the kingdom of God before others.'[21]

The current opinion is that foreigners and unbelievers are bad
people and are excluded from the kingdom of God. But Jesus says:
'Many strangers will sit at table with Abraham, Isaac and Jacob in
the kingdom of God.'[22]

Current opinion scorns sexually impotent and castrated men.
But Jesus says: 'There are those who are castrated from birth, those
who are castrated by human intervention and those who are
castrated for the kingdom of God. God does not despise them.'[23]

The current opinion is that people who cannot assert themselves do not count because they always fail to get their share. But Jesus says, 'Blessed are the meek, for they will possess the earth.'[24]

I thought that I had collected enough provocative statements to make some agitation about Jesus understandable. Granted, these were provocations which did not worry the Romans. To stress the harmlessness of Jesus I added in conclusion:

Much that Jesus says is reminiscent of the teaching of known philosophers. Jesus no more represents a danger to the state than do the Greek and Roman philosophers.

I read my report through once again. Was it accurate? Certainly. Everything that I had written down was based on information about Jesus. But did my account also sound innocuous enough not to arouse any unnecessary suspicion about Jesus?

If anyone wanted to denounce Jesus to the Romans he would have an easy enough time. All he had to do was to report what I kept quiet about.

I kept quiet about Jesus' negative statements on the family. About his dismissal of the duty to bury one's own father with words like 'Let the dead bury their dead.'[25] Throughout my studies I nowhere found an analogy to this harsh saying.

I kept quiet about the fact that Jesus attacked state rule as oppression and exploitation: 'The rulers oppress their people and misuse their power over them. It must not be like this among you.' Wasn't it illuminating that I had not found any analogies to such statements either? Nowhere else was there a saying which stated: 'Whoever would be first, let him be last and slave of all.'[26] Nowhere else was there a saying which put in question the basis of the state in a similar way.

I kept quiet about Jesus' criticism of our religious institutions. Jesus had prophesied that the present temple would disappear. A new temple created by God would take its place.[27] One could hardly say more clearly that the present priests and temple officials had God against them. These attacks on the temple were attacks on the most important institutions of our religion.

Wasn't all that enough to have Jesus arrested? He was not a harmless itinerant philosopher. He was not directly engaged in rebellion, but he was a prophet steeped in the thought that God would soon bring about a great rebellion against the lords of this world. Wasn't that enough for arrest and the death sentence?

There was no doubt about it. Jesus was in danger. So I felt the need to protect him all the more. He rejected violence. He did not preach hatred against the Romans. The Zealots kept their distance from him. Certainly he was a rebel, but he was a rebel like Joanna, not like Barabbas. Certainly sharp words came from his mouth. But his stories were even more impressive; small poems full of grace and humanity. I could write something more about them for Metilius. He was interested in books and literature. So I sat down again and began a new sheet of papyrus with the title:

On Jesus as a Poet

Jesus is a peasant poet who has enriched Jewish literature with marvellous stories. These stories do not presuppose any city education on the part of the hearer. They tell of seedtime and harvest, seeking and finding, fathers and sons, masters and slaves, hosts and guests. Although they come from everyday life they set out to say something extraordinary: that God is utterly different from our ideas of him. Jesus' stories are parables of the relationship between God and humanity.

The fact that Jesus clothes his teaching in stories is connected with the conviction of our people that one cannot make any picture of God. One can only compare him with something else. And even that is often inappropriate. For no single thing, no human being, no object, can serve as a parable of God – only an event can convey some idea of him. Only stories can be parables of him.

That is bound up with a second conviction. We believe that we can find God only if our attitudes change. Parables of God are therefore stories in which something changes, or, more accurately, parables are stories in which the hearer is so involved that he or she changes. Only then does one detect something of God.

Other peoples narrate myths about their gods which take one

into another world. But we tell our own story. We tell of events in this world. Jesus, too, tells of the everyday life of men and women. He thinks that God is near in this everyday life. He wants to open people's eyes to him.

If one wants to find a place for Jesus in the history of literature he comes close to the writers of fables. They too tell short stories which anyone can understand. Their narratives, too, are meant as images. Sometimes Jesus rewrote fables. One example is the fable of the tree which doesn't bear fruit. A father censures his son for being a good-for-nothing and tells him the following fable:

'My son, you are like a tree which brought forth no fruit, although it stood by the water, and its lord was compelled to cut it down. But it said to him: "Transplant me, and if I do not bring forth fruit even then, cut me down." However, its lord said to it: "When you stood by the water you did not bring forth fruit; how will you bring forth fruit if you stand anywhere else?"'[28]

For Jesus that becomes the following story:

'A man had a fig tree in his vineyard, but when he looked for fruit he found none on it. Finally he said to the gardener: "Look, I've been waiting three years for this fig tree to bear fruit, but I can't find any. Cut it down; why should it use up the soil time and again for nothing?" But the gardener said: "Master, leave it standing for one more year. I will dig up the soil around it well and fertilize it. Perhaps it will bear fruit next year. If not, then have it cut down."'[29]

Jesus' parables differ from fables in that plants and animals do not speak in them. Only human beings speak. A further difference is that many fables try to reconcile people to the harshness of life. They say that if you don't adapt, you go under, get devoured or crushed. In the parables of Jesus people have a chance, even if others have pronounced the death penalty on them.

On another occasion Jesus transformed the theme of the father and the two sons into a new story. Here, first, is a version of the theme from our philosopher Philo:

'A father had two sons, a good one and a bad one. The father wanted to bless the bad one, not because he preferred the bad one to the good one, but because he knew that the good one already deserved a blessing on his own merits. But the bad one had only his father's prophecy as a hope for a successful life. Without it he would inevitably become the unhappiest of all men.'[30]

Other versions of this theme are current. The father always prefers the worse brother to the better. Jesus made one of his finest compositions from such material:

'There was a man who had two sons; and the younger of them said to his father, "Father, give me the share of property that falls to me." And he divided his living between them. Not many days later, the younger son gathered all he had and took his journey into a far country, and there he squandered his property in loose living. And when he had spent everything, a great famine arose in that country, and he began to be in want. So he went and joined himself to one of the citizens of that country, who sent him into his fields to feed swine. And he would gladly have fed on the pods that the swine ate; and no one gave him anything. But when he came to himself he said, "How many of my father's hired servants have bread enough and to spare, but I perish here with hunger. I will arise and go to my father, and I will say to him, 'Father, I have sinned against heaven and before you; I am no longer worthy to be called your son; treat me as one of your hired servants.'" And he arose and came to his father. But while he was yet at a distance, his father saw him and had compassion, and ran and embraced him and kissed him. And the son said to him, "Father, I have sinned against heaven and before you; I am no longer worthy to be called your son." But the father said to his servants, "Bring quickly the best robe, and put it on him and put a ring on his hand, and shoes on his feet; and bring the fatted calf and kill it, and let us eat and make merry; for this my son was dead, and is alive again; he was lost, and is found." And they began to make merry. Now his elder son was in the field, and as he came and drew near to the house, he heard music and dancing. And he called one of the servants and asked what this meant. And he said to him, "Your brother has come, and your father has killed the fatted calf, because he has received him safe and sound." But he was angry and refused to go in. His father came out and entreated him, but he answered his father, "Lo, these many years I have served you, and I never disobeyed your command; yet you never gave me a kid, that I might make merry with my friends. But when this son of yours came, who has devoured your living with harlots, you killed for him the fatted calf!" And he said to him, "Son, you are always with me, and all that is mine is yours. It was fitting to make merry and be glad, for this your brother was dead, and is alive; he was lost, and is found." '[31]

Jesus told many parables about God and humanity in this way. They teach that God is not as we imagine him, and that people therefore may behave quite differently if they want to act in accord with God. It emerges from all these parables that Jesus is a poet who commends love and tolerance. His parables and sayings will long be read and loved.

Everything that I had written about Jesus fitted. He was an itinerant philosopher and a poet. But it was clear to me that he was more. He was a prophet. And that was difficult to make clear to foreigners. They thought of a prophet as someone who made statements about the future. Other people also had such prophets. But our prophets were a unique phenomenon. What other peoples had prophets who threatened their own folk with disaster? What other people believed in a God alongside whom there was no other? The uniqueness of our prophets was connected with the uniqueness of our God. I had to think about that again. Was this perhaps the key to understanding Jesus?

Only our God called on those who worshipped him to turn away from all other gods. Only our God required those who acknowledged him to change their behaviour in a radical way.

All over the world the strong win through. But our God has chosen weakness: he helped slaves fleeing from Egypt and made them his people. He supported the prisoners of war who were deported to Babylon. To turn towards this God means to turn towards the poor and weak. And for that reason the strong and the rulers feel threatened by our God and hate us.

Even if I managed to make it clear to Metilius that Jesus was a prophet of this God, would he not have to reject Jesus even more? Must he not have learned from our writings that prophets have always been involved in politics? Would he not notice that if Jesus were a prophet he was dangerous to politicians?

What did the prophets do, then? They drove our people to recognize the one and only God and change our behaviour. They did this as one brings up children, by threatening punishment and making promises. And they were fierce and inexorable in so doing.

Jesus, too, threatened a judgment on this world. A mysterious man would judge all men. This judgment would break in suddenly and unexpectedly on this world – not only on villains and scoundrels but also on the normal life of the world:

> *As it was in the days of Noah,*
> *so it will be in the days of the Son of man.*
> *They ate, they drank,*
> *they married, they were given in marriage,*
> *until the day when Noah entered the ark,*
> *and the flood came and destroyed them all.*
> *Likewise as it was in the days of Lot –*
> *they ate, they drank,*
> *they bought, they sold,*
> *they planted, they built,*
> *but on the day when Lot went out from Sodom*
> *fire and brimstone rained from heaven and destroyed them all.*[32]

This judgment will befall each individual, not particular groups or peoples. It will separate those who lived closely together:

> *I tell you, in that night there will be two men in one bed;*
> *one will be taken and the other left.*
> *There will be two women grinding together;*
> *one will be taken and the other left.*[33]

Such a judgment must have been deeply disquieting. Each individual must have asked, What shall I do? How can I survive? According to Jesus there was only one criterion in the judgment: whether or not one had helped others. In the end the 'Man' would judge all nations

– and he would not ask what religion or philosophy one had, or what colour skin. He would say to those who withstood the judgment:

> *Come, O blessed of my Father,*
> *inherit the kingdom*
> *prepared for you from the foundation of the world;*
> *for I was hungry and you gave me food;*
> *I was thirsty and you gave me drink,*
> *I was a stranger and you welcomed me,*
> *I was naked and you clothed me,*
> *I was sick and you visited me,*
> *I was in prison and you came to me.*[34]

Beyond question Jesus threatened like all the prophets. But he did it in a remarkable way. He did not threaten with the judgment of God but with the judgment of the mysterious 'Man'. No one was certain of withstanding his judgment. But everyone had a chance. For the only criterion the judge laid down was whether a person had helped others, not in order to be rewarded in the judgment, not out of a concern to serve this mysterious man, but simply in order to help. The righteous would reply at the judgment in amazement:

> *Lord, when did we see you hungry and feed you,*
> *or thirsty and give you drink?*
> *And when did we see you a stranger and welcome you,*
> *or naked and clothe you?*
> *And when did we see you sick or in prison and visit you?*
> *And the King will answer them,*
> *Truly, I say to you,*
> *As you did it to one of the least of these my brethren*
> *you did it to me.*

Could one make that clear to the Romans? Could one explain to them what even many among our own people could not understand? Wouldn't the Romans feel deeply disturbed when they heard that a 'Man' would judge all human beings, even the Romans! A 'Man' would judge every human violation, humiliation and oppression perpetrated by others as though it had been done to him? It was clear that Jesus' preaching of judgment had to be kept secret from the Romans.

And what about the promises? Like most prophets Jesus promised a change for the better and gave hope. Many people at that time believed that the wickedness and misery they endured showed that God had abdicated his rule over the world and Satan. Evil ruled in the world. It was the underlying cause of the state of the many possessed people who could not lead a life worth calling human. It underlay oppression by foreign soldiers. It underlay everything that harmed people. But Jesus held out hope that the rule of evil was being overcome. He said:

> *I saw Satan fall like lightning from heaven.*
> *Behold, I have given you authority*
> *to tread upon serpents and scorpions,*
> *and over all the power of the enemy;*
> *and nothing shall hurt you.*[35]

Most people were as it were under the spell of evil. They said: 'Isn't the world full of fighting and war? Don't wars show that evil prevails?' But Jesus gave another explanation. Precisely that was a sign that evil was collapsing.

> *If a kingdom is divided against itself,*
> *that kingdom cannot stand.*
> *And if a house is divided against itself,*
> *that house will not be able to stand.*
> *And if Satan has risen up against himself and is divided,*
> *he cannot stand,*
> *but is coming to an end.*[36]

The kingdom of God will replace the rule of evil. It comes into being where evil loses its power over human beings, where demons are driven out and sick people are cured, where the hungry are filled and the desperate are consoled. It begins where people leave behind everything to respond to this great turning point.

The kingdom of God is like a treasure hidden in a field,
which a man found and covered up;
then in his joy he goes and sells all that he has
and buys that field.
Again, the kingdom of heaven is like a merchant
in search of fine pearls,
who, on finding one pearl of great value,
went and sold all that he had and bought it.[37]

Jesus was more than an itinerant philosopher and poet. Jesus was a prophet, a unique prophet. Most people use divine judgment as a threat when existing norms are violated. With Jesus it was different. For him rule would pass to people who were worthless by existing standards: children, foreigners, the poor, the meek, the castrated. Here only one criterion was to apply, namely how one had behaved towards these people, indeed towards all in need of help. Jesus was a unique prophet.

Or was Jesus more than a prophet? Had not Jesus compared himself with Jonah the prophet and Solomon the wise man and said, 'More than Jonah is here, more than Solomon is here'?[38] Had he not called blessed those who experienced what prophets and kings had longed for?[39] Did not what they had longed for necessarily transcend all prophets and kings? So was Jesus' saying right: 'The law and prophets apply up to John. From then on the kingdom of God is taken by force'?[40] Was something new beginning with Jesus which transcended even the prophets?

The people were whispering that he was the Messiah. Could he be the Messiah? There was nothing to indicate that he wanted to drive out the Romans by force! But was he not after some sort of rule? Only a few things had trickled out. He must in fact have promised his disciples that they would sit with him on twelve thrones and rule all Israel.[41] I had also heard the rumour that there had been a dispute among the disciples about who was to occupy the places of honour on his right hand and on his left.[42] But Jesus rejected such considerations out of hand. There was no hierarchy in the new kingdom of God. Whoever wanted to be first there had to be the slave of all. There would be a restored people: the twelve tribes of Israel would be gathered together again. Along with the Gentiles they would stream to Palestine from all four points of the compass. A new temple would stand in the centre of the kingdom. There would be a great banquet. The poor would become rich, the hungry would be filled, the mourners would be full of joy.

These and similar rumours went the rounds. But it was all very mysterious. The only thing that was clear was that Jesus would play a decisive role in the great change, along with his disciples. Perhaps he would become that Son of man of whom he spoke now and then. For the moment he and his followers went through the land like the partisans of another kingdom. He once even called his disciples robbers who seize the kingdom of God for themselves by force.[43] No wonder that the people saw him in the role of Messiah.

But I wanted to present him to the Romans merely as an itinerant philosopher and poet. I wanted to conceal the prophet, not to mention that figure which Jesus had become in the longings and hopes of the people! But what if he now appeared as a prophet? What if the Romans should find him something other than the person whom I had described?

What role did he really play? That remained a mystery. Did I even know what role he played in my life? For a long time he had been more than the subject of my investigations. Otherwise I would not find so intolerable the idea that as a result of my investigations he could fall into the hands of the Romans – find it as intolerable as the idea that I could endanger Barabbas by what I was doing. In either case I would be betraying and handing over something of myself.

What was I really looking for in Jesus? In my reading of Greek and Roman literature the thought had occurred to me that perhaps I was in fact looking for a doctrine for all peoples, Jews and Gentiles. Didn't Jesus offer such a doctrine? Wasn't what he preached as an itinerant philosopher also comprehensible to Greeks? And didn't the Romans, too, understand what he said as a poet? Wasn't there perhaps a purpose behind the way in which Jesus relativized the commandments which separate us from other peoples, the commandments about the sabbath and purity, while at the same time heightening the commandments which bind us to all humanity; the prohibition of killing, infidelity, perjury? Everyone could understand this prophet, but he was deeply rooted in our people. Everything that he said and did took place in the name of God, who had chosen the weak and outcast and was more powerful than Pharaohs and rulers.

Could Jesus solve my problems, problems which all arose out of the prejudices and tensions between Jews and Gentiles? Didn't I live in a no man's land on the frontier? Somewhere between Pilate and Barabbas? Between Gentiles and Jews? In this frontier area I had found myself in humiliating dependence on the Romans. And wasn't it precisely the point at which Jesus encountered me – as a free man who remained faithful to himself and his people.

Or even in his case was there the danger that one day people would appeal to him who saw in him only the itinerant philosopher and poet? Those who saw only what could easily have influence beyond the bounds of our people? Those who would play off Jesus against our people? Those who no longer wanted to see that he was the prophet of an oppressed people?

Fortunately I did not have to clarify these questions all at once. Now the only thing was to send a realistic but innocuous report about Jesus to the Romans. As I was aware that I was saying only half the truth I added to my reports a short letter to Metilius in which I mentioned in passing that my report was only an interim one. One could say even more about Jesus. Then I sealed my reports and the letters. It was convenient that Baruch had expressed a desire to spend the Passover in Jerusalem. I could hand him the letters to Metilius. He might think that they were business letters dealing with the next deliveries of corn to the Roman cohorts.

Baruch asked for a longish holiday. He had done my work for several weeks while I was educating myself by reading many books. He had become efficient. But I noted that his thoughts were elsewhere:

'Once one has learned as an Essene to despise riches, it's difficult to pile them up,' he sighed.

I noticed in our conversations how much he missed his community. He knew that they would never take him back now. He was an outcast. But he still hadn't found a new home. Even in our family.

Dear Dr Kratzinger,

You draw my attention to an interesting point: Andreas has to play down the 'uniqueness' of Jesus for tactical reasons. Now according to the 'criterion of difference' this is decisive for distinguishing between authentic and inauthentic Jesus tradition. Should I not have brought out the incomparability of Jesus more strongly right from the start, instead of relativizing his preaching by using many analogies?

I doubt whether the criterion of difference is a practicable one. The fact that we cannot recognize any dependence of a saying of Jesus on the Jewish tradition does not mean that there could never have been such dependence. Jesus could have been influenced by oral traditions. Or by traditions contained in writings which have been lost.

Moreover the criterion of difference neglects all that Jesus has in common with Judaism, as though – in contrast to other men – he could not be understood from his historical environment. The 'criterion of originality' (another name used for the criterion of difference) is dogma in disguise; Jesus seems to drop directly from heaven. And this dogma has an anti-Jewish slant: what puts Jesus in opposition to Judaism cannot be derived.

So let me reformulate the criterion of difference: traditions about Jesus have a claim to authenticity when they are historically possible within the framework of the Judaism of his time but at the same time have a special accent which enables us to understand how primitive Christianity later developed out of Judaism. Not only Jesus but the whole of primitive Christianity can be derived from Judaism.

Otherwise you are right when you assume that the disguising of Jesus as an innocuous itinerant philosopher and country poet is also meant to be a criticism of innocuous modern pictures of Jesus.

Your comments were very illuminating. I look forward to your next letter.

Yours,
Gerd Theissen

15

Reforming Temple and Society

A few days after Baruch had set off with the report for Metilius, news reached me which changed everything. I had to go to Jerusalem as quickly as possible. Barabbas and two Zealots had been put in prison. They had resisted arrest. A Roman soldier had been severely wounded and had died as a result. I had to go Jerusalem immediately. Perhaps I could do something for Barabbas when I reported to Metilius. I had to help him; I owed my life to him.

With Timon and Malchus I went through Samaria to Judaea without going round by Peraea, as Baruch had done.[1] I wanted to get on as quickly as possible so as to arrive in Jerusalem before the Passover.

During the journey I brooded on how I might help Barabbas. Should I present him as one of the moderates among the Zealots who had to be spared? Should I report how he had pleaded for me? Or would it be better to keep quiet about all that? Was it better to argue for all three imprisoned Zealots and keep quiet about my connections with Barabbas? But in any case wouldn't the Romans execute them in retaliation for the dead Roman soldier? Had my efforts any prospect of success? These thoughts occupied me for three days all the way from Galilee to Jerusalem. Finally I had an idea.

As soon as we arrived in Jerusalem I called on Metilius. He received me in his office in the Praetorium. There was a mood of alarm among the Romans. Metilius seemed tense. But he greeted me like an old friend.

'You've come just at the right time. We must get down right away to this Jesus of Nazareth. I've read all that you wrote. But now there's been a new development, an episode in the temple forecourt. Have you heard about it?'

'I've only just arrived in Jerusalem.'

'Yesterday Jesus disrupted the business in the temple.'

Metilius paced up and down restlessly.

'Our soldiers in the temple forecourt report that Jesus arrived in the temple court, which is open to Jews and Gentiles, along with some followers. There he caused a disturbance by driving away those who sold sacrificial animals, turning over tables and preventing the workmen from carrying tools through the temple. It was only a minor episode. Since the business about the aqueduct our soldiers have orders to hold back and avoid any provocation. The Jewish temple authorities seem to have some grip on things. At least after the episode there was further discussion between them and Jesus.'[2]

I considered feverishly how I could sell this episode as the wild actions of an itinerant philosopher. I had to try, simply to preserve my own credibility:

'Probably the provocative actions were chiefly intended to make discussions with the temple authorities possible. Itinerant philosophers sometimes resort to spectacular means of drawing attention to themselves.'

'That could be. But I must investigate. It's not the only episode in the last few days. We recently caught a few Zealots who were certainly not innocuous.'

He definitely meant the arrest of Barabbas and his two companions. Here I could truthfully assure him that there was no connection with the incident in the temple. However, first I asked:

'Is there any knowledge of a connection between Jesus and these Zealots?'

'That's what I want to talk to you about. What do you think?'

I paused for a moment, then I said: 'The activity of the Zealots is directed against the Romans, and the episode in the temple is directed against the Jewish authorities.'

'Nevertheless there could be a connection: the Zealots are fighting against the aristocracy who are connected with the temple. Criticism of the temple is criticism of the temple aristocracy. At least it must suit these terrorists if the high priests get into difficulties.'

'And what might this action in the temple mean?'

Metilius stopped pacing, shrugged his shoulders and said: 'I've only suggestions.

First, Jesus prevents workers carrying tools through the temple. That's a protest against the rebuilding of the temple. They've been working on it now for half a century and it still isn't finished. Perhaps Jesus is rejecting the building of this temple.

Secondly, Jesus overthrows tables. Does he mean to say that the temple will be overthrown and will collapse in this way? Is he announcing a destruction of the temple? At all events I see this action as a blatant attack on the temple.

Thirdly, he prevents moneychangers and those who sell sacrificial animals from going about their business. The money which is changed is used to buy animals. Without these businesses there would be no sacrificial cult. So is Jesus against bloody sacrifices? Is he against the temple in principle? What use is it if you don't sacrifice in it?

As I've said: these are all guesses.'

As always, Metilius was astute. Wasn't he right? Even though he didn't know the prophecy of Jesus that the existing temple would be destroyed to be replaced by a new temple not made with hands?[3] The episode in the temple must be connected with this prophecy. This cleansing of the temple was probably one of those symbolic actions with which our prophets make their prophecies more vivid. It was all the more important to give the whole thing an innocent interpretation. So I said:

'I doubt whether Jesus wants to do away with temple worship. He probably wants merely to do away with some abuses, above all the involvement of the temple in business. Hence his action against merchants and workmen, against all those who serve the temple. He wants the temple to be accessible without money. That corresponds to his support of poor people.'

Metilius shook his head. He wasn't completely convinced: 'I must also tell you what I was able to discover about the discussion following this episode. Jesus was asked to say what right he had to disturb temple business. He replied with a counter-question: the temple representatives should say whether or not God was behind the baptism of John.'

'And what answer did he get?'

'None. His opponents kept quiet. So he said, "If you don't say whether God is behind John the Baptist or not I shan't tell you what right I have to disturb temple business."'[4]

'Perhaps he did this to dodge an awkward question.'

'I think differently. You once told me what the temple meant to your people and the whole of society: it removed the sins of the people through sacrifice. John the Baptist offers forgiveness of sins through his baptism. If the temple officials said that John's baptism came from God they laid themselves open to the question, Why do you then perform sacrifices for the forgiveness of sins? Why do you kill animals? Why don't you go down to the Jordan and as it were sacrifice yourselves, by being baptized in water. In short, I believe that basically Jesus wants to do away with what the temple stands for at present. Anyone who thinks that forgiveness of sins can be achieved independently of the temple has undermined its position.'

'Perhaps you're right. A series of itinerant philosophers, particularly of the Pythagorean school, reject bloody sacrifices.'

'If my interpretation is right, Jesus would only be a threat to the temple: a threat to the high priests bound up with it and the people of Jerusalem, but not for the Romans. We want to steer clear of disputes within a religion. But I must investigate whether there are connections with the Zealots. Why are Zealots active in Jerusalem at about the same time? Have you discovered anything about relationships between Jesus and the Zealots?'

I was ready for this question. On the way I had considered what to say: 'According to my information,' I began, 'among the people who go with Jesus from place to place there is one Zealot, and possibly even two others. The one I'm certain about is a follower called Simon the Zealot, because of his name. Judas Iscariot could be another, since Iscariot could be a version of *sicarius*.[5] Finally a Simon Bar Jonah might also be suspect. Some call the Zealots Baryonim, i.e. people who move around in desert areas. However, the surnames of Judas and Simon are also open to other interpretations.'[6]

Metilius felt his views confirmed.

'So there are connections between Jesus and the Zealots.'

I had reckoned on this reaction and replied: 'I've investigated things and come to a surprising conclusion. First I had my doubts because the immediate followers of Jesus also include a publican named Levi, i.e. one of those hated tax collectors and excise men who are fought against by the Zealots. Secondly I felt that if one of the followers of Jesus was called "the Zealot", one could certainly conclude that not all of them were Zealots – otherwise it wouldn't make sense to distinguish one of these by this nickname.'

'But that goes against my suspicions,' thought Metilius.

'That was my view, too. I've gone into the matter thoroughly. I managed to make contact with some Zealots. I learned from them that Simon the Zealot had been one of their number but was now regarded as a traitor because he had attached himself to Jesus. This Jesus is felt by the Zealots to be a threat: he argues for non-violence. He rejects Zealot methods. If he gains any more supporters among them and in the population it would be a serious blow to the resistance movement.'

'If I understand you rightly, then, there are two kinds of troublemakers competing for one and the same lot of supporters and sympathizers: on the one hand the Zealots and on the other Jesus.'

'That's how I would put it. The Zealots indicate the problem in our land. Jesus could be the solution to this problem, or more exactly, he has brought me to a solution.'

'You must explain that to me more clearly.'

Metilius looked at me with interest. Evidently he didn't know how the Roman administration should act in this situation. He seemed grateful for any idea.

I took a deep breath. This was the opportunity I had been waiting for. Perhaps the only chance of saving Barabbas. Everything depended on whether I could convince Metilius.

'In the villages of Galilee I've been investigating the reasons why young people leave house and home to join the Zealots in the hills. They do so because of the oppressive economic situation of ordinary people: when they have to incur debts because the harvest fails or because of other blows of fate they cannot pay their taxes and prefer flight to the Zealots to slavery and imprisonment. None of these young people are born as terrorists; they become terrorists because of their circumstances. If one were to offer them an alternative to the terrorist life, a realistic prospect of returning to normal life, many of them would turn away from their life as bandits.

Hence my proposal, which contains three points.'

Metilius was extremely tense. He leant on the table with hands outstretched, turning his head towards me as if he didn't want to miss a word I said. I continued:

'First, the Roman prefect of Judaea and Samaria proclaims a general amnesty for any criminal acts committed by any member of a Zealot band; this amnesty to apply to all those who are prepared to return to normal life.'

Metilius sagged. He got up and again began to pace restlessly up and down. The brief glance that he gave me expressed deep disappointment. I knew that I had lost. Nevertheless I continued:

'Secondly, a general remission of debts will see to it that ordinary people who might flee to the Zealots have a new chance.[7]

Thirdly, the state should settle landless people – above all former Zealots – in frontier areas. These people are used to fighting and could serve as a defence force against external enemies.

Only if we fight the real cause of our ills can we bring lasting peace to the land.'

After a pause Metilius said: 'And what has Jesus to do with this solution?'

I replied: 'His movement is an indication that a large number of Zealots would in fact be ready to give up their way of life if only they had the opportunity. The way back to normal life is closed to them either because they've committed a crime or because in the meantime their smallholding has been sold. Jesus' free itinerant life-style offers them the possibility of leaving their bandit existence. Life with Jesus is hard: it presupposes that you can get by on very little. If former Zealots prefer it to a Zealot existence, how much more will they welcome a return to normal life.'

'But does this Jesus offer them an amnesty and remission of debt?'

'He cannot speak for the state or for their creditors. But he assures them all of God's amnesty. God writes off all debt if a person is converted and begins a new life. And he also obliges us to forgive one another our debts.'[8]

'Itinerant philosophers often have good ideas. But political reality is rougher than these ideas.'

'Wouldn't an amnesty also be a good thing from a political point of view? The situation is tense. The people are still disturbed about the killings during last year's demonstration, they haven't come to terms with the butchering of innocent Galilean pilgrims, nor can they yet excuse the execution of John the Baptist. To ease the situation, a clear sign of good will would be appropriate. The Romans must show that they want to draw a line under the conflicts of the past. Otherwise violence escalates and there is encouragement for those forces among the people who feel that violence can only be held back by counter-violence. A festival would be the best opportunity to proclaim a general amnesty for Zealot criminal acts.'

Metilius shook his head with resignation.

'But isn't a general remission of debts utterly unrealistic? How is the state going to persuade all creditors in the land to write off their debts?'

'In our country that would be possible. We have an old law which says that all debts are to be remitted every seven years.[9] The law is rarely practised, but it exists. It just has to be enforced again. Negotiations could be carried on about that with the high priest and the Sanhedrin. The Sanhedrin is interested in easing the situation.'

Metilius looked at me with irritation: 'Your proposal is so radical that I don't know what to say.'

'An amnesty seems to me to be the most urgent thing. It must be announced soon, before any new unrest.'

'Only the prefect himself can decide about that. And even he has quite limited powers.'

'At least my suggestions should be put to him.'

Metilius hesitated. 'Do these ideas come from Jesus?'

'They're my ideas.'

'I see a similarity between your proposals and the aims of this Jesus. You want to reform society and Jesus wants to reform the temple – and perhaps all your religion. Jesus says that the temple no longer functions as the central place where sins are forgiven. Forgiveness is also offered outside the temple, by baptism or by following him. You say that society stops functioning when burdens are distributed in an intolerable way and that we must look for new ways of remitting debt. Jesus offers a divine amnesty. You want a state amnesty. There's certainly some connection between these ideas.'

'Can I reply in a parable?' I asked, and I told a parable of Jesus, leaving out any reference to the coming kingdom of God.

'God is like a lord who wanted to settle accounts with his stewards. When he began the reckoning, one was brought to him who owed him a million. As he could not pay, the lord ordered him to be sold, with his wife and children and all that he had, in order to wipe out the debt. But the steward fell on his knees, imploring him, "Have patience with me. I will pay everything back." Then the lord had pity on him; he released him and also forgave him his debt.

Just as he got out, this man met a fellow steward who owed him a small sum. He seized him by the throat, throttled him and said, "Give me back what you owe me." The debtor fell on his knees and begged him, "Have patience with me and I will pay you back." But the creditor would not listen. He had him thrown into prison straight-away until he had paid the debt.

When the others saw what had happened they were greatly distressed. They ran to their master and told him what had happened. He had the man brought to him and said, "What a wicked person you are. I forgave you all your debts because you asked me. Should you not also have had pity on your fellow steward as I had pity on you?"

Then in anger he handed him over to the torturers for punishment until the whole debt had been paid back.'[10]

Metilius had listened attentively. He asked somewhat sceptically:

'That's a parable. Does it really call on us to release those who owe us money?'

'No,' I said, 'but the little people in debt to whom Jesus tells his parables will inevitably think of the money they owe.'

Metilius rolled up the papyrus sheets with my reports on and stowed them carefully in a leather case. He clearly regarded the official part of my visit at an end. But he didn't let me go yet. Rather, he gave himself breathing space by putting the leather case with my reports on the shelf of a tiny cupboard and looking out briefly into the street, which was thronged with pilgrims, as it was every year at Passover. Now he came over to me, put his hand on my shoulder, and asked me a question which I hadn't expected just then.

'Andreas, why doesn't your great philosophy of God liberate you from all the trimmings of your religion?'

I was speechless. Had Metilius now nothing more important to do than to discuss religious questions with me? He continued:

'You've presented a radical proposal for reform to me which would produce a change in our policy. May I now make some suggestions to you about how you might change your religion?'

He sat down on a chair opposite me. He concentrated.

'Since our last conversation I met a Jew from Alexandria with whom I had a long conversation about your religion. In his view the laws are to be understood symbolically. The commandment to rest on the sabbath means that you need inner tranquillity in order to turn to God. Circumcision is a symbol of the control of passions and desires. Neither sabbath nor circumcision need be practised in the literal sense.[11] If such views became established, Judaism could be an influential philosophy. It would have as devotees many people who want to worship one God, a God who calls us to be generous towards the weak, people who are now deterred by circumcision and the sabbath rules.'

'This Alexandrian Jew speaks for a constantly diminishing group in Judaism,' I said cautiously.

Metilius brushed away the thought with a wave of his hand.

'What even a few Jews in Alexandria think interests me. What do you think?'

I looked him straight in the face. Was this an interrogation? Metilius seemed to guess my thoughts.

'I'm not interested as a Roman official. I'm personally interested. I want to be clear about your philosophy.'

'The problem is,' I began hesitantly, 'that Jewish faith is not a philosophy. It's not something of which you're convinced only in your heart, but something which you're seen to practise. It's a life-style. We delight in being able to worship God in many specific actions, great and small. We worship God even by observing regulations about food and following many little customs which have been handed down to us. It's not enough to hear God's commandments and understand their deeper meaning: they must also be obeyed.'[12]

'But all these commandments contain a good deal which hinders dealings between Jews and non-Jews. Why don't you distinguish between two groups of commandments: the moral commandments which are absolutely necessary for human social life and the ritual commandments, which rest on tradition but are not necessarily bound up with the worship of the one and only God? Doesn't the preaching of Jesus point in this direction?'

'Nowhere does Jesus say that children are not to be circumcised. Nowhere does he cast radical doubt on the sabbath.'

'But couldn't he prompt such thoughts?'

'People like this Alexandrian Jew may already have arrived at such ideas. But they certainly wouldn't be able to convince us. You underestimate how important the many traditional commandments are – even those which we only observe because they're contained in our tradition. By fulfilling them together, openly and visibly, we assure ourselves that we are true to our faith.'

'But couldn't you do that in another way? When I asked one of your great teachers what the most important thing was, he said to me, "Do not do to your neighbour anything that you would not like to have done to you. That is the whole Torah and the rest is exposition; go and learn it."[13] So what use are the many other commandments? Why circumcision and food laws?'

I had to think. Was Metilius really interested in our religion? Or was he just looking for new trends in it which might make possible a less conflictual relationship between Jews and Gentiles? Did the Romans want to encourage such tendencies for political reasons? Finally I said:

'What would happen if we allowed Jews to marry women who didn't share our faith? Or uncircumcised Gentiles to marry Jewish women?[14] The Gentile partner would go on worshipping his or her old gods. He would bring up the children in his faith. Our God would become one god alongside others, even if he were recognized as the supreme god. Faith in the one and only God can only survive along with a life-style adopted by anyone who marries into a Jewish family. As long as our faith differs so radically from our environment, we must also differ in our life-style.'

'But won't all peoples worship the living God one day?'

'That's what we hope for.'

Metilius got up and pointed outside through the window with his hand.

'And then these pilgrims from all countries will not be just Jews but people from all the nations? Everyone would have access to the temple?'[15]

'Even today the temple is open for anyone who is converted to God.'

Metilius thanked me for the conversation. He promised to present my idea of an amnesty to Pilate. If necessary, Pilate would give me a personal audience. Then he said good-bye. If only all Romans were like Metilius! There was no doubt that since our first meeting he had understood more and more about our religion. Was he, too, someone in no man's land?

Dear Dr Kratzinger,

I had to chuckle over your kind letter. You looked up my dates and discovered that I was the right age to be a rebel in 1968. Yes, I was shaped by that rebellious time. I've never denied it. Nor would I want to, though the tactless actions against the older generation at that time were not to my taste.

The content of your letter has made me think. When I was writing I was not aware of something that has struck you on reading it, namely that I am using the experiences of my generation, the exaggerated hopes for reform, the failure of the existing power-structures and people's illusions, the great sobering up which took place among some and the resort to violence and terror which was the response of others. Is my picture of Jesus a projection of my generation? It's tactful of you to leave me to draw the conclusion that it might well be out-of-date.

However, one thing is important to me. The experiences of my generation may be expressed in the framework. My picture of Jesus is less affected by it. It's open to various interpretations. It only becomes a unity from Andreas' perspective. The narrative has deliberately been structured so that no one could come to the conclusion that this is another picture of Jesus as he was. It is Jesus from the perspective of particular social experiences.

Is this perspective arbitrary? The narrative framework is set in a world which has been reconstructed historically from Josephus. Those could also have been Jesus' experiences. The question is even whether one must not see him in that light if one interprets him in the light of the biblical traditions of exodus and exile? And whether one mustn't look at it in that way if one takes a positive view of our own exodus out of an immaturity for which we ourselves are responsible: the 'Enlightenment'. Wouldn't there be an irreplaceable loss if religion withdrew again into the conversation between God and the soul?

Be this as it may, I assume that even you once went through a rebellious period. How did you feel? Of course you needn't answer this indiscreet question!

With thanks and all good wishes,
Yours,
Gerd Theissen

16

Pilate Afraid

The next day was the day before the Passover. To my amazement I was summoned to Pilate very early on. The messenger said that it was urgent. I hurried to the Praetorium. Was Pilate going to issue an amnesty? Had my connections with Baruch become known? I hovered between hopes and deep forebodings. It was going to be a bad day; I wished I didn't have to face it.

Pilate looked serious. He welcomed me in a friendly way and took me into a small room with only one window. He sent his bodyguard out and told them to wait at the door till he called. Evidently he wanted to discuss something that he didn't mean everyone to hear. When we were alone he began:

'I've looked with interest at your proposal for an amnesty and a remission of debts. It reminds me of ideas which I had in my youth – of Solon's remission of debt for the citizens of Athens and the struggle of our two Gracchi to reduce the differences within society.[1] So you see that I'm not just turning down your ideas. But to get to the point: a general amnesty is beyond my competence. It would be so significant politically that only the Emperor could announce it.'

I couldn't hide my disappointment. Pilate continued.

'What is in my power, though, is an amnesty for individuals. In addition to the three Zealots imprisoned recently a further case has arisen. A fourth arrest took place during the night. The case is to be heard today. You'll be familiar with the man. Jesus of Nazareth. He is suspected of stirring up messianic movements. The high priest thinks it best to settle the case before the Passover, so that it doesn't attract too much attention.'

I was terrified. They had imprisoned Jesus. My heart raced and I trembled. Everything had come to a threatening climax.

Pilate continued. 'I've read your notes on Jesus. On that basis I would regard him as harmless. Philosophers and poets should be allowed to live in this land. But if he's a messianic pretender he's a danger to the state.'

Now every word was important. What a good thing it was that I had continually turned over in my thoughts all the arguments with which I might defend Jesus. I went straight to the main argument.

'A central teaching of Jesus is not to resist evil. Rather, if someone strikes you on the left cheek you are to offer him the right. Anyone like that is harmless.'

Pilate remained unimpressed: 'That kind of behaviour is not a danger to the state in the usual sense. But it can throw it into disarray, indeed it can make it more helpless than whole cohorts of rebellious Zealots.'

'But if everyone in the land behaved like Jesus there could be no more resistance fighters,' I interjected.

'I've learned from experience. What you say recalls an event at the beginning of my rule which had incalculable repercussions.[2] When I was sent to Judaea by Tiberius I had images of the emperor, which served as standards, brought to Jerusalem during the night, secretly and under cover. The next day this caused great excitement among the Jews. They were convinced that their law would be trampled underfoot; it forbade the setting up of any images in the city. Not only were the city dwellers in an uproar, but the population of the country streamed in in large crowds. They made their way to me in Caesarea and begged me to remove the standards from Jerusalem and to respect their ancient customs. I refused, whereupon they fell prone all round my house and remained motionless for five days and nights. The next day I took my seat on the tribunal in the great stadium and summoned the mob on the pretext that I was ready to give them an answer. Then I gave a prearranged signal to my soldiers to surround the Jews. The unexpected sight of the armed soldiers three deep which surrounded them made the Jews dumbfounded. I threatened to cut them to pieces unless they accepted the images of Caesar, nodding to the soldiers to draw their swords. But the Jews as though by agreement fell to the ground in a body and bent their necks, shouting that they were ready to be killed rather than transgress the Law. Amazed at the intensity of their faith I ordered the standards to be removed from Jerusalem.

Andreas, I began my period of office with a defeat – not at the hands of an armed host or dangerous resistance fighters but at the hands of a host of defenceless people. They offered me not only their backs but their necks. They invited me not only to hit them but to kill them. This unfortunate beginning to my rule caused me many problems. I've always had to be careful to maintain my authority. Believe me, a state can be more helpless in the face of people who show that they are defenceless than in the face of legions of soldiers.'

'But didn't this Jesus of Nazareth say "Do not resist evil"?'

'Did he? In that case he doesn't observe his own teaching. A few days ago he drew attention to himself in the temple as a troublemaker. He drove out merchants, and overturned the tables of money-changers and those who sell doves. That was violence against people and things![3] Isn't he a Zealot?'

'But he clearly dissociated himself from the Zealots. He said, "You should give to the emperor what is the emperor's and to God what is God's."'[4]

'All right, I've read your report,' said Pilate somewhat tetchily, 'but is that an argument in the other direction? Doesn't this story about the coins fit that incident in the temple court admirably? There he fell upon the money-changers. They sit there in the temple in order to change money of all currencies into coins of Tyre which are the only legitimate coinage in the temple. Of course, coins of Tyre don't have the emperor on them – they're far worse: they have the Tyrian God Melkart, whom we call Heracles. If one is to give back the silver coins to the emperor because the picture of the emperor is on them, it would only be logical to ask that the coins with the idol Melkart on should be given back to him. It could be argued: at all events don't give them to our God, that God in the Jerusalem temple who tolerates no other alongside himself.'

'But couldn't one also argue that Jesus would have nothing against using the sacred temple money for so secular a use as aqueducts?'

Pilate laughed, 'One could even use his teaching profitably in that connection!'

I wouldn't give up. 'And from another aspect it helps the Romans. He rejects the Zealot campaigns to boycott the taxes.'

Pilate shrugged his shoulders. 'What does that add up to? To want to give the emperor back his coins doesn't go very far. In your view the emperor has transgressed the commandment of your God. He has allowed himself to be portrayed on coins. Readiness to give him back his wicked coins doesn't amount to loyalty to the state. One could just as easily see it as contempt. Give this blasphemous emperor back his blasphemous coins! God is more than the emperor! I sense something like that behind what Jesus says.'

I had to start all over again: 'And yet this Jesus shows the only way out of the crisis in our land.'

'The only way? I can tell you the only sure way. We need two legions here instead of 3,500 soldiers. Then people would see reason and the land would have peace.'

'But it can also be done without legions.'

'Nothing can be done in the Roman empire without legions.'

'But it would work with us. The cause of the unrest in the land is the hostility between the native inhabitants and the foreigners: the Greeks and Syrians in the neighbouring city states and the Romans. The native Jews feel oppressed and hate the foreigners. Because things go badly for them economically, whereas the cities of the foreigners flourish, this hatred is constantly refuelled. Only when it disappears will there be no more terrorist attacks, no violent demonstrations and no unrest. Foreigners say that everything would be better if we Jews recognized their gods. If we saw that our God belongs in the great family of gods then we would be accepted into the great family of nations in which everyone feels related. But that's not the way for us. Our religion obliges us to hold firm to this one God – even if that isolates us among the nations. Nothing can move us from our faith. Even your best philosophers know that there is only one God.'

'And what will this God replace our legions with?'

'Jesus teaches that this God wants us to love not only those who are native here but also strangers. He says, Love your enemies! This God makes his sun shine on everyone: Romans and Greeks, Syrians and Jews. We imitate him when we break down the barriers between the peoples.'

'Impossible. Love one's enemies! Every child among us knows that a virtuous man does good to his friends and harm to his enemies.'[5]

'Jesus teaches a new doctrine. Is it impossible because it's new? For us Jews it would be a way of hanging on to our faith and becoming open towards all people, as the old promises foretold.[6] Among us this doctrine has a chance.'

'Among you! You don't have to defend your land! We Romans look after that. Our army sees to it. I've served in it long enough to know that only if we confront our foes firmly can we keep the peace. Such doctrines as Jesus teaches are suitable for a subject people. For us they're useless. They would demoralize our soldiers. So this Jesus is crazy. A dangerous lunatic of whom people whisper that he's the new king.'

I protested. 'Everything that I've discovered about Jesus indicates that he doesn't want to become king or Messiah.'

'But others hope that he will become the new king. And there's the problem. As far as I'm concerned any lunatic can be regarded as a king. I've nothing against that. He only becomes dangerous when others believe in him. He also becomes dangerous when he personally doesn't believe that he's a king. Mere expectation about him creates unrest, since everyone thinks that the great revolution is on the way. Even muddle-headed innocents then become security risks.'

'All right, perhaps he's muddle-headed. But if that's the case you should let him go, not secretly, but in the context of an amnesty. Even if people expect him to become the new king – how could he be dangerous if he puts forward teaching which is demoralizing to soldiers? Where will he get his troops from? And what use are troops who love their enemies? Who don't defend themselves?'

Pilate wasn't listening to me. He had got up and gone to the window. I saw what was happening to him. His eyes looked in my direction – and past me. His hands moved as he spoke, but no sound came from his lips. Finally he sat down on his chair with a sigh. He said quietly,

'I'm afraid . . .'

I looked at him in amazement. He said once again:

'I'm afraid that this matter is slipping out of my hands. No, I cannot.'

Was Pilate talking to me or to himself? He fell to brooding. I almost had the impression that he had forgotten me. I cleared my throat. He looked up. His gaze had become clear again. His voice sounded firm and resolute:

'I seriously considered whether I shouldn't set these three bandits I mentioned free at Passover. Yes, I had decided to do that. But then I heard of this new messianic movement around Jesus. The festival is approaching. The masses are streaming to Jerusalem. The situation can become critical. The risk is too high.'

'But can't you put off the execution of the three bandits? If the festival went well, perhaps lots of things would look different.' Even as I spoke, I felt how hopeless my suggestion was. Pilate shook his head.

'The risk is too high. I cannot release everyone. That could be misunderstood – indeed it could make some fanatics think that we were weak. We mustn't give that impression – particularly at a time when there's uproar among the people. Nevertheless I will adopt your proposal. Not all of it, but part. One person can be released. One – that's a limited risk. I can see whether gentleness pays off.'

Once again I ventured a suggestion: 'Couldn't you release two? A Zealot and Jesus? That would go some way towards meeting the feelings of different parts of the population.'

'No, one is enough. I shall leave it to the people whom they choose. I shall offer them Jesus or a Zealot. Then I can see who has more supporters among the people. Then it will become evident whether this Jesus and his ideas has a chance here, or whether I must go on expecting violent resistance among the people.'

I was terrified. Pilate was turning my idea of an amnesty to reconcile the people into an experiment in assessing his chances of power. I felt my stomach contract. There was a lump in my throat. A cold shudder ran down my back. Again I felt myself in the jaws of the beast. I attempted not to show any of this. Pilate looked at me and said:

'It would only be just if I had them all executed. But during our conversation it has dawned on me that there are two different kinds of trouble-makers. I believe that both are dangerous. I shall test which of them has the mood of the people behind them. You see, I'm giving your ideas a chance.'

'And who is the alternative to Jesus?'

'A certain Barabbas.'

I was a helpless spectator as events moved towards a catastrophe. I could no longer conceal my dismay. My whole body trembled. Pilate looked at me in amazement.

'You can really be content. You gave me an idea with your talk of amnesty. You've convinced me that there are different movements here. A choice must be made between them. This alternative is your idea. A good idea!'

I controlled myself as best I could, summoned up all my strength and thanked Pilate for taking up my idea of an amnesty, while at the same time wishing that I had never had this idea which had put me in such an impossible dilemma. Pilate found more appreciative words for my work. He said that it was good that he had been able to speak to me before he had to pass judgment in the Jesus case.

I don't know how I got home from the Praetorium. I was in a turmoil. Whatever happened, it would be terrible. Everything in me rebelled against this end, an end in which I was involved in an uncanny way, an end which I had not wanted. Nevertheless Pilate had said, 'It's your idea. A good idea.' I heard his voice in me and winced as though every word were a whiplash.

The houses shimmered before my eyes. Their dark doors turned hostile faces to me. Everywhere I heard the whispering of people whose voices rose up from within me. There he goes, the traitor, the one who thought that he could deceive Rome! Now the trick's rebounded on him! He's achieved nothing. Whatever the decision, I felt a share in the fate of the one who had to die. Even though I kept telling myself that I didn't betray them, I didn't have them arrested, I pleaded for everyone, I wanted everyone to have an amnesty, I was innocent.

Was I really innocent? Perhaps at the beginning of our conversation Pilate had wanted to let both Jesus and Barabbas go free? Perhaps it had only dawned on him during our conversation that the two of them represented alternatives?

There was no doubt that I was involved in the final outcome, this choice between Jesus and Barabbas. Was I also guilty? No, I cried, no!

Everything in me rebelled. I'm innocent! But as soon as my voice rang out, other voices rose up within me and whispered, 'You're guilty.' I couldn't stifle them. The way home was torture.

As soon as I arrived, I sent Malchus to discover how things went. He was to stay near the Praetorium and report the decision to me. I felt too weak to get personally involved.

Anxious hours went by. Finally Malchus returned with the news: at the request of the people Barabbas had been released. He had immediately disappeared. They had crucified Jesus in front of the city. Along with two other Zealots.

The decision had been made. I was somewhat calmer. I felt strong enough to go to the edge of the city. I wanted to see Jesus at least from afar. I had kept coming upon traces of him in Galilee. I had never met him. Now would be my only meeting: with a man who had been executed as a criminal. Timon and Malchus accompanied me.

We could see the place of execution from the second wall of the city. Three crosses were standing there. Three tortured and humiliated men hung on them – in the anguish and pain of death. The people were whispering that one was already dead. The Romans had executed him because they feared that he could be the Messiah.

I looked from afar at the cross on which Jesus hung. It was the one in the middle. To the left and right of him hung the two condemned Zealots. Perhaps they were two of the young men we had met in the caves of Arbela. Perhaps the two who had brought us out of the caves. Who knows? The sun was setting behind them. It cast its brightness on the cross of Jesus and the Zealots, the dead man and the two dying men. It lit up the Roman soldiers and the onlookers who were following events, partly out of curiosity, partly in dismay.

We were standing in the shadow of the Galilean. We felt that these people were not criminals. We had come to know the Zealots. We had heard of Jesus. Malchus said, 'If the sun could see and feel as we do, it would go dark for grief. If the earth could feel, it would quake with anger.'

But the sun did not go dark, and the earth remained at rest. It was a normal day and the darkness was only in me. Only in me did the foundations of life shake; only in me did the voices whisper: 'You're guilty. You're guilty.' The voices got louder and louder, more and more urgent. I couldn't keep them back. They drowned any reply. Things grew blurred, then I lost consciousness.

Timon and Malchus brought me home. Later they told me that I had sunk into a fever for three days and nights. Sometimes I had imagined a beast which threatened me. I had cried out and tossed restlessly to and fro.

I myself had only confused memories of my state. Tormenting scenes kept going through my head. I kept seeing the three crucified men before me. Their pain was my anguish. When I became more peaceful, disconnected sentences turned into prayers in my mind. I lamented:[7]

My God, my God,
why have you forsaken me?
Why are you so dumb?
Why so distant?
Day and night I have called on you for help.
But you are relentless.
I know that our forefathers were delivered.
But that is as a dead memory in me.
I am hardly a man.
I am a beast, a worm, nothing.
Everything mocks me.
Everything triumphs over my downfall.
Many enemies encircle me,
surround me.
The jaws of beasts threaten me.
I am in their power.
I am collapsing.
My bones are falling apart.
My heart hurts,
my throat is dried up,
My tongue sticks to my gums.
I lie in the dust,
as if I were dead.
Surrounded on all sides,

I see no way out.
But you gave me the task of living.
Without you I cannot draw breath.
Be near,
for there is no one to help me.

For three days I hovered between life and death. But after three days and nights I became calmer. The decision had been made for life. It had been made without involving me. It still took a long time for me to accept it. For a long time I was torn apart by images of the last events. Again and again all these things kept running through my imagination. At night I often cried out when anxious dreams of an uncanny beast raged through my disturbed soul.

Dear Dr Kratzinger,

To your comments on the last chapter you added some personal remarks which moved me deeply. You too once rebelled, in the 1950s when the rearmament of our country was discussed. At that time you argued that the Sermon on the Mount was a basis for political decisions. Today you are sceptical about such an approach. You share Pilate's scepticism about Andreas' arguments. You too have known what it is to have your hopes crucified.

Of course you're right. No defence minister can assure an attacker that he would not fight back. The finance minister may not just pile up treasure in heaven. The economics minister must not take lilies and birds as an example. No justice minister can abolish the courts. So are the demands of the Sermon on the Mount only for the personal sphere? Should we simply recognize our inadequacy in the mirror of its radical demands?

I have come to the conclusion that these demands should indirectly determine our political action. A society should be run in such a way that the experiment of radical discipleship is possible. A society only becomes human when those who turn their backs on accusations and trials are not lost. It is only human when it allows a demonstration of love of one's enemies. It is only human if it contains outsiders who can exist without cares. Political action cannot use the Sermon on the Mount directly as a criterion, but it can provide conditions in which individuals and groups can use it as a criterion by which to take their bearings.

To avoid a misunderstanding: I don't think that the Sermon on the Mount should have even a remote niche reserved anywhere in society, as an 'ethical nature reserve'. Rather, all society should be structured in such a way that the experiment of radical discipleship becomes possible. Then groups of disciples can have an effect on society as a whole and be the light of the world, the salt of the earth.

Perhaps you don't entirely reject the dream of your rebellious time.

All good wishes,
Yours,
Gerd Theissen

PS   So far the fictitious narrative and the story of Jesus have been separate. In the last two chapters they overlap. This is meant to stress that what is said about Pilate's reasons for setting Barabbas or Jesus free belongs to the realm of fiction, not to historical reality.

17

Who was Guilty?

I spent another three days in Jerusalem. Then, as neither Metilius nor Pilate sent for me, I regarded my task as over. I avoided visiting the Praetorium again of my own accord. Perhaps I could withdraw from the affair unnoticed.

I was glad to be able to get back to normal business. So I travelled through the country as a grain and olive dealer and found distraction in my everyday negotiations, purchases and sales. I did not find liberation from my inner tensions. There was a paralysing pressure on my life. I kept busy all the time in order to tire myself out.

The next time I was in Caesarea, I went to the synagogue service there – and met Metilius. I wanted to hide. But he had already seen me. To my amazement he seemed to be joining in the shema. At least his lips were moving when we were expressing the belief of all Jews in the one and only God.[1]

'Hear, O Israel, the Lord your God is one God. And you shall love the Lord your God with all your heart and all your soul and all your strength.'

Metilius listened devoutly to the reading of the Torah, a section from the five books of Moses, in the second part of the service; this was followed by a reading from the prophets. He also followed the short address given by the preacher attentively. Was Metilius a godfearer? Or even a proselyte?[2] Or was he there as a spy? Did he just want to make contact with Jews? I found it uncanny that the head of the Roman espionage system should be taking part in worship in a Jewish synagogue.

After the service he greeted me in a friendly way. He invited me into his house – privately, as he said. He had recently learned that he was being posted to the Legio IV Ferrata, the 'iron legion', in Antioch, and was glad that he was able to bid farewell to me.

I was still mistrustful: it could all be a trick to gain confidence. Of course anyone would be inclined to say more to an officer who would soon be out of the country than to others. I decided to be careful, but gladly accepted his invitation, not least in the hope of learning more about the reasons for the condemnation of Jesus.

Metilius's house was not far from the harbour of Caesarea, which Herod had had built. We had a marvellous view of the city and sea.[3] The harbour-mouth faced north, as in that locality the north wind is the gentlest, and on either side rose three colossal statues standing on pillars. Adjoining the harbour were houses of limestone, and to the harbour led the streets of the town, laid out the same distance apart. On rising ground opposite the harbour-mouth stood Caesar's temple, of exceptional size and beauty; in it was a colossal statue of Caesar, in no way inferior to the one to Zeus in Olympia on which it was modelled, and a second statue of the goddess Roma. Because Herod had built the city in honour of the emperor, he had called it Caesarea.

It was a splendid view. And Caesarea generally was a fine city, with amphitheatre, theatre and market place. The Romans could feel at home here.

Metilius had his slave bring fruit. We ate and talked.

'So you're visiting our synagogue services?' I asked.

'Why not? I've now got to know some Hebrew and Aramaic.'

'Did you learn it to get to know our religion – as a student?'

I took a date. It was marvellously sweet. Metilius nodded.

'That's how it began. I had to learn about your faith for professional reasons. I read the holy writings. Much in them attracted me a great deal. Above all belief in the one God. He is not unknown to us. One of our philosophers referred me to a Greek, Xenophanes, who lived round about the time of Etruscan rule over Rome; he is already said to have stated: "There is only one God, the greatest among gods and men, like to mortals neither in form nor thoughts."[4] Your writings are even more radical. For example, in the last half of the book of Isaiah I read an oracle of your God which says, "I am the Lord, and none other; there is no God beside me."[5] Xenophanes, however, spoke of gods in the plural.'

'Do you want to become a Jew?' I asked provocatively.

'Not exactly,' he replied. 'If I were a Jew I could no longer go on being a soldier. How could I keep the sabbath if the troops were on duty then? How could I avoid the sacrifices?[6] I shall visit your synagogues now and then and just take from you what makes sense to me, belief in the one God. But even there I have difficulties.' He hesitated and then continued. 'May I ask you something? Perhaps soon I shall have no one with whom I can talk about your religion.'

'Of course,' I said, and added with a smile: 'But I'm not the best conversation partner. No theological training and from a family with an idol in the house!'

'That doesn't matter,' Metilius reassured me. 'Perhaps you'll understand my problem all the better. I've learned from Stoic philosophy that all things are permeated by divine reason. You can detect it everywhere: in the ordering of nature, in the alternation of day and night, in the orbits of the stars. We Stoics call this reason god. It's a god one can experience. But you say that God once created the world from nothing. How can one believe that? No one could have been present at creation. No one can be your witness. No one can provide the sort of evidence there is for omnipresent reason.'

'At every moment you're a witness to creation. Creation from nothing can be experienced as universally as reason in things.'

'I don't understand.'

'It's hard to describe because it's so obvious – so obvious that one can no longer perceive it. For it includes a self: one's own seeing, perceiving, thinking; one's own existence.'

'I still don't understand.'

'At every moment there is a transition from being to nothing. Every moment goes past before we have wholly registered it. It's now. But as soon as I have noted it it has gone.'

'But it was there once.'

'What was, is no longer. It is finally past. Everything sinks into nothing. Our ancestors who once were, are no more. We shall perish. Even the hills will no longer be there one day.'

'But creation would be the opposite. A transition from non-being to being.'

'And you also witness that every moment. The future moment is not yet. We ourselves are not yet what we shall be. A transition from nothingness to being takes place every moment. That's what we mean when we say that God creates every moment from nothing. And he preserves it until it sinks back into nothingness.'

'That sounds as though things could change at any time. But they remain the same. And according to Stoic philosophy, that is in fact a sign of the divine reason: it is to be found in all that is regular, ordered, abiding.'

'According to our faith God has also created the world order. And he recreates it every moment. He does not allow it to sink into chaos.'

'But couldn't God change something at any moment?'

'Of course! We don't believe that the ordering of the world is already final. It is God's reason which is evident in it. But it is that reason which must constantly realize itself anew throughout the world. It points beyond present circumstances.'

Metilius sighed deeply. He leant over the table by which we were reclining and reached for a bunch of red grapes. After a while he said: 'Questions like this make me feel terribly giddy. I can understand people who say that this is abstract speculation, with no bearing on real life.'

'It's very important for our life,' I retorted. 'A Stoic will say, "My task in this world is to live in accord with nature." By that he means living in accord with the eternal divine order which is evident in it. He accepts the world as it is. But we don't believe in an eternal order. It's created anew every moment. Every moment it's snatched from chaos and nothingness. We believe in the task of living in accord with the true God whose creation is aimed at a new order.'

'That's why you're so rebellious. That God who creates everything from nothing can also turn losers into winners, and outcasts into conquerors.'

'That's so. We sing in a hymn:

He has put down the mighty from their thrones
and exalted the humble.
He has filled the hungry with good things
and sent the rich empty away.[7]

Can you understand why a Roman officer has difficulties with this

God? And yet something attracts me. I don't know what. I want to go on investigating, even in another land.'

'Would you rather stay in Palestine?'

'I've come to love this land. But it's paradoxical. Precisely because I've gained sympathy for Jewish belief, I want to get away.'

I kept quiet.

'As a soldier I live here in an atmosphere which is hostile to the Jews. Our soldiers aren't Romans. They're Syrians and Greeks from Palestine. They hate the Jews. If I could advise the emperor, I would tell him to post them elsewhere and send Roman soldiers instead.'[8]

'But aren't many Roman soldiers antisemitic?'

'Certainly, but here it's a firm tradition. I've asked myself how it came about. The last independent kings of the Jews, the Hasmonaean kings, conquered and enslaved the surrounding Syrian and Greek cities. Since then these cities and their inhabitants have feared nothing more than a powerful Jewish monarchy. They're particularly suspicious of all Jewish kings.'

'But there are no more Jewish kings!'

'Not directly, but there are people who either claim to be the long-awaited Jewish king or whom others hope may emerge as kings and messiahs – like this Jesus whom we recently executed.'

'And are such pretenders hated by the soldiers!'

'And how! Our soldiers did everything you could think of to mock this Jesus. After he had been condemned and disfigured by torture they called the whole cohort together and put a purple robe on him, wove a crown of thorns and put it on him. Then they began to greet him: "Hail, king of the Jews!" They hit him on the head with a reed, spat at him and knelt before him and did him homage.[9] They mocked the poor man. All their hatred of the Jews came out in this ill-treatment.'

'Why didn't your officers intervene?'

'Not all of them think as I do. Pilate himself is not very good at speaking to the Jews. And the strong man in Rome, Sejanus, is said to be decidedly antisemitic.'

'But that means that hatred of the Jews is also behind the execution of Jesus,' I exclaimed.

'That's so. But many factors came together there,' Metilius replied. 'You may well know more about the reasons than I do.'

Again I became suspicious. Did he want to interrogate me about Jesus? The Romans must have been interested in gathering information about his movement. Could there be a resurgence? Could it find new followers? But Metilius went on: 'Why did the people in Jerusalem decide for Barabbas and not for Jesus?'

I shrugged my shoulders. I really didn't know. Metilius said:

'Since then I've learned more about that remarkable episode in the temple. Jesus spoke an oracle about the temple: "This house made with hands will be destroyed and another house not made with hands will be built."[10] The driving out of some money changers and people selling sacrificial animals in the temple is said to be an illustration of this prophecy. But such oracles and provocations haven't made any friends in Jerusalem. Almost all the city lives on the sanctity of the temple. All the priests and high priests profit from the offerings to the temple, as do all the temple craftsmen who do building work in it. Add to that all the hostelries which lodge masses of visitors and all those who deal in sacrificial animals, including the tanners who use the skins of sacrificed beasts. Anyone who attacks the holiness of the temple attacks the economic basis of these people and their families in Jerusalem. Pilate had a bitter experience of it when he wanted to introduce imperial standards into Jerusalem and use money from the temple for secular purposes.'

It struck me that Jesus' teaching about what was clean and what was unclean could also lead to a good deal of uncertainty. If there were no longer clean foods, clean vessels, clean goods, clean people – then everything could be bought just as well from Gentiles as from Jews. I thought of our profitable trade in pure olive oil with the diaspora communities in the cities of Syria. But I steered the conversation round to another point.

'The Jewish council of state, the Sanhedrin, handed Jesus over. Couldn't they simply have let him go? Why did they do that?'

Here, too, Metilius could only offer conjectures. 'It is certain that many members of the Sanhedrin profit from the temple. All high priests live on tithes and other offerings to the temple which are prescribed in the law. So they have an interest in the impregnable sanctity of temple and law. But Jesus was critical of the temple and didn't observe all the precepts of the law. Wouldn't they inevitably be afraid that the law, the basis of their existence, would be destroyed?'

'But surely he was executed on political grounds, as a messianic pretender?'

Metilius confirmed this: 'That's true. The oracle against the temple and its role in religious questions was not a factor for Pilate. Pilate condemned Jesus as someone who endangered Roman rule by virtue of being a royal pretender. That was the decisive reason.'

'And the Jewish council handed him over to the Romans on this charge! Why?'

'The motives of the council of state are quite clear. Like any political authority it is interested in holding on to power. It knows that this power is limited. As far as we Romans are concerned its existence is justified only if it is better at keeping the peace in the land than if we were directly responsible for keeping it ourselves. So it must avoid unrest at any price. That is its decisive interest. The Romans would intervene the moment it could no longer control the situation. If need be, we would abolish the council.'[11]

'But was this fear of Jesus justified? Was he really a troublemaker?'

'Perhaps he was quite harmless. But his movement could easily have led to unrest. People who had poured into Jerusalem with him at the Passover hailed him as Messiah.[12] He had disrupted the traders in the temple courts. He had aroused the expectation that something decisive was about to happen. The kingdom of God was coming. The situation was tense.'

'People didn't think that he himself was particularly dangerous?'

'No, the danger lay in the great crowds at Passover. We've had experiences of it. Because of these crowds the Roman prefect comes at festivals with a cohort to reinforce the standing garrison, so as to damp down unrest from the start. Don't you know the story of that fart that almost sparked off a war?'[13]

I shook my head. Metilius told the story. 'The people had gathered in Jerusalem for the feast of unleavened bread, and the soldiers stood on guard over the temple colonnade, armed men, as I said, always being on duty at the feasts to forestall any rioting by the vast crowds. One of the soldiers pulled up his garment, bent over, and displayed his backside to the Jews, making a noise as indecent as his attitude. This infuriated the whole crowd, who noisily appealed to the prefect to punish the soldier. Some of the less restrained young men and others from the people who had a tendency to rebel joined in the struggle, raised stones and began to throw them at the soldiers. The prefect was now afraid that the whole people would attack him, so he sent for more heavy infantry. When these poured into the halls the Jews were seized with uncontrollable panic, turned tail, and tried to flee from the temple into the city. So violently did the dense mass struggle to escape that they trampled one another down and three thousand people were crushed to death.

That kind of thing can happen at any Passover. The people are excited. Certainly their high spirits are kept in check by the soldiers. On the other hand the presence of the soldiers excites the people even more, especially when these soldiers cause antisemitic provocation. So I think that the emperor should remove them and replace them with Roman soldiers. Such unnecessary provocations as that fart would certainly be less frequent.'

'But Jesus didn't provoke the people in that way!'

'His disruption of those selling sacrificial animals and the money changers was a provocation, though of a quite different kind. But if a fart can cause a war, think what can arise from the provocation of merchants in the temple forecourt. The Jewish council, the Sanhedrin, certainly did right to hand Jesus over.'

'Was he arrested straight after the disturbances in the temple forecourt?'

'No, that would have been unwise. That would have caused even more unrest. We know that in himself this Jesus was quite harmless. But if an excited crowd had been there, anything could have happened. For that reason the Sanhedrin arrested him by night when he was alone with his closest followers.'

'How did people know where he would be?'

'A follower betrayed him for money.'

'Do you think that this Jesus was guilty?', I asked. 'Was it right to impose the death penalty?'

Metilius hesitated: 'I think that he was innocent. He caused many difficulties. But he wasn't a criminal.'

'So who do you think was guilty of the death of Jesus?'

Again Metilius reflected for a long time. 'It's wrong to look for culprits. Perhaps it's wrong to seek to attribute guilt. There were many causes of his death. One was the tensions between Syrians and Jews. Without antisemitism in the Roman cohorts, right up to the prefect, things would have gone differently. The tensions between Jews and Romans were another. Without Roman anxiety about messianic unrest Jesus would not have been arrested. The tensions between the population of the city and countryfolk were another cause: perhaps the people of Jerusalem would have asked for Jesus to be freed had they not been distrustful of all country people who attack their holy temple. The tensions between the aristocracy and ordinary people were yet another. The aristocracy want to maintain their power. So they hand over to the Romans those they suspect of causing unrest. And the Romans want to control the Jews. So they look with suspicion at the law, which is the basis of their income and power. Everything comes together here. This Jesus was caught up in the wheels. He was torn apart by the tensions under which this whole people suffers.'

'But wasn't Pilate the chief culprit? Isn't he guilty?'

'If you want to make one person responsible, then it was Pilate. He passed sentence. He was responsible in the legal sense.'

'Why did he condemn him? Why didn't he let him go as a madman?'[14]

'I think that Pilate was worried that all these tensions and conflicts would prove too much for him. He preferred to have Jesus die to further his own survival.'

'Do you think that he'll be successful? That now he can continue his rule untroubled?'

Metilius shrugged his shoulders. 'Much is possible in this country. I've often had to change my estimation of the situation. I've had to relearn a great deal. I don't venture any more forecasts. I'm not even certain that this Jesus business is finished.'

'What can come of it now that he's dead?'

'He has followers. After the death of John the Baptist, to begin with people also thought that the matter was over. But then Jesus appeared.'

'Do you know anything about his followers?'

'They've gathered in Jerusalem. They believe that Jesus isn't dead. They claim to have seen him alive in visions.'

'After the death of John the Baptist some people said that Jesus was John the Baptist risen from the dead.'

'In that case the sorry business would begin all over again from the beginning. But these followers believe, not that he has returned to life, but that he has gone to God. God has raised him from the dead.'

'But that's absurd!'

'Why? It's no more absurd than belief in the God who at any moment makes the world from nothing. I have to confess to you that when I asked you about creation from nothing I already had this question about Jesus at the back of my mind. Can there be such a thing as the recreation of someone from the dead? Is there a creation in the present? But perhaps all these ideas are going much too far. Perhaps this is just a defiant reaction of the disciples, who cannot accept the death of their master. Or something else.'

This conversation with Metilius had one positive consequence. I hoped that with the posting of Metilius I would get no more commissions from the Romans. At some point Pilate too would be recalled. Perhaps soon, if he did not assert himself in all the conflicts, small and great. Then I would finally be free.

Dear Dr Kratzinger,

You think that there are very different kinds of sections in this last chapter: on the one hand a sober analysis of the possible factors which led to the execution of Jesus and on the other an interpretation of Easter faith in terms of the idea of 'creation from nothing'. You are right that here I didn't want just to portray a past belief but to interpret it for the present.

Of course there is evidence of the idea of a creation from nothing from the second century BC on. It can first be found in II Macc.7.28. Philo is familiar with it. Paul presupposes it (Rom.4.17), indeed in II Cor.4.17 he probably interprets the 'appearance' before Damascus with images from creation faith.

I gladly concede that I could not have written these sections on creation and resurrection without knowledge of Danish creation theology. From it I have learned that existence and non-existence, creation and annihilation, are present in time at any given point. Here we centre upon that mystery with which all theologians and philosophers are concerned, which raises the question 'Why is there something and not nothing?' We celebrate this mystery in the Easter faith.

My narrative exegesis here turns into narrative hermeneutics. In other words, I am concerned not only with the significance which was once attached to Easter faith but with the meaning that we could see in it today.

With all good wishes,
Yours,
Gerd Theissen

18

The Man: A Dream

In conversation with Metilius I had learned that any group and any individual seeks to assert itself at the expense of others. All of us have learned that we must spare the weak. But in conflicts we are ready to sacrifice others for ourselves – for fear that we ourselves may perish.

The Jewish council had taken this view: it is better for a man to die than for the whole people to lose its independence. They sacrifice the one man in the interest of the whole.[1]

Pilate followed the same motto: better for another to die than for his own rule to be threatened. He was worried that unless he executed Jesus he would not be able to control the next messianic movement.

The people had precisely the same feelings. To protect their own interests they called for the crucifixion of Jesus. They feared the economic ruin that would follow if temple and city were no longer regarded as holy places, to which pilgrims streamed from all over the world.

Barabbas, too, benefited from this law. Someone else had died in his place.

And so I saw everyone caught up in a concern to secure their survival at the expense of others, at the expense of the outcast and the condemned.

Certainly I had had only an incidental role in this cruel game. But this recognition removed little of the burden. Were we not all like animals who live at the expense of the weaker members of the species? Indeed, do we not continue amongst ourselves that eating and being eaten that we observe in nature – usually between different species? Everyone lives by suppressing others. No one can escape that. And yet I would never accept it. Even if I had it demonstrated to me a thousand times that God had arranged this world in such a way, I would never be content with that.

Disgust overwhelmed me that I was involved in this game, abhorrence that I would go on being involved in it. I saw no way out unless it were possible to change the basic ordering of the world! I had spoken of precisely that with Metilius. But now the idea seemed to me to be absurd. Who would bring about this change? Were we human beings to revise creation? Was it to be expected that God would make it anew?

I had returned to my house. My thoughts became increasingly gloomy. I brooded without getting anywhere.

I was in this mood when I had an evening visit: Baruch was at the door. We hadn't seen each other for almost six months. He came just at the right time. My work for the Romans had had at least one good result: I had been able to bring Baruch back to life. I had found him a human wreck and now there he was, whole and healthy. This time I was the one who was disorientated, confused and at my wits' end.

We sat in the upper room. It had gone dark. An oil lamp gave light. Baruch said that he had looked for me in Sepphoris and then gone after me. He had brought a sealed letter from home which had been left there for me by strangers. Everything else poured out from him in a disconnected way. In Jerusalem he had joined a new commune. They led an underground existence. They had all goods in common. The hungry were fed, the mourners consoled; husband and wife, free men and women and slaves had the same rights.[2]

Was Baruch again dependent on a sect? Had I also failed here? But I was only half listening. Something else had caught my attention. I thought that I had recognized the writing on the outside of the letter. Was it a letter from Barabbas? Excitedly, I broke the seal.

Baruch kept talking. He went on and on. About meals together. About peace and love. About miracles. About healings. My ears pricked up when he said:

'Our commune goes back to Jesus of Nazareth, in whom you used to be interested.'

I objected: 'Jesus is dead. Failed like so many other prophets.'

'No, he's not dead. He was seen in changed form after his death.'[3]

There was no stemming Baruch's flood of words.

I had once brought Baruch back to life, but not to the life of a merchant. I couldn't give him what he had sought in the wilderness community, security in a community which had withdrawn from the wickedness of the world. Now he had found what he had been looking for.

I should really have been delighted at his enthusiasm. What a contrast it was to his self-destructive behaviour in the wilderness! Or was it a relapse into that dream of a completely different life of which he had dreamed as an Essene? Did he want to infect me with his dream? But all he managed to do was to make me aware of my own vulnerability and wounds. Anything to do with Jesus opened up wounds and caused pain. It simply reminded me that with the best will in the world one can be entangled in a disastrous chain of events. Baruch couldn't guess what was going on in my mind.

But perhaps Barabbas had found a way out. Perhaps at least I had brought him back to life. Undisturbed by Baruch's flow of words I read the letter.

Barabbas to Andreas
Shalom
Burn this letter as soon as you have read it, for no one must find it on you. No one is to know what is in it. I'm writing above all to thank you. I've heard how much you did for me. I barely escaped death. The price was high. Another died in my place. Two of my friends were crucified with him. Since then I've been asking myself: Why the other? Why Jesus? Why not me?
I know that Jesus is close to your heart. You defended his gentle way of rebellion and rejected my way of resisting. Now I'm indissolubly bound up with him. I keep thinking what that means for me.
If he has died in my place, then I am obliged to live for him. You would probably say that I am in debt to him, that I should follow his way. But I've come to another conclusion. Our two ways are opposed, and yet the one points to the other.
The gentle rebellion of Jesus is only taken seriously by the powerful when they know that the alternative would be violent rebellion, involving incalculable risks. Only in such a situation do

people like Jesus have a chance. Only with us in the background are they important.

But the same is true of us. Our harsh way has a chance only if the other way can still be followed. We can shake the existing order, but we cannot build up a new order with our methods. We run the risk of being overwhelmed by the consequences of our action. Violence begets more violence. Once we have established ourselves we have to look for forgiveness and reconciliation.

We must go our own ways vicariously for one another. They are different and often opposed. I know that Jesus would not approve of our way. Nevertheless we depend on each other. His way is in danger of being exploited by the powerful. We are in danger of losing sight of our goal.

At the end our ways will bring us together; indeed they have already become one. Two of my friends were crucified with Jesus. They belong to him. He died as 'king of the Jews', with our people as his companions.[4] I recognize that he is superior. But he needs us. He needs our dirty work. He needs his following. We were there dying with him when his disciples had forsaken him. If I ever fall into the hands of the Romans and suffer his fate, I shall be united with him.

God be gracious to us all.

Your friend
Barabbas

Baruch had gone on talking while I was reading. My attention was divided. The voice of the distant Barabbas came nearer, Baruch's voice went further away. And yet both were important for me. For without Baruch's presence helpless despair would have overcome me. I immediately knew that Barabbas would meet the same fate as Jesus. Neither his way nor the way of Jesus was viable. Even my ideas were illusions. I had dreamed of reforms. But for that one needed power, and this lay with the Romans. As long as they thought they could quell any disturbance with troops, they had no interest in improving conditions. Nothing worked. It was all senseless. Once could do nothing.

Fortunately at this moment there was at least one thing that I could do: burn the letter. I held the papyrus sheet over the flame of the oil lamp. The top of it began to burn. Flickering light illuminated the room. Baruch's shocked face came and went in a sudden shadow. For the first time he noticed that I was preoccupied with something completely different.

'What are you doing?' he asked in confusion.

'I'm burning this letter.' I was filled with disgust and abhorrence, any faith I had in ashes. A destructive lust against everything overcame me.

'What do you mean?'

How far our thoughts were removed from each other! I doubted whether we would find any way of getting into conversation this evening.

'Baruch,' I said, 'don't forget why the Essenes expelled you. You unmasked the stories about their treasures as an illusion. You saw that it serves to deliver men into the hands of the society and lead them to give up their possessions. Don't you see that the followers of Jesus have similar illusions?'

'None of them claims to have hidden treasures.'

'Instead they talk of a treasure in heaven. They believe in a dead man who has seized power for them in heaven. Without this faith they would never get anyone voluntarily to hand over all his possessions to society.'

'A living man has seized all power in heaven and on earth on our behalf. Now if God can make a dead person alive, can he not fill our dead hearts with living spirit and enable us to do things that no one has thought possible?'

'What's the difference, then, between hidden treasure on earth and a hidden representative in heaven. Neither can be verified. Both could be illusions. Any group needs a few lies to keep them all together, first the Essenes and now you.'

'You overlook one difference. None of the Essenes has seen the treasure. But Jesus was seen by many people. Many people found truth in his words. He appeared to many people after his death.'

'And what if these appearances were fantasies and hallucinations?'

'Why shouldn't God use fantasies and hallucinations to address a message to us?'

'What message?'

'That God is again taking Jesus' side – even after his death.'

'Wouldn't it be more correct to say that the disciples are again taking Jesus' side?'

'God's spirit is driving them to it.'

'How can you recognize God's spirit here?'

'Because God has always acted like this with us. He has always chosen the weak and outcast. In the same way he has now chosen the crucified Jesus!'

'I doubt whether this spirit of God can ever seize a group of people. Every group needs sacrifices and scapegoats. Wouldn't your community send me out into the wilderness, as the Essenes sent you, for asking sceptical questions?'

Baruch protested. 'We have no hidden treasure with which to entice people. Once a couple did in fact want to keep some treasure secret. But it came out.'

'And what happened to them?'

'They had sold a field and pretended to give the community the whole proceeds, but in fact kept half of it back. A meeting of the community ruled that they had offended against the spirit of our community.'[5]

'Were they forgiven?'

'The verdict came as a shock to them. They dropped down dead.'

I leapt up in agitation and exclaimed, 'Haven't you yourself seen what happens when someone offends against the holy spirit of a community? You were cast out to die of hunger. And now you drive two of your members to death because they didn't do something as perfectly as you wanted.'

'No one wanted them to die. Everything happened by itself.'

'Baruch,' I cried out, 'how can you belong to such a commune? Is that acting in the spirit of Jesus? Didn't he often eat with toll collectors? They regularly hide money. Did he ever use his power to cause people to die?'

That got home to Baruch and he kept silent.

Then he said quietly, 'Perhaps you're right. We, too, are not perfect. Nevertheless there is a good deal of love and readiness to help in our community. Why do you speak so harshly against it? Do you want to extract me from it, too?'

Did I? What had I tried to shake Baruch's faith with such violence? Was it because I myself was wounded. I look a long time to answer.

'When I got you out of the Essene community everything was different. At that time things were going badly with you. Now I have problems. Something was destroyed in me when this Jesus died. I had pinned a good deal of hope on him, including the solution of some personal problems. Now I've lost all my illusions and don't want to persuade myself to adopt new ones.'

That must have been quite incomprehensible to Baruch. But it did me good when he said, 'Join us.'

I shook my head. 'I'm not right for your commune. I'm a rich merchant. What would I do in a community which despises the acquisition of possessions and deals so strictly with its members?'

Baruch's enthusiasm and my sorrow were worlds apart. We went on trying to lessen the comfortless aftertaste of talking at cross purposes by agreeing over unimportant everyday matters. Our conversation ran on into the night. Finally we lay down to sleep: Baruch in a room on the ground floor, I above. I knew that I wouldn't go to sleep very quickly, despite my tiredness. For a long time I stared into the night.

The clear starry sky spread its arch over me. Millions of stars flickered an infinite distance away from me. My own life was so tiny: a speck of dust on this earth. So what was this whole world? Was it anything other than a random collection of dirt and dust, light and darkness, earth and water on which lived a variety of collections of dust which tortured one another in the struggle for life by oppressing, exploiting, humiliating and sacrificing one another? And the people who became aware of that despaired. They rebelled. They wanted to escape. Some rebelled violently, and found themselves in the vicious circle of violence and counter-violence. Others made the world go up in flames in their bloody fantasies – and in so doing conjured up greater suffering than that because of which the world deserved destruction. Others went into the wilderness, constructed an alternative world, wanted to be holy amidst the unholy doings of the world. But they, too, sent their scapegoats into the wilderness when they thought that necessary. Not even the victims learned a lesson! Not even they refused their assent when others became the victims! And all those involved in this cruel game gave good reasons for it. Some wanted to preserve law and order, others to establish justice; a third group wanted to fulfil God's commandments. All had their reasons. And all were caught up in the cruel logic of this world.

I was again seized with disgust at everything. And again words from our scriptures occurred to me:

> *Again I saw all the oppressions*
> *that are practised under the sun.*
> *And behold, the tears of the oppressed,*
> *and they had no one to comfort them.*
> *On the side of their oppressors there was power,*
> *and there was no one to comfort them.*
> *And I thought the dead who are already dead*
> *more fortunate than the living who are still alive;*
> *but better than both is he who has not yet been,*
> *and has not seen the evil deeds that are under the sun.*
> *Then I saw that all toil and all skill in work*
> *come from a man's envy of his neighbour.*
> *This also is vanity and a striving after wind.*[6]

Was that the truth? But if it was the truth, the whole truth, why should one join in this senseless game? Why not go on strike? Why not say, 'I don't want this life. I voluntarily give it up'? Wouldn't that be consistent, if the dead are happier than the living?

I looked at my hands and imagined how dead hands look. I felt my face, to get some idea of the form of the dead skull which was in me. I tried to imagine myself as a cold and lifeless corpse. But as I touched my body, I felt how warm it was. My heart beat regularly. My breath went in and out. My eyes saw the starry sky. My ears heard the lapping of the lake. My nose smelt the smell of sand and salt water. I saw, heard, smelt. I lived, breathed and felt. Wasn't it a miracle that dust and earth could live, think and feel, doubt and despair? Think how many processes in my body had to take place regularly for me to be able to experience this moment without bodily pain! And if it was only a transitory moment – was it any the less worthwhile for that?

I thought of Barabbas. Mustn't he have felt the same way? What would become of this body which was now still alive but which was doomed to execution? He had been given life again. Wasn't that a good thing, even if everything which had led to it seemed so meaningless? Wasn't it a good thing continually to be given life, even if there was a dark connection with all the victims? With all those who, like Jesus, were torn apart by the conflicts of this world?

I felt that my life was part of the life that was given. In me lived on something of all men and women, the happy and the unhappy, Jesus who went freely through Galilee and the crucified victim. I seemed to have an obligation to preserve this life. Wasn't it betrayal to throw it away? And if my own life were sacrificed, somewhere in the cellars of the Romans or the terrorists' caves, wouldn't it live on in all those who rebelled against the idea that life is possible only at the expense of another life? Wasn't there deep within me the intimation of a life which could not attain fulfilment by being against others but only by being alongside them? In which everyone, the fortunate and the unfortunate, were bound together as closely as the members of a body. Where there was a fulfilment of Baruch's dream that everyone had everything in common?

I went to sleep. In my sleep I again dreamed that dream which had pursued me for so long. So far I had dreamed only fragments of this dream. But now it came together into a unity.[7]

I was standing by the sea. A storm stirred up the water. Foam-flecked waves broke and rushed up the shore. A figure detached itself from the chaos. Outlines became visible. A lion with a flowing mane went up the shore, raised its paws and roared: 'The land is mine. It belongs to me and no one else.' I looked around and saw a great many people hiding from the lion in terror. Some didn't move. Then the lion sprang upon them, seized one of them and crushed him with its teeth, quickly silencing his agonized cries. Immediately the other people fell down and begged to be spared. The lion enjoyed this homage from the men and women in triumph. Then it noticed a group of people who were not all on their knees. It attacked them with rage. Two of them attempted to flee as it approached. But they were caught and killed. Then it had attained its purpose. All were on their knees before it. The lion reared up and roared: 'I'm not a monster! I'm not a monster. I make peace! Peace on earth.' And then it vanished.

Again I was standing by the raging sea. A new monster emerged from the breaking surf. A broad-shouldered bear came out of the water. It approached the people and separated them into two groups. One group was given whips and the other was fettered. Those with whips began to drive the other people to work. Again and again some of those with fetters collapsed from exhaustion. The bear immediately leapt up and devoured them. Others succeeded in loosening their fetters. They tried to slip away unnoticed but with swift strides the bear fell upon them and killed them. Sometimes the two groups of people joined forces, threw the whips away and tried to escape, but the bear was quicker: with angry gestures it attacked the group and massacred those in it. Then it reared up and growled: 'I'm creating order! I'm creating order!'

Yet again I was standing by the raging sea. The waves sprayed up so high that they seemed to want to flood heaven. A new monster was born from them. An eagle emerged from the sea. In its claws it held a round sphere. On it was a cross with hooks bent upwards. It spread its wings and overshadowed the whole land. People ran in panic. Shrieking they sought refuge in caves and holes. But not all found protection. Some attempted to join those who had already found shelter but they were violently repulsed. No one wanted to take them in. So they wandered helpless up and down in the open air: women, children, men, old people. Only rarely did someone take one of them in and provide shelter. All the time the eagle kept hovering threateningly over the scurrying people until they were out of their minds with worry. Then he dropped his sphere. A loud explosion resounded over the plain. Black smoke obscured the sky. There was a stench of foulness and blood. When the smoke cleared, the plain was full of bodies and bones. The eagle crowed, 'I'm making space. Space for life, life on this earth.' Then he faded away to nothing.

However, the terror was not yet at an end. The sea raged and continued to break over the land. Its thunder continued. New monsters emerged on the shore. This time they were two giant octopuses which settled side by side and with long grasping tentacles sought to span the whole world. At the ends of each tentacle were two holes, one large, one small, supervised by overseers. Forced by these overseers, people got money and put it in the large holes. The octopuses devoured it eagerly. A little money rolled back for the overseers through the small holes. In return they drove the others with whips in order to satisfy the octopuses. A great many people were hungry, many were sick, many naked, many wandered around lost. With the courage of despair, those who were maltreated sometimes attacked their guards. Then the octopuses provided the overseers with swords and spears for them to remedy the situation. Many of the rebels were put in prison, and many were murdered. And the tentacles were again supplied. Now and then one group of guards would be replaced by another. Then one of the octopuses would withdraw a tentacle so that the other could put a tentacle in the gap that had been left. Next the octopuses drew themselves up against each other and made threatening gestures. They caused many little monsters to emerge from the sea. First of all long tubular mouths emerged, then round heads which slowly turned to and fro on clumsy backs. These were dragons or giant tortoises which crept on to the land. They took up position in two groups. Each time one side was reinforced by a new giant tortoise, the other was, too. Monsters clad in more and more armour confronted one another; they breathed fire. A red flame emerged from every tube. The fire threatened to consume the earth. The people who so far had hidden behind the armed monsters were thrown into a panic. They fled headlong in all directions. I expected a great catastrophe.

Then darkness suddenly obscured my gaze. For a moment I could see neither sea nor land, stars nor moon, trees nor shrubs. The human lamentation had fallen silent and the beasts had disappeared. A light from the land appeared in the sky. A figure with a human form became visible. It emanated a warm light. In this light one could once again see the maltreated earth. I saw the beasts from the abyss. They were dead. The octopuses had drawn in their tentacles and collapsed. The armoured monsters had been scrapped. Everywhere people were getting up, breathing again. They looked expectantly at the figure from heaven. I could not yet recognize it, but it seemed familiar. Suddenly it came to me. This was the man of whom I had dreamed in Pilate's cells. The one who had once freed me in a dream from the claws of the beast. And it seemed that scales fell from my eyes as I heard his voice:

Blessed are the peacemakers,
for they shall be called sons of God.
Come, O blessed of my Father,
inherit the kingdom prepared for you
from the foundations of the world,
for I was hungry and you gave me food,
I was thirsty and you gave me drink,
I was a stranger and you welcomed me,
I was naked and you clothed me,
I was sick and you visited me,
I was in prison and you came to me.[8]

It was Jesus, a changed Jesus. I had only seen him once – from the city wall of Jerusalem. At that time he was hanging dead on the cross, but now he radiated life, peace and freedom. The rule of the beasts was at an end. I woke up, happy but confused.

I got up from my bed, went out into the open air and looked at the sea from the upper story of our house. Behind a white strip of sand increasingly deep darkness spread westwards, that darkness from which my confused dreams had arisen. Now it lay calm and still. No monster was creeping to land. No storm was disturbing the surface of the sea. No thunder burst against the shore. Something else happened. From the land the light grew more intense. Where sky and sea had merged, pale strips appeared on the horizon, coloured shadows met the invisible sun in the east. Rays broke out from the depths of the land. Then the sun appeared over the hills and covered the sea with glowing light.

The city shyly reflected the first brightness. The buildings emerged increasingly clearly from the shadow of the streets. Temple and synagogue, the houses of Jews and Gentiles, all were bathed in the dawning light. The sun arose on good and evil, just and unjust. I felt it, bright and warm.

The chaotic monsters of the night had been overcome. My anguish at the harshness of life was over. In me the rule of the beasts had come to an end. The true man had appeared to me. And I had recognized the features of Jesus in him. He had given me back the earth. It had not got better since the previous day. Today, as yesterday, the struggle for a chance to live would continue. But that wasn't everything. This battle need not dominate all my action and thought. I made a new covenant with life.

I could clearly feel a voice coming to me from all things, a voice which offered me this covenant with life. Never again would I wish the earth away, never again deny life. Never again would I allow myself to be overcome by beasts from the abyss. I heard the voice, and it was one with the voice of Jesus. I had the certainty that wherever I went it would always accompany me. I could not escape it anywhere. And I responded and prayed:

> God,
> *you have searched me and know me.*
> *You know when I sit down and when I rise up;*
> *and know all my thoughts from afar.*
> *Whether I am active or resting, you know me;*
> *you are acquainted with all my ways.*
> *Even before a word is on my tongue,*
> *O God, you know it altogether.*
> *You enfold me on all sides*
> *and lay your hand upon me.*
> *Such knowledge is too wonderful for me,*
> *it is too high, I cannot attain it.*
> *Where could I flee from your spirit*
> *Or where could I escape your presence?*
> *If I ascend into heaven, you are there,*
> *if I make my bed in the underworld, you are there also.*
> *If I take the wings of the morning,*
> *and dwell in the uppermost parts of the sea,*
> *even there your hand shall lead me,*
> *and your right hand shall hold me.*
> *If I say, Let darkness cover me,*
> *and the light about me be night,*
> *even the darkness is not dark with you;*
> *the night is as bright as the day.*
> *For darkness is as light with you.*
> *For you formed my inward parts,*

you knitted me together in my mother's womb.
I praise you, for you are fearful and wonderful.
Wonderful are your works.[9]

For a long time I stood like this on our house and let the dream of the man echo in me. The rule of the beasts could not last for ever. Some time the man had to appear, the true man. And everyone would recognize in him the features of Jesus.

Then I went to the downstairs room and woke Baruch. We ate breakfast, shared the bread, drank from the same cup and rejoiced at being together.

In Place of an Epilogue

Dear Dr Kratzinger,

Now that the book is finished you ask whether I can give you a brief book list. You're curious about the academic literature on which my picture of Jesus and his time is based. I shall mention only the most important titles.

In my view the best account of Jesus is still that by Günther Bornkamm, Jesus of Nazareth *[Hodder and Harper and Row 1960]. I also found E.P. Sanders,* Jesus and Judaism *[SCM Press and Fortress Press 1985] very important. I've learned a great deal from it. Benedict Otzen,* Den antike jødendom *[Kopenhagen 1984], is a good summary account of ancient Judaism which combines religious and social history. The writings of Martin Hengel are indispensable for the history of Palestine at the time. I'm thinking particularly of his book* Die Zeloten *[E.J.Brill 1961,[2] 1976], and his big book on* Judaism and Hellenism *[SCM Press and Fortress Press 1974]. It will certainly not have escaped you that many insights from my own works on the social history of the Jesus movement and early Christianity have found a place in this book – just as I have learned a great deal from the researches in social history by my colleagues, male and female.*

I also have to thank the many people who have read and criticized the first outlines of this book on Jesus: Daniel Burchard, Gerhard and Ulrike Rau, Elisabeth and Katharina Seebass, Gunnar and Oliver Theissen and above all my wife. Wega Schmidt Thomee typed the manuscript many times and made critical comments on it. David Trobisch offered many valuable suggestions for improvement in style and content.

Of course I also have to thank you, Dr Kratzinger. While I've been writing this book you have constantly held my narrative fantasy in check with your strict scientific attitude. You have relentlessly insisted that I should not confuse the historical with the fictional, poetry with truth. So you will probably be pleased if to end with I tell the reader that you too are a figment of my imagination – and a good example of the way in which fictitious figures can embody the truth!

So good-bye!
Yours,
Gerd Theissen

Appendix:

The Most Important Sources on Jesus and his Time

1. The Gospels and their sources

(*a*) The Gospel of Mark is the oldest Gospel. It served as a basis for Matthew and Luke. It was written after the beginning or shortly after the end of the Jewish War (AD 66–70), since 13.1ff. combines a prophecy of the destruction of the temple with prophecies about events in the war. There is dispute as to where it was written. The early church tradition holds that it was produced in Rome, but in my view it comes from Syria, in fact from the same kind of Christianity as that on which Paul is dependent. Like Paul it puts forward the view that all food is clean (7.18ff.), quotes comparable words of institution at the Last Supper to his (14.22–24), and like Paul describes the message of Jesus as *euaggelion*, 1.1 – clearly taking over pre-existing terminology. However, it is theologically independent of Paul. It will come from communities in which John Mark had such a high reputation that a gospel could be attributed to him, even though he was not an apostle. John Mark was particularly active in the East (cf. Acts 12.12; 12.25; 13.5) and belongs with Barnabas to that kind of Christianity within which Paul began but from which he parted company (cf. Acts 15.37; Gal.2.11ff.). The community to which the Gospel of Mark is addressed must have had a large number of Gentile Christians in it: Jewish customs are explained (7.3), and a Gentile centurion is the first to confess the 'Son of God' (15.39).

(*b*) The Logia source (= sayings source, abbreviated as Q = German *Quelle*, source) has been reconstructed from the Gospels of

Matthew and Luke. In addition to the material from Mark that they have in common these two Gospels contain series of words of Jesus which agree so strikingly in what they say and the order in which this is put that we have to assume that there is a common written model or a common oral tradition which has taken an improbably fixed form. I think that the former alternative is more likely. As the linguistic background of the sayings is Aramaic, the source may have originated in Aramaic-speaking Syria or Palestine. It reflects a time when Christianity had yet to detach itself from Judaism. All the sayings can be understood as addressed to Israel. This collection of sayings of Jesus came into being before the Jewish War. The coming of Jesus as Son of man is expected in a peaceful world (Luke 17.26). Instead of the temple being destroyed, the prophecy is that it will 'be forsaken' by God (Luke 13.35f.; Matt. 23.7ff.). On the other hand the temptation narrative – the only narrative in Q other than that of the centurion of Capernaum – presupposes the self-deification of Gaius Caligula (AD 37–41): he is the ungodly ruler of the world who requires obeisance. The Logia source may have come into being between 40 and 65. As the Gentile mission officially recognized by the Apostolic Council between about 46 and 48 is not yet in prospect, it would be possible to date the source to the beginning of that period.

(c) The Gospel of Matthew was quite definitely written in Syria. It has Jesus' fame extending as far as 'Syria' (4.24). The author seems to be looking at Palestine from the (north-)east: for him Judaea is 'beyond the Jordan' (19.1). The temple has been destroyed, as is shown by the Matthaean insertion into the parable of the great supper in 22.7. The Gospel was written after Mark, but must have been in use in Antioch (in Syria) around 110: Bishop Ignatius of Antioch quotes from it. So it may have been written between 80 and 100. The evangelist is writing for a community with a Jewish-Christian tradition. Some passages that are not in Mark or Q (the 'special material') have a Jewish-Christian stamp. Matthew 5.17–19 asserts that the Torah will always be valid. These Jewish-Christian communities had become open to the Gentile mission without taking Paul's course of criticizing the Torah. This openness to the Gentiles is reflected in the structure of the book: Jesus rejects the mission to the Gentiles in his lifetime (10.6), but after the resurrection he sends the disciples to all nations (Matt. 28.18ff.). The apostle Matthew can hardly be the author. He would have had to have been very old. It is probable that only when there were several Gospels were they attributed to different authors in order to distinguish them. In the circles in which that happened the Gospel of Matthew was the most popular of the Synoptic Gospels (Matthew, Mark, Luke). Only this Gospel – and that of John – was attributed to an apostle.

(*d*) The Gospel of Luke hardly comes from the East. For the author the hot desert wind is not in the east wind, as it is in Palestine, but the south wind – as in all Mediterranean countries west of Palestine (cf. Luke 12.55). The author was probably much travelled. A travel narrative in Acts written in the first person plural begins in Asia Minor (16.11ff.) and leads via Jerusalem to Rome. He has an amazingly good knowledge of the temple. He may once have visited Jerusalem, coming from Caesarea (and crossing Samaria). That would explain his positive attitude to the Samaritans (cf. 9.51ff.; 10.30ff.; 17.11ff.). In view of his picture of Paul it is hard to imagine that he was one of Paul's companions, but that cannot be ruled out completely. There is a dispute as to when the Gospel was written. It is certainly aware of the destruction of Jerusalem. That is prophesied in more detail in Luke 21.20–24 than in any other Gospel. The author is deeply moved by the fate of the city: Jesus weeps over Jerusalem (19.41) and calls on the women of Jerusalem to bewail their own fate (23.27ff.). This indicates a time not too far from AD 70. It will have been written around the same time as the Gospel of Matthew (80–110). Whereas the Gospel of Matthew represents a Jewish Christianity which is open to the Gentiles, the Gospel of Luke is a writing for Gentile-Christian communities to remind them of their Jewish origin.

(*e*) The pre-Synoptic traditions (the first three Gospels are called Synoptic). Luke 1.1–3 and Bishop Papias from Asia Minor (beginning of the second century) bear witness to the existence of oral tradition about Jesus. The Gospels fixed this oral tradition in writing where they did not resort to written sources (Mark; Q). The age, origin and interests of each of these traditions have to be investigated. Here are some arguments indicating why we cannot deny the Jesus traditions a historical background.

(i) The locality of the Jesus traditions. Many traditions about Jesus have the stamp of a Palestinian setting. Here are some examples of a local Palestinian colouring. Only someone who knows that the Jordan flows directly through the wilderness can talk of a 'Baptist in the wilderness' (Mark 1.5). Otherwise it is hard to see how one could baptize in the wilderness! The story of the Syro-Phoenician woman presupposes knowledge of conditions in the border territory between Galilee and Tyre. The abrupt saying about 'the dogs' (= Gentiles) to whom one should not throw 'the children's' (= Jews) bread becomes comprehensible once we know that the Jews of Galilee provided the bread for rich Tyre.

(ii) The dating of the Jesus traditions. Many traditions about Jesus can be dated back before the earliest written sources to which we can gain access. The saying about the 'reed in the wind' (Matt. 11.7) may presuppose a coin minted by Herod Antipas in AD 19/20, which he never minted again. The Marcan passion narrative presupposes an audience with precise knowledge: who were Alexander and Rufus (Mark 15.21)? What were the family circumstances of the second Mary mentioned in Mark 15.40? Is she thought to be the mother of James and Joses? Or just the mother of James? What was 'the' insurrection in which Barabbas was taken prisoner (Mark 15.6)?

(iii) The sayings of Jesus were partly handed down by itinerant missionaries and preachers who continued Jesus' style of having no home. They have preserved for us the spirit of the radical commands of Jesus: only itinerant preachers, like Jesus without a home, possessions or family, could credibly put them forward and hand them on without having to adapt them to the needs of a 'bourgeois' life. On the other hand the needs of the local communities left far less mark on the sayings of Jesus than one might assume. Nowhere are local authorities (presbyters, episcopi and deacons) legitimated by a saying of Jesus. Nowhere does a saying of the earthly Jesus call for baptism as an initiation rite before entering the community. Nowhere is circumcision rejected as a condition of entry for Gentiles.

(iv) The inner coherence of the Jesus tradition! We may assume that the Jesus traditions from Q and Mark, from the special material in Matthew and Luke, and from the Gospel of Thomas came down through different channels of tradition. Nevertheless they present a uniform picture. That also goes for the form of Jesus' sayings. Since within any synoptic form of sayings of Jesus we can usually demonstrate that one or more saying is 'authentic', we are quite certain that Jesus used the forms that are contained in the sayings tradition, in other words that he used admonitions, proverbs, beatitudes, woes, parables and so on. Nowhere else is there this combination of wisdom sayings, poetry and prophecy. It is distinctive and produces a coherent whole.

(*f*) The Gospel of John differs so markedly from the other three Gospels, not only in the style of Jesus' sayings but also in its account, that here we would seem not to have a picture of Jesus as it was regularly handed down, but the strongly stylized portrait of a special group. Knowledge of Synoptic narratives is presupposed (e.g. the arrest of John the Baptist, 3.24, or the calling of the Twelve, 6.70); possibly even whole Gospels (Luke?). The group speaking as 'we' whom we meet at the beginning and end of the Gospel (1.14ff.; 21.24) want to give the community a deeper understanding of Jesus: he is seen as the pre-existent ambassador who comes from the Father and returns to him. The Gospel of John was written at the end of the first century. It was already known in Egypt in the first half of the second century, as a papyrus (P52) shows. The death of Peter (AD 64) is presupposed (cf.21.18f.) Peter was long survived by a 'disciple' of whom rumour had it that he would not die before Jesus returned. But he, too, died (21.20–23). All this indicates the end of the first century. It is hard to determine where the Gospel was written: early church tradition mentions Ephesus. But it is hardly conceivable that in this port the tiny Galilean lake could be described as a 'sea' (John 6.16ff.). Therefore many scholars suggest Syria as the place of origin. Because the message is received positively in Samaria, there could be a connection with the Samaritan mission. But that belongs in the prehistory of the Gospel.

2. *Josephus*

Josephus is the most important source for the history of Palestine in the time of Jesus. He was born in Jerusalem in 37/38, was in Rome between 64 and 66, and on his return led the Jewish revolt in northern

Palestine as military governor of Galilee, being taken prisoner by the Romans in 67. He was spared, since he prophesied that the Roman general Vespasian would become emperor. When Vespasian really did become emperor, Josephus was given his freedom. His important works are:

(*a*) *De bello Judaico (BJ)*, 'The Jewish War', a history of the Jewish revolt between AD 66 and 73, first published in 73; this also contains an account of Jewish history from the second century BC. The book is meant to demonstrate that there is no point in opposing Roman rule over the world. In the Jewish war Josephus mentions Pilate, but not Jesus. The silence about Jesus and the Christians is understandable. It was AD 66 before the Christians were accused of arson in Rome. Moreover Josephus tends to keep quiet about the messianic movements in Palestine.

(*b*) The *Antiquitates Judaicarum* (= *Antt.*), 'Jewish Antiquities', are a history of the Jews which was written in the nineties; it begins with creation and ends with the Jewish war. A section on Jesus (*Antt.* 18,63f.) has either been inserted by Christian copyists of Josephus or (more probably) revised by Christians. In *Antt.* 20,200 Josephus mentions 'James, the brother of Jesus who is called Christ', who was executed in Jerusalem in AD 62. This mention of Jesus is completely above suspicion and all the more reliable since as an inhabitant of Jerusalem Josephus can give trustworthy evidence about the execution of James.

(*c*) The *Vita* or 'Life of Josephus' contains no more than a brief outline of Josephus' youth and is particularly concerned with describing his activity as military governor of Judaea during the Jewish war. In it he defends himself against charges laid against him. The work is particularly interesting because it gives us a first-hand account of Galilee in the first century AD. Granted, this information comes from a time forty years after the death of Jesus. But the conditions generally will also have applied in the time of Jesus.

(*d*) *Contra Apionem* (Against Apion) defends Judaism against attacks made by a writer of that name.

The historical value of Josephus as a source varies depending on what sources he himself had at his disposal. Where he was an eyewitness and contemporary he often reports at first hand. Much of his information has been confirmed by excavations (e.g. at Masada). For the periods before his own he of course depends on sources. The *Antiquities* in particular contain valuable accounts of conflicts in Pilate's day which fit well with other sources about Pilate (Philo, the New Testament, coins and an inscription). But we must remember that Josephus is always strongly pro-Roman (more so in the Jewish War than in the *Antiquities*). As Josephus tells an exciting story, he is worth reading. His works are the best commentary on the Synoptic Gospels.

3. Philo

Philo was a well-educated Jewish theologian and philosopher who lived in Alexandria from about 15/10 BC to around AD 40. He wrote perceptive interpretations of the Old Testament in which he read the philosophical insights of antiquity into the Bible. But he was also active as a politician. He led a delegation of Alexandrian Jews to the emperor Gaius Caligula in AD 40 to counter outbursts of antisemitism in Alexandria. He wrote an extremely interesting work about this delegation, the *Legatio ad Gaium* (Delegation to Gaius). We are indebted to Philo not only for information about the Essenes but also for an important note about Pilate. He does not mention Jesus, but he does mention unjust executions under Pilate (among which he would certainly have included the execution of Jesus had he known about it). His silence about Jesus does not mean much; he is also silent, for instance, about John the Baptist.

4. The Qumran writings

In 1947 ancient scrolls were found in caves by the Dead Sea which come from a settlement at Qumran that was later excavated. This was settlement of so-called 'Essenes' (probably = 'Pious'), who formed monastic community there in the wilderness. The writings are referred to by the number of the cave in which they were found, the letter Q (= Qumran) and the initial of the title.

(*a*) 1QS is the Rule of the Qumran community, found in Cave 1; it contains strict regulations about admission to the community and various punishments, going as far as expulsion. The Qumran community regarded itself as the temple of God. They wanted to be as holy as if they were constantly in the temple in immediate proximity to God.

(*b*) 1QM (from *milhamah* = war) is the War Scroll, also found in Cave 1. It describes the dream of a great war in which the Qumran people fight against the Romans and Satan, supported by God and his angels.

(*c*) CD (= Cairo Documents) is the term used for the so-called Damascus Document which had already been found in a Cairo synagogue before the discoveries at Qumran. In particular it contains rules of life for Essenes who were not living at Qumran and therefore were not subject to such strict regulations.

(*d*) 1QpHab is a commentary on the book of the prophet Habakkuk (p stands for *pesher* = commentary) found in Cave 1. From the Habakkuk commentary we learn something about the Teacher of Righteousness who founded the Qumran community in the second century BC.

Nowhere do the Qumran writings mention Jesus and the Christians; nor do they mention e.g. Herod and his sons or Pilate. But they are important for research into Jesus in providing a contrast to his preaching. Like Qumran, Jesus intensifies some Jewish commandments, but he combines this intensification with a message about the grace of God which is particularly directed towards sinners. By contrast, in the Qumran writings we find consistently strict regulations.

5. Tacitus

The Roman historian Tacitus was born about 55/56 and lived into the second century. In his *Histories* he too reports the Jewish revolt. His general observations about the Jews are very important for an assessment of Jews in the first century. In the *Annals* he mentions the 'Christiani' in connection with the burning of Rome in AD 66. 'The man from whom this name is derived, Christus, was executed during the reign of Tiberius on the orders of the procurator Pontius Pilate; suppressed for the moment, the pernicious superstition broke out again, not only in Judaea, the place where this evil originated, but also in Rome, where all the filth and abominations from all over the world come together and are fashionable' *(Annals* XV,44,3).

Notes

1. The Interrogation

1. Cf. Josephus, *De Bello Judaico* (The Jewish War = *BJ*), 2,175–7 (II,9,4): 'After this he (= Pilate) stirred up further trouble by expending the sacred treasure known as Corban on an aqueduct . . . This roused the populace to fury, and when Pilate visited Jerusalem they surrounded the tribunal and shouted him down. But he had foreseen the disturbance, and had made the soldiers mix with the mob, wearing civilian clothing over their armour, and with orders not to draw their swords but to use clubs on the obstreperous. He now gave the signal from the tribunal and the Jews were cudgelled, so that many died from the blows, and many were trampled to death by their friends as they fled. The fate of those who perished horrified the crowd into silence.'

2. Josephus reports riots in Caesarea shortly before the outbreak of the Jewish war, i.e. in AD 66 (*BJ* 2,284–292 = II,14,4ff.). This city had certainly been founded by Herod, a Jew, but he had had it endowed with pagan temples from which the non-Jews derived a claim to the city. There is already evidence of a struggle over civil rights in the fifties (cf. *BJ* 2,266–70 = II,13,7), but it may have much older roots.

3. For the rebellion in Sepphoris cf. Josephus, *BJ* 2.56 (II,4,1); for the destruction of the city and the enslaving of its inhabitants by Quintilius Varus cf. *BF* 2,68 (II,5,1).

4. In contrast to almost all of Galilee Sepphoris was pro-Roman in the Jewish war; cf. Josephus, *Vita* 346 (= 65).

5. The coins minted to mark the foundation of Tiberias do indeed have reeds on them as an emblem of Herod Antipas.

6. The animal statues in the palace of Herod Antipas were destroyed by rebels at the beginning of the Jewish war. They were a public scandal:

Josephus had been ordered by Jerusalem to remove them. When he got to Tiberias other rebel groups had already been there before him (Josephus, *Vita* 65f. = 12).

7. There are several variants on this antisemitic version of the exodus of the Israelites from Egypt. The one given above is a free paraphrase of Tacitus, *Histories* V.3.

8. These words (*pacique imponere morem, parcere subiectis et debellare superbos*) are used by the Roman poet Virgil (70–19 BC) to describe the historical mission of the Roman empire (*Aeneid* VI, 852f.).

9. In fact the shadow of war often lay over the land: when in AD 40 the emperor Gaius Caligula wanted to set up a statue of himself in the temple, many Jews took up arms. Only the sudden death of the emperor in January 41 prevented a war. In AD 66 a great revolt broke out. After the initial successes of the rebels against the Syrian legate Cestius Gallus, this revolt was put down in two great campaigns under Vespasian and Titus. Jerusalem was captured in AD 70 and in AD 73 (or 74) Masada, the last bastion of the rebels, fell. Josephus took part in this war first as a Jewish general on the rebel side and after his capture by the Romans on the Roman side; he wrote about it in his *magnum opus, De Bello Judaico*.

2. Blackmail

1. The prayer takes up themes from Psalm 26.

2. An inscription of Pilate's found in Caesarea shows that he had the rank of 'prefect' and not procurator. We often find representatives of the *equites* (literally 'knights') in both ranks. The *eques* was a citizen who had a capital of 400,000 sesterces. Above the *equites* came the senators with a minimum capital of a million sesterces. These figures hold for the first century AD.

3. Gymnasia are Greek schools. They could be found in all the Hellenistic cities of Palestine. Herod the Great himself had the gymnasium in Ptolemas built *(BJ* 1,422 = I,21,11). That there was a gymnasium in Sepphoris is guesswork. But this city later had a theatre, another institution closely associated with Greek education. There were certainly already Torah schools in Judaism at that time. The high priest Jesus, son of Gamaliel, probably carried out a reform of Jewish schools in about 63 to 65.

4. Josephus himself can serve as an example of how the sons of well-to-do families retreated into the wilderness for religious studies. In his 'biography' he tells how as a result of dissatisfaction with his study of the various religious trends in Judaism he spent three years with a desert hermit called Bannus who fed on wild plants and performed frequent religious ablutions (probably in the Jordan, *Vita* 11f. = 2).

5. In tractate Shekalim (= On the temple tax) in the Babylonian Talmud the water supply is explicitly included among the works which are to be paid for from the temple tax (cf. Shekalim IV,2).

6. The last two sentences are a literal quotation from the work 'On Anger' by the Roman philosopher Seneca (*c*.4 BC – AD 65), II, 34,4.

7. Judas Maccabaeus, the leader of the revolt against the Syrians, made a defensive alliance with the Romans in 161 BC (I Macc.8, Josephus, *Antiquities* 12,414–19 = XII, 10, 6), which was later renewed under Simon (*c*. 139 BC: I Macc.14.16ff.; 15.15ff.).

8. The successors to the Maccabees, especially Alexander Jannaeus (103–76 BC), had conquered the neighbouring non-Jewish cities in Judaea (and Galilee). A dispute between Aristobulus II and Hyrcanus II over the succession to the throne in 63 gave the Romans under Pompey a welcome opportunity to bring the small Jewish kingdom under their control and to 'liberate' the non-Jewish cities of Judaea.

9. This is the view of things put forward by Josephus (after the Jews had lost the war of AD 66–70). He attributes it to Herod Antipas II in a long speech to the rebel leaders at the beginning of the Jewish war (cf. *BJ* 2,345–401 = II,16,4).

10. The quotation comes from Philo, *Legatio ad Gaium* (= The Delegation to Gaius), 302. Philo was a contemporary of Jesus who lived in Alexandria.

11. Philo describes this episode and the protests in *Legatio ad Gaium* 299–305.

12. Pilate was the first prefect of Judaea who dared to use pagan symbols on his coins: the augurs' staff and a libation vessel. The prefects before and after him carefully avoided hurting the religious feelings of the Jews with pagan emblems, which were associated with idolatry.

13. Cf. the illustrations in A.Ben-David, *Jerusalem und Tyros*, 1969.

14. Following themes from Ps.12.

3. Andreas' Decision

1. Stoic philosophy was widespread among the educated upper classes of the Roman empire. It taught self-control and doing one's duty. Suicide was regarded as a legitimate option and was indeed recommended as an escape from a hopeless situation. There was also similar thinking among the Jews: the Jews besieged in the fortress of Masada during the Jewish war killed one another in their hopeless situation in AD 73 (or 74) so as not to fall alive into the hands of the Romans. According to Josephus *(BJ* 7,400 = VII,9,2), 960 men, women and children met their end at that time.

2. Such a train of thought can be found in the Wisdom of Solomon, 13.6–9, a work which can be dated back to the second or first century BC. It comes from the Jewish diaspora, perhaps from Egypt.

3. In fact in the first centuries AD Judaism developed a flourishing art in which the radical prohibition against images was disregarded. The frescoes in the synagogue of Dura Europos on the Euphrates are a high-point.

4. This takes up themes from the Sibylline Oracles III, 767–95, a Jewish section in this book of oracles which was widely circulated in antiquity. Like the whole of the third book in this collection it was probably written in the second century BC. The themes in this prophecy go back to Isa. 11.1ff.

5. Here Barabbas represents the 'philosophy' of Judas of Galilee, whose rebellion against the Romans dragged down Sepphoris with it. Josephus gives an account of him in his *Antiquities* (= *Antt)* XVIII.1ff. and *BJ* 2,117ff. = II,8,l. The following statement is typical: 'The deity would only contribute to the success of this plan (the achievement of freedom) if human beings themselves played an active part in it' *(Antt.* 18.5 = XVIII, 1,1).

6. Cf. Gen.12.10–20.

7. Cf. Gen.27.

8. Cf. I Sam.27.

9. Cf. Dan.7.

4. The Commission

1. Following themes from Ps.19.

2. The description of the Essene settlement by the Dead Sea comes from Pliny the Elder, *Natural History* V, 73. Excavations by the Dead Sea (at Qumran) have brought the Essene settlement to light. In addition numerous Essene writings have been found in neighbouring caves, so that we have good information about this community in the wilderness.

3. Cf. Philo, *Quod omnis probus liber sit* (= On the Freedom of the Virtuous), 75–87: 'One cannot find among them anyone who makes arrows, spears, daggers, helmets, breastplates or shields, nor any armourer, builder of machines of war, nor any other person who makes things that are used in war' (78). 'There are no slaves at all among them, but all are free and serve one another. They look with scorn on masters who have slaves, not only as being unjust because they violate equality but also as being godless because they destroy the ordinance of nature which gave birth to all in the same way and fed them as a mother and made them real brothers, not only in name but in fact' (79). This is one of the few passages in antiquity in which slavery is clearly rejected as being unjust.

4. Cf. Josephus, *BJ* 2,141 = II,8,7.

5. In contrast to the Essenes by the Dead Sea (in Qumran), who lived a celibate life, there were also Essenes living scattered through the country who married (cf. *BJ* 2, 160,161 = II,8,13).

6. The high priest expelled from office is the so-called 'Teacher of Righteousness' who, according to the writings of the Essenes found at Qumran, had founded the Essene community and given it its normative form. A wicked priest appears in the Qumran writings as his counterpart; he is certainly to be identified with one of the Jewish high priests. The only dispute is over which high priest it was. It may have been Jonathan, who became high priest in 152 BC, or perhaps his successor Simon (143–135 BC).

7. Cf. Josephus, *Antt.* 15,373–4 = XV,10,5.

8. Cf. Luke 23.12.

9. In the *Legatio ad Gaium*, 299–305, Philo describes the attempts to put up shields in the Antonia fortress, without pictures, but with a dedication to the emperor.

10. This is taken almost word for word from Josephus, *Antt.* 18,117 = XVIII,5,2. Josephus describes John the Baptist in such a way that the Greek and Roman readers of his work can understand him.

11. Josephus gives this reason for the arrest and execution of John the Baptist (cf. *Antt.* 18,118 = XVIII,5,2).

12. Thus Tacitus, *Histories* V,5,1f. The charge of 'being haters of the human race' also occurs elsewhere. It even appears in connection with the Jew Paul, who connects this antisemitic prejudice with his own people (cf. I Thess. 2.15).

13. Hecataeus of Abdera (*c.* 300 BC), who has a positive attitude towards the Jews, also derives their 'unsociable way of life which does not welcome strangers' from their expulsion from Egypt (in Diodore XL,3,4).

14. Lev.19.33f.; cf. Deut.10.18f.

15. This version appears in the *Geographica* (XVI, 2,35ff.) of Strabo of Amaseia (born 64/63 BC).

16. The argument that the philosophers had true knowledge of God but, unlike Moses, did not have the courage to draw consequences from it, can be found in Josephus, *c. Apionem* 2,168–171 = II,16.

17. The Aristotelian Theophrast (372–288/7 BC) sees the Jews as a 'race of philosophers' (in Porphyry, *De abstinentia* II,16). But for the Jewish writer Aristobulus (second century BC), too, Jews are a 'philosophical school' (in Eusebius, *Praeparatio Evangelica* XIII, 12,8).

5. The Wilderness Community

1. A pottery workshop and a scriptorium have been found at Qumran. Presumably the community sold manuscripts of the Bible. Salt and asphalt had long been got from the Dead Sea. And they certainly practised agriculture.

2. According to Josephus, *BJ* 2,137ff. = II,8,7, a new member first had to follow their life-style for a year outside the community (probably in the wilderness); he was then admitted as a probationer for two years. Only after three years was he admitted to all the life of the community as a full member.

3. Josephus writes about the Essenes: 'Men convicted of major offences are expelled from the order, and the outcast often comes to a most miserable end; for bound as he is by oaths and customs, he cannot share the diet of non-members, so is forced to eat grass till his starved body wastes away and he dies. Charity compels them to take many offenders back when at their last gasp, since they feel that men

tortured to the point of death have paid a sufficient penalty for their offences' (*BJ* 2,143–4 = II,8,8).

4. Cf. Josephus, *BJ* 2,141 = II,8,7.

5. Josephus says of Bannus *(Vita* 11) that he fed on what grows 'of itself'. The food of John the Baptist should also be compared with this (Mark 1.6).

6. Cf. 1QS 1.9–11: according to this the Essenes are enjoined 'to love all the sons of light, each according to his lot in the divine council, but to hate all sons of darkness, each according to his guilt in God's vengeance'.

7. In fact three copper plates, the so-called Copper Scroll, were found in one of the Qumran caves (= 3Q 15). This contains information in Hebrew writing about the size and location of hidden treasure. No one has yet found it. Either this is Essene or temple treasure, or imaginary treasure which never existed.

8. These rules for punishment come from the 'Community Rule' (= 1QS; cf. 1QS VI,24–VII,25).

9. The last paragraph paraphrases Philo, 'On the Freedom of the Virtuous', 79. The Essenes in fact got the reputation of also rejecting the most inhuman form of possession, that of other human beings. This point has no place in the writings found at Qumran; there was no slavery in the desert community itself.

10. The songs of praise (Hodayot, hence the abbreviation 1QH) found at Qumran contain marvellous religious poetry in the style of Old Testament psalms. Some of these songs go back to the 'Teacher of Righteousness'. The text is a free paraphrase of 1QH III, 19ff.

11. Josephus describes these Essene meals in *BJ* 2,129–133 = II,8,5. The future meal with the Messiah is described in the 'Community Rule' (1QSa II,11–21).

12. The reasons for the solar calendar appear in the 'astronomical book' of I Enoch (I Enoch 72–82), which was also found in Qumran. However, the book (and other writings which presuppose the solar calendar) was also circulated outside Qumran.

13. According to Josephus (*BJ* 2,142 = II,8,7) the Essenes had to swear 'not to commit any robbery'. According to *BJ* 2,125 (= II,8,5) they took nothing with them on their journeys 'but weapons as a protection against robbers', as they could expect to be welcomed everywhere by other Essenes.

14. These marriage laws appear in the 'Damascus Document', CD IV.20–V.2, V.7–11.

15. The description of the eschatological struggle appears on one of the writings found in the caves of Qumran, the so-called 'War Scroll' (= 1QM).

6. Analysis of a Murder

1. Leviticus 18.16 reads: 'You shall not uncover the nakedness of your brother's wife; she is your brother's nakedness.' In her first marriage Herodias had been married to a son of Herod called Herod.

2. In Mark 6.17–29 we can read the result of this 'court gossip' which then went on to reach ordinary people and was further elaborated: this is roughly how ordinary people in Palestine saw the events which led to the death of John the Baptist. Josephus is probably nearer to the truth when he gives as the real reason Herod Antipas' fear of a rebellion (Josephus, *Antt.*18,118 = XVIII,5,2).

3. King Herod had a winter palace built in Jericho; it has been excavated.

4. All the mosaics in the Herodian palaces have only plants as motives. Herod clearly observed the prohibition against images in his palaces. It is a historical fact that Herod had walls painted to look like real marble; this can easily be seen by anyone who visits Masada by the Dead Sea (one of his fortified refuges).

5. The list of this food follows Pliny the Younger (*Letters* I, 15).

6. Cups with this inscription are known from Syria in the first century AD. Cf. A.Deissman, *Light from the Ancient East*, Hodder and Stoughton 1927, 129.

7. Ecclesiastes 9.7.

8. According to Josephus (*Antt.*13,293 = XIII,10,6) the Sadducees had a following among the well-to-do. They did not believe in fate (*Antt.*13.173 = XIII,5,8) nor in survival after death (*BJ* 2,165 = II,8,14; cf. Mark 12.18–27: Acts 23.8) and recognized only the five books of Moses as holy scripture.

9. Cf. Luke 13.1ff.

10. Herodias acted like other wives of the Herods; Salome, the sister of Herod I, and Drusilla were divorced, which Josephus brands as an offence against the Jewish law (cf. *Antt.*15,259 = XV,7,10 and *Antt.*

20,143 = XX,7,2). Josephus says expressly of Herodias that by being divorced she had broken ancestral laws (*Antt.*18,136 = XVII,5,4); this sounds as though Herodias was aware of the basic significance of this step. Possibly she was following not only the Hellenistic and Roman legal tradition but also Aramaic traditions: there is also evidence of a wife's right to obtain a divorce in the fifth century BC from the Egyptian colony of Elephantine. There is also evidence for Palestine for the time of the Bar Kochba revolt. (AD 132–135).

11. As Josephus relates (*Antt.*18,111f. = XVIII,5,1).

12. For what follows see Josephus (*Antt.*17,349–353 = XVIII,13,4).

13. For levirate marriage (from the Latin *levir* = brother-in-law) cf. Deut.25.5–10.

14. According to Josephus, Antipas had John the Baptist executed because he feared a rebellion (*Antt.*18.118 = XVIII,5,2). That may be historically credible, and in no way contradicts the New Testament tradition according to which John the Baptist was executed because of his criticism of Antipas' marriage. The marriage and criticism of this marriage were beyond question political factors of the first order.

15. Isa.40.3 (cf. Mark 1.3).

16. Antipas in fact suffered an annihilating defeat from his former father-in-law because of deserters (cf. Josephus, *Antt.*18,114 = XVIII,5,1).

17. For the Nabataean war between Antipas and Aretas cf. Josephus, *Antt.* 18.113ff. = XVIII,5,1. The Syrian legate Vitellius had to intervene (18,120ff. = XVIII,5,3). A more major war was avoided by the death of Tiberius in AD 37.

18. The account of the fall of Antipas and his exile here is based on Josephus, *Antt.*18,240–256 = XVIII,7,1f.

19. Mark 10.11–12.

20. It could be that such an attempt was in fact made, cf. Luke 13.31–33.

21. Song of Songs 4.1.

7. *Jesus – A Security Risk?*

1. Following themes in Ps. 137. 'Babylon' at that time was a widespread code name for Rome (cf. Rev.18; I Peter 5.13).

2. Such an episode could underlie the report in Luke 13.1ff. that Pilate had Galilean pilgrims and the animals they were bringing to sacrifice killed.

3. The attack on the emperor's slaves took place under Cumanus (AD 48–52). 'On the Beth-horon high road bandits swooped down on one of the emperor's slaves, a certain Stephen, and robbed him of the baggage that he was carrying. Cumanus sent out men with orders to bring the inhabitants of the neighbouring villages in chains to his headquarters, blaming them for their failure to pursue and capture the bandits' (Josephus, *BJ* 2,228f. = II,12,2).

4. According to the Letter of Aristeas the Septuagint (abbreviated as LXX) was prepared for the famous royal library in Alexandria on the orders of King Ptolemy II (283–246) by seventy-two translators from Jerusalem in 72 days. This translation of the Old Testament was to be used in the liturgy by Jews living outside Palestine, who often knew only Greek and no Hebrew.

5. The prophetic oracle is Isa.40.3. Not only John the Baptist but also the Qumran community referred to this oracle (cf. Mark 1.3). They intended to prepare the way for God in the wilderness by strict observance of the law (cf. 1QS VIII.12–14).

6. When the great rebellion against the Romans broke out forty years later the Essenes also took part in it. One of them, called John the Essene, was military governor of the rebels in the district of Thamna (Josephus *BJ* 2,567 = II,20,4). The Essenes probably believed that the time of the last struggle between the children of light and the children of darkness had come. They went under in this struggle. Excavations in Qumran have shown that their settlement by the Dead Sea was destroyed at that time. Many Essenes were cruelly tortured and executed. They refused to the last to acknowledge the emperor as their master and showed amazing courage and steadfastness in enduring torture (cf. Josephus, *BJ* 2,152 = II,8,10).

7. Cf. Josephus, *BJ* 2,56 = II,4,1: 'At Sepphoris in Galilee Judas son of Hezekiah – a bandit chief who once overran the country and was suppressed by King Herod – collected a considerable force, broke into the royal armoury, equipped his followers, and attacked the other seekers after power.'

8. In fact in AD 66 an alliance between the younger members of the upper classes and the resistance movement in the country led to the outbreak of the Jewish war.

9. Cf. Josephus, *BJ* 2,118 = II,8,1: 'In his time (i.e. that of Coponius,

AD 6–9) a Galilean named Judas tried to stir the natives (namely of the territory of Archelaus, Judaea and Samaria) to revolt, saying that they would be cowards if they submitted to paying taxes to the Romans, and after serving God alone accepted human masters.'

10. The violent death of Judas the Galilean is not reported in Josephus, but we hear of it in Acts 5.37. The report in Acts probably accords with the facts.

11. Two sons of Judas the Galilean called James and Simon were crucified under the procurator Tiberius Alexander (AD 46–48) (Josephus, *Antt*.20,102 = XX,5,2). So the resistance was carried on by the family of Judas the Galilean after his death. His grandsons played a leading role in the Jewish war (66–70) and include defenders of Masada, which was not conquered by the Romans until AD 74.

12. Foreigners could have sacrifices offered for them in the temple in Jerusalem; they bought the animals and the priests performed the sacrifice in their absence, since they could not enter the holy precinct. The institution of these sacrifices in AD 66 had been the signal for revolt against the Romans (cf. Josephus, *BJ* 2,409f. = II,17,3). The sacrifices instituted at that time also included sacrifices for the emperor and the Roman people twice a day (Josephus, *BJ* 2,197 = II,10,4). The emperor once ordered sacrifice to be made for himself at his own expense (Philo, *Legatio ad Gajum* 157). The costs had later been devolved to the Jewish public (this can be inferred from Josephus, *c.Apionem* 2,77 = II,6).

8. *Researches in Nazareth*

1. In the Jewish war the rebel leader John of Gischala made substantial profits by selling pure oil to Jews living in Syria. He sold it at eight times the price that he had paid for it (Josephus, *BJ* 2,591f. = II,21,2).

2. Jewish slaves had to be released without payment in the seventh year, unless they voluntarily chose permanent slavery (cf. Deut.15.12ff.). They might not be sold to non-Jews – for in that case they would have no hope of legitimate release. By contrast Gentile slaves remained in permanent slavery. However, many of them were converted to Judaism. As a result they came to enjoy the privileges of Jewish slaves. Generally speaking it must be noted that Judaism

restricted slavery to a degree that was amazing in antiquity. Its duration was limited, and within this period there was one day of rest, the sabbath, which was laid down by law.

3. The following story comes from Philo, *Depecialibus legibus* (On individual laws) II,159–62. This story is certainly based on typical happenings in Egypt. Matthew 5.25–26; 18.23–35 shows that even in Palestine the situation of people in debt was often hopeless. The debt presupposed here is unknown to Jewish law and indicates that Jews had come under the competence of alien jurisdiction.

4. Such incidents are presupposed in the parable of the wicked men in the vineyard (Mark 12.1–9). Letters on papyrus are preserved from the middle of the third century AD, written by a certain Zeno, who was vainly trying to recover debts: the collector whom he employed was driven out of the village (cf. CPJ I, no.6, 129f.).

5. Unemployment is presupposed as a social problem in Matt.20.1–16.

6. Cf. Luke 6.20–21. The parallel version in Matthew turns the poor in the economic sense into 'poor in spirit' (Matt.5.3) – certainly a reformulation of the beatitude which does not correspond to the original wording.

7. Matt.8.21f.

8. Luke 14.26.

9. Mark 3.21,31–35. It may be a historical fact that Jesus' family had a tense relationship with him during his lifetime. Later, however, members of the family belonged to the Christian community (e.g. James the brother of Jesus, cf. Gal.1.19).

10. Micah 7.6. Luke 12.53 presupposes that the prophecy of the book of Micah has been fulfilled in the proclamation of Jesus.

9. In the Caves of Arbela

1. Mark 10.25: the saying states that it is impossible for a rich man to enter the kingdom of God.

2. Matt.6.24.

3. Luke 6.24. The underlying idea is that everyone is assigned a particular portion of 'happiness'. The rich have already received theirs, so it is now the turn of the poor.

4. Cf. the description of Galilee by Josephus: 'The whole area is excellent for crops or cattle and rich in forests of every kind, so that

by its adaptability it invites even those least inclined to work on the land. Consequently every inch as been cultivated by the inhabitants and not a corner goes to waste. It is thickly studded with towns, and thanks to the natural abundance the innumerable villages are so densely populated that the smallest has more than 15,000 inhabitants' (*BJ* 3,42–43 = II,3,2). The numbers are probably somewhat exaggerated.

5. Based on themes from Ps.104.

6. What follows is taken almost word for word from Josephus, *BJ* 1, 310–313 = I,16,4. The caves of Arbela are very much smaller than those presupposed above. However, in the wilderness of Judaea there are cave-systems which were used by the resistance fighters. Here they have been as it were 'transposed' to Galilee.

7. Eccles.4.1–3.

10. Terror and Love of One's Enemy

1. According to Josephus (*Antt.*18.5 = XVIII,1,1) the Zealots taught: 'God would only readily contribute to the success of this venture (achieving freedom from the Romans) if they contributed to it themselves, or even better, if those who in their view had become supporters of a great cause also did not avoid the trouble which was involved (in its implementation).'

2. Mark 4.26–29: the parable of the seed that grows by itself.

3. Cf. Luke 6.15. Matthew calls Simon the 'Cananaean' (from Hebrew *kana*, be zealous). So he confirms the information in Luke that Simon is a 'Zealot' (cf. Matt.10.4). Furthermore the fact that a Zealot is mentioned in the New Testament shows that the 'Zealots' did not first form a resistance group in the course of the Jewish War, though one might get this impression from Josephus.

4. Matt.5.38–41.

5. Matt.5.43–45.

6. Mark 10.42–43.

7. One can clearly infer the connection between tax debts, paupery and recourse to 'banditry', i.e. to the resistance struggle, from Josephus (*Antt.*18.274 = XVIII,8,4): because people did not look after their land because of long-drawn-out protest demonstrations they feared 'that the neglect of agriculture would inevitably lead to banditry

because they (i.e. the farmers taking part in the demonstration) would not be able to pay the taxes'.

8. Mark 12.13–17. In the present version of the story in Mark it is the Pharisees and the Herodians who put the question. It is possible that originally Jesus' conversation partners were people sympathetic to the resistance fighters.

9. Neh.5.

10. Hecataeus of Abdera, who lived in the time of Alexander the Great, reports of the Jews that Moses gave each of them a piece of land, and the priests a rather larger one so that they could devote themselves to worship. However, the Jews were forbidden to sell their land, so that the richer could not oppress the poorer (in Diodorus Siculus XL, 3,7).

11. The story of the Maccabaean revolt is told in I and II Maccabees.

12. Based on themes from Ps.73.

13. Eccles. 4.3.

11. Conflict in Capernaum

1. According to the chronological divisions of the time a day ended at dusk, when the next day began.

2. Matt.11.5–6.

3. Mark 5.25–34.

4. Mark 7.24–30.

5. The Essenes in fact held this strict opinion, as we know for example from the Damascus Document found in Qumran (abbreviated CD): 'No man shall assist a beast to give birth on the sabbath day. And if it should fall into a cistern or pit, he shall not lift it out on the sabbath' (CD XI, 13f.). The same rule is also applied to human beings: 'Should any man fall into water or fire, he shall not be pulled out by a ladder or rope or any other tool (on the sabbath)' (CD XI, 16f.). The view of the Pharisees on this point was less strict: 'If an animal falls into a waterhole (on the sabbath), then you are to bring branches and pillows and put them under it. If it comes out, it comes out' (i.e. there is therefore no need to worry about the desecration of the sabbath (bShab 128b). Matt.12.11 even presupposes that in the first century AD it was held that one can give active help to an animal on the sabbath.

6. Mark 3.1–5.

7. Mark 2.27.

8. For the foundation of Tiberias on a cemetery cf. Josephus, *Antt*.18.38 = XVIII,2,3.

9. Cf. Mark 7.1ff.

10. Mark 2.23–28.

11. Mark 7.15.

12. Matt. 23.25–27.

13. A blessing which is spoken in the morning before reading from the Bible. For Jewish prayers (in English and Hebrew) see e.g. *The Authorized Daily Prayer Book*, translated S.Singer, Eyre and Spottiswoode (1890)[26] 1960.

14. Ex.19.5f.

15. Tacitus *(Hist.* V,5) and Juvenal *(Sat.* XIV, 105f.) think that the Jews observe the sabbath out of laziness.

16. Cf. Matt.8.5–13.

12. Men on the Frontier

1. For the foundation of Bethsaida Julias see Josephus, *BJ* 2,1,8 = II, 9,1; *Antt*.18.28 = XVIII,2,1.

2. The toll collectors in the ancient world were not state officials but entrepreneurs who leased tolls from the state, paid an agreed sum to the treasury and put the rest in their own pockets. Understandably they were very unpopular.

3. It is striking that the two largest towns in Galilee, Sepphoris and Tiberias, are never mentioned in the Synoptic Gospels.

4. For Levi's feast see Mark 2.13–17; the story as we now have it sees Levi's meeting with Jesus and his decision to follow him as a single event. It is quite possible that this decision came to maturity over a period. The narratives in the Gospels compress the most important events into a short space.

5. This must already have been said of Jesus in his lifetime, as Matt. 11.19 shows.

6. Jewish care for the poor was well organized. Sufficient for two meals a day was distributed every week to the poor living in a locality. Strangers were given enough for two meals on the actual day. Toll collectors were so despised that it was forbidden to receive gifts from them to pass on to the poor. They were allowed to give in another way.

7. Luke 14.12–14.
8. Matthew 11.28.
9. Luke 14.16–24.
10. This addition to the parable appears only in the version in the Gospel of Matthew (where the householder has also become a king). Most scholars are generally agreed that this is a later addition to Jesus' parable.
11. Mark 10.15.
12. Cf. Mark 10.14.

13. *A Woman Protests*

1. Cf. Mark 6.45–52.
2. Cf. the two versions of the 'miraculous feeding'. Mark 8.1–9 speaks of seven loaves for four thousand, Mark 6.35–44 of five loaves for five thousand. Here is tangible evidence of the growth of the miraculous.
3. According to Luke 8.3, 'Joanna the wife of Chuza, a steward of Herod Antipas' is one of the women who supported Jesus out of her own resources.
4. The so-called Psalm of Solomon 17 (from the first century BC) gives us an insight into messianic expectation in the time of Jesus. The Messiah will drive out the enemy (PsSol.17.25), gather and sanctify the people. 'And no stranger and foreigner shall continue to dwell among them' (PsSol.17.28).
5. Cf. Mark 6.14. The fact that Jesus is taken to be John the Baptist redivivus presupposes that previously he was completely unknown. Therefore this note about the anxiety of Herod Antipas may well be a very old reaction to Jesus' ministry even during his lifetime.
6. For the teaching of the Sadducees cf. Josephus, *Antt.*18.16–17 = XVIII,1,4, which is taken up in the phrases that follow.
7. The Sanhedrin was the Jewish council in which the high priests (with Sadducean leanings) and representatives of the lay nobility sat. Since the time of Queen Salome Alexandra (77–67 BC) the Pharisees had also been represented in it. That probably contributed greatly towards turning the Pharisees into a movement which was at least provisionally accepted by the existing order, whereas originally they had been an opposition party.
8. Eccles.3.19.
9. Eccles.9.7.

10. Matt. 11.28.

11. Luke 17.21. The translation 'The kingdom of God is in you' is disputed. Many scholars translate it 'in your midst'. In the saying of Jesus which is quoted below Jesus asserts that the kingdom of God is abolishing the rule of demons. If demons depart from within human beings, the kingdom of God is beginning. So this kingdom of God clearly begins within human beings – even if it is not something inward. It is bound up with a miraculous transformation of the whole world.

12. Matt.12.18.

13. This miracle story was handed down by the ancient satirist Lucian of Samosata (c.AD 120–180) in his dialogue 'The Lying Friend', chapter 16.

14. Cf. Mark 5.34; 10.52; Luke 7.50; 17.19; Matt.9.29.

15. Cf. Mark 2.18–19. Jesus differed here from John the Baptist. The latter fasted, whereas Jesus rejected at least excessive fasting.

16. Luke 10.23–24.

17. Cf. Matt.12.42.

18. Matt.6.25–26.

19. Matt.5.44–45.

20. Matt.5.21–22.

21. Cf. Song of Songs 8.6–7.

14. Report on Jesus, or Jesus in Disguse

1. Josephus compares the Pharisees to Stoics (Vita 12), the Essenes to Pythagoraeans (*Antt.*15.37 = XV,10,4). 'The Pythagoraeans also formed a kind of secret society and had sharing possessions as their ideal.

2. The Cynics, so called after the nickname of Diogenes in the barrel (*kyon* = dog), taught extreme modesty in needs and little sense of shame, i.e. they departed pointedly from usual customs. In the first century AD there were many cynic mendicant philosophers wandering around the Roman empire with long shaggy beards, dirty cloaks, satchels and staffs.

3. Matt.10.10. In teaching that the disciples are to travel without satchel and staff Jesus is perhaps deliberately distinguishing them from the Cynic itinerant philosophers with whom they could easily be confused.

4. Cf. Matt.12.28–34. Jewish scribes and Jesus are agreed in this doctrine, as history shows. There are similar summaries e.g. in Testament of Issachar 5.2: 'Love the Lord and your neighbour.' That piety towards the gods and justice towards fellow human beings were the most important virtues is shown by Xenophon, *Memorabilia* IV,8,11; Philo, *De spec.leg.* II, 63.

5. The 'golden rule' is virtually proverbial throughout antiquity. We find it even before Jesus in Jewish writings, cf. Tobit 4.15; Letter of Aristeas 207.

6. Matt.5.39.

7. For the teaching of Socrates cf. Plato, *Crito* 49Aff. The following anecdote is told of Socrates: 'When Aristocrates kicked him, Socrates did not retaliate or rebuke him except by saying to a passer-by, "This man suffers from mule's disease"' (Themistius, *On Virtue* 46). The philosopher Epictetus taught that the Cynic itinerant philosophers had to 'let themselves be kicked like a dog and even when being kicked go on loving like a father of all, like a brother' (Epictetus, *Diatribes* III, 22,54).

8. Seneca, *Beneficiis,* IV, 26,1. However, Seneca added a qualification: 'God cannot give some gifts to the deserving without also automatically giving them to the undeserving' (*Beneficiis* IV, 28,1).

9. Matt.7.3–5.

10. Matt.6.25ff.

11. Cf. Matt.5.21f. Cleanthes taught: 'A robber is someone who, even before he stains his hands with blood, arms himself for murder and has the intent to rob and kill. His wickedness is carried through and made manifest by his action, but it does not begin there' (quoted in M.Pohlenz, *Stoa und Stoiker*, Zurich 1950, 128).

12. Matt.5.27ff. Cf. Cleanthes, Fragment 573.

13. Epictetus, *Handbook of Morality*, 33.5.

14. Mark 7.15.

15. In the first century BC a Hellenistic Jew by the name of Phocylides wrote proverbs; No.228 reads: 'Purification does not make the body clean, but only the soul.'

16. Cf.Matt.6.5ff.

17. Cf.Matt.6.1ff.

18. Cf.Matt.6.16ff.

19. Cf.Mark 3.1ff.; 2.23ff.; Luke 13.10ff.; 14.1ff.

20. Cf. Mark 10.13–16; Matt.18.3.
21. Matt.21.31.
22. Cf.Matt.8.11ff.
23. Cf.Matt.19.10–12.
24. Cf.Matt.5.5.
25. Cf.Matt.8.21–22.
26. Cf.Mark 10.42–43.
27. Cf.Mark 14.58.
28. This fable appears in the so-called Ahikar romance, and many versions were already widespread in pre-Christian times.
29. Cf. Luke 13.6–9.
30. Philo, *Quaest in Gen.IV*, 198.
31. Luke 15.11–32.
32. Luke 17.26–30. The 'Man' is a heavenly figure who according to Dan.7 replaces the kingdoms of 'beasts'.
33. Luke 17.34–35.
34. The following quotations come from Matt.25.31–46.
35. Luke 10.18f.
36. Mark 3.24–26.
37. Matt.13.44–46.
38. Matt.12.41–42.
39. Cf.Luke 10.23–24.
40. Cf. Matt.11.12–13; Luke 16.16.
41. Cf. Matt.19.28; Luke 22.29f. This promise to the 'twelve disciples' could hardly have originated after Easter: after the betrayal by Judas it is hard to imagine that a promise would have been invented which also assigns him rule over Israel as one of the Twelve.
42. Mark 10.35–45.
43. Matt 11.12.

15. Reforming Temple and Society

1. According to Josephus, by this route it took three days to get from Galilee to Jerusalem *(Vista* 269). Samaria was often avoided because of the tensions between Jews and Samaritans. According to the Gospels of Mark and Matthew Jesus, too, does not go up to Jerusalem through Samaria (cf. Mark 10.1; Matt.19.1). According to the Gospels of Luke and John, however, he does travel through

Samaria (cf. Luke 8.51ff.; John 4.1ff.).

2. Cf. Mark 11.15–19, 27–33.

3. Cf. Mark 14.58.

4. Cf. Mark 11.27–33.

5. All robbers and resistance fighters were called *sicarii* in the Roman empire. Josephus uses this term for a special group in the Jewish resistance against Rome. He describes how they stabbed their victims with short knives in the market place and immediately afterwards protested against the crime in the uproar at the top of their voices. One of their first victims was a high priest. Cf. *BJ* 2,254 = 2,13,3.

6. In Aramaic 'Iscariot' could simply mean 'man from Carioth'; Barjonah – as Peter is called in Matt.16.17 – is most probably to be translated 'son of Jonah'.

7. One of the first actions of the Zealot rebels in the Jewish war was to burn the debt archives. In so doing they hoped to win over all those in debt and all the poor to the revolt against the Romans (cf. Josephus, *BJ* 2,427 = II,17,6).

8. Cf. the Lord's Prayer, Matt.6.12. When Jesus says that one must ask for forgiveness and be ready oneself to forgive one's debtors, he is certainly also thinking of financial debts.

9. Deut.15.1ff.

10. Matt.18.23–25.

11. In his work 'On the Travels of Abraham' Philo criticizes Jews who interpret the Law symbolically. As an example he gives the view of the sabbath and circumcision which are sketched out above *(De migr.*89–93).

12. When King Izates of Adiabene (first half of the first century AD) was converted to Judaism, he was first assured by a Jewish merchant that circumcision was not absolutely necessary if he wanted to be an adherent of Jewish faith. But then a certain Eleazar came from Galilee and put forward the view that it was not enough to read the laws, but that it was vital 'to do what was commanded by them. Thereupon the king had himself circumcised' Josephus, *Antt.*20.38–48 = XX,1,4).

13. This statement is attributed to Rabbi Hillel (about 20 BC, bShab. 31a). Whether he really did it is another matter. But the fact that the golden rule is attributed to the most famous teachers shows how highly it was regarded.

14. Even the Herodian royal house required that sons-in-law should be circumcised (cf. Josephus, *Antt.*20.139 = XX,7, 1).
15. A pilgrimage of the nations to Zion was expected in the messianic age (cf. Isa. 2.2f.; Micah 4.2; Isa.56.7; 60.3; Tobit 13.13).

16. Pilate Afraid

1. Solon carried through comprehensive social reforms in Athens in 594–63 BC. Among other things he abolished slavery for debt. He stopped creditors selling bankrupt debtors as slaves or binding them by any form of partial tenancy. The two Gracchi were concerned to bring about a more just distribution of land in Rome in 133 or 123/2 BC.
2. The following story follows Josephus *BJ* 2, 169–74 (changed into the first person).
3. Cf. Mark 11.15–17.
4. Cf. Mark 12.13–17.
5. Xenophon, *Recollections of Socrates,* II,67,35, is an example: one had to excel in doing good to friends and ill to enemies.
6. Cf. e.g. Isa.2.2–5: the prophetic oracle promises that one day all peoples will go on pilgrimage to Jerusalem.
7. Following themes from Ps.22. The passion narratives in the Gospels have quotations from and allusions to this psalm.

17. Who was Guilty?

1. The *shema* takes its name from the first word of the Jewish confession of faith: 'Hear, O Israel' = *Shema yisrael.* It is spoken three times a day and has a fixed place in the synagogue liturgy.
2. In particular people from the upper classes sympathetic to Judaism remained godfearers without going over completely to Judaism; i.e. they did not have themselves circumcised. The centurion Cornelius in Caesarea (Acts 10.1ff.) is one such godfearer sympathetic to Judaism.
3. The following description of Caesarea is based closely on Josephus, *BJ* 1,413.f = I,21,7.
4. Xenophanes, Fragment 23. Xenophanes lived about 570–475/70 BC. He was one of the so-called pre-Socratics.

5. Isa. 45.5. Chapters 40–55 of the Book of Isaiah do not come from Isaiah but from an unknown prophet at the time of the Babylonian Exile (Deutero-Isaiah = Second Isaiah). This prophet is the first to formulate unmistakably the belief that there is only one God.

6. For these reasons the Jews were exempt from military service.

7. From the so-called Magnificat of Mary (Luke 1.52–53).

8. The very cohorts involved in the execution of Jesus openly expressed their hatred of Jewish kings on the death of the Jewish King Herod Agrippa about fifteen years later, in AD 44. They dragged a statue of the king's daughter into a brothel and publicly celebrated his death in Caesarea. At that time the emperor Claudius seriously considered disbanding the cohorts (cf. Josephus, *Antt.*19,356–90, 364–6 = XIX,9,1f.).

9. Mark 15.16–20.

10. Mark 14.58.

11. At this point the judgment of the Gospel of John is amazingly realistic: the Sanhedrin uses against Jesus the argument: 'If we let him go on thus, every one will believe in him, and the Romans will come and destroy both our holy place and our nation.'

12. Cf. Mark 11.1ff.

13. The following episode – based on Josephus, *BJ* 2,22–7 = II,12,1 – took place under the procurator Cumanus (AD 48–52).

14. The Romans would certainly have let a madman go. In AD 62 a country prophet called Jesus son of Ananias caused a stir with a prophecy of impending disaster on Jerusalem, the temple and the people. The Jewish aristocracy arrested him, interrogated him and handed him over to the Romans. However, the procurator came to the conclusion that the prophet was mad and let him go (Josephus *BJ* 6,300–309 = VI,5,3). The parallel to the case of Jesus of Nazareth is unmistakable. Jesus, too, caused offence with a prophecy which criticized the temple. He, too, came from the country. And he, too, faced hearings from both authorities.

18. The Man: A Dream

1. Cf. John 11.47–50.

2. Cf. the accounts of the earliest community in Acts 2.42–47; 4.32–37; and Acts 1–6 generally.

3. The earliest tradition about the appearances is contained in I Cor. 15.3–7. Here Paul is quoting a tradition handed down to him. He got to know the witnesses Peter and James who he mentions there personally three years after his conversion – that is, in the thirties. There can be no doubt about the subjective authenticity of the appearances tradition.

4. Two 'robbers' were crucified with Jesus.

5. Acts 5.1ff.

6. Eccles.4.1–4.

7. This dream is a very free rendering of Daniel 7. In the book of Daniel the four beasts depicted in it are interpreted in terms of the world empires of the Babylonians, Medes, Persians and Greeks. A Jewish apocalyptic writing from the end of the first century – so-called IV Ezra – narrates this dream again. There it ends with the Romans.

8. Matt.5.9; 25.34–36.

9. Ps.139.1–14.